FOR CALVINISM

FOR CALVINISM

MICHAEL HORTON

ZONDERVAN

For Calvinism

This title is also available as a Zondervan ebook. Visit www.zondervan.com/ebooks.

This title is also available in a Zondervan audio edition. Visit www.zondervan.fm.

Requests for information should be addressed to:

Zondervan, *3900 Sparks Drive SE, Grand Rapids, Michigan 49546*

Library of Congress Cataloging-in-Publication Data

Horton, Michael Scott.
For Calvinism / Michael Horton.
p. cm.
ISBN 978-0-310-32465-2 (softcover)
1. Calvinism. 2. Reformed Church—Doctrines. I. Title.
BX9422.3.H67 2011
230'.42—dc22 2011007934

Cover design: Tobias Outerwear for Books
Interior design: Cindy LeBreacht

Printed in the United States of America

To my mother, who taught me to expect to find wonderful truths—
and not a few surprises—in the Scriptures

CONTENTS

FOREWORD

When asked to write this foreword to Michael Horton's book *For Calvinism*, I feared that, as a committed Arminian, I would not be able to write anything good about it. I should have known better. I've known Mike for about twenty years, and we have had many constructive conversations about our theological differences. I like to think I have influenced him (to think better of Arminianism), and I know he has influenced me—to think better of Calvinism and Calvinists.

I have always found Mike to be a generous and yet devoted adherent of what he calls the "doctrines of grace" (Reformed theology). Don't get me wrong; I still strongly disagree with some of his characterizations of Arminianism and especially with the "five point" Calvinist system he espouses. Anyone who doubts it should read my companion volume *Against Calvinism* (Zondervan, 2011). However, I regard Mike as one of the kindest, gentlest true Calvinists around. By "true Calvinist" I mean one who believes those doctrines correctly and argues that they are crucial to the gospel.

Mike is truly a scholar and a Christian gentleman—and this book demonstrates it. Its exposition and defense of Calvinism is uncompromising without arrogance or hostility toward those who disagree. Even where he disagrees with classical Arminianism, he does not offer the sort of willful misrepresentations that I so often find in treatments by Calvinists. They are matters of perspective. Mike accuses Arminianism mainly of inconsistency, which I appreciate because that's better than the accusations that it is simply a false gospel or a "different worldview."

My basic complaint about the Calvinism Mike expounds and defends is likewise its inconsistency. Some readers may wonder how important that complaint is, but I'm sure Mike and I agree that there is no such thing as "foolish consistency." As Mike is fond of saying (and I agree): "If we are going to get the message out, we had better first get it right." Part of getting it right is making sure it is intelligible.

In my opinion, of course, high, federal Calvinism, the theology expressed in this book, necessarily makes God the author of sin and evil by "good and necessary consequence" of its claim that everything, including the fall of Adam, was and is foreordained by God. In other words, I worry that this theology undermines the goodness of God's character. Nevertheless, I realize from this book (and, to a lesser extent, from other books defending high Calvinism) that Calvinists do not intend to undermine the goodness of God's character. The view of God espoused here is of a God both incomparably great and good. Unfortunately, some elements of it take back some of that goodness. Nevertheless, this theology has an impressive historical pedigree and, as Mike demonstrates, much biblical support.

Anyone interested in reading the best case possible for Calvinism *must* read this book. It is informative, engaging, clear, and self-critical. It helpfully contributes to the ongoing discussions and debates about God's sovereignty among evangelicals. I need not have worried about having nothing good to say. After reading the book I can recommend it wholeheartedly with the reservation that I strongly disagree with its central claims. In today's climate of theological controversy many people will think that inconsistent. Well, they're simply wrong. It is possible to be committed and fair, critical and generous. *For Calvinism* proves it and my hearty endorsement reveals it.

Roger E. Olson

ACKNOWLEDGMENTS

I'm grateful to my brother Larry for introducing me to the book of Romans, as well as the books and audio tapes of R. C. Sproul, James Boice, J. I. Packer, Roger Nicole, and others; and to my other brother, Gary, for paying my way to their conferences. I'm also grateful to these great Christian leaders for taking the time to encourage and mentor me in a variety of ways over many years.

I also want to thank Derek Buikema for helping track down the data for this book's chapter on missions.

As always, I'm grateful to my wife, Lisa, for her constant companionship in the gospel and to our children not only for providing occasions to teach them but to learn from their insights into God's Word.

ACKNOWLEDGMENTS

INTRODUCTION

CALVINISM AND ARMINIANISM: WHY BOTHER?

Calvinists are "the chosen frozen." Become one and you're sure to lose not only your evangelistic and missionary zeal, but also the heartfelt joy of a personal relationship with Christ. The pursuit of holiness will wane. Calvinism is a religion of the head, not the heart or the hands.

Many people have certain assumptions about what Calvinism will lead to on the basis of misunderstandings about what it teaches and therefore where it logically leads. Calvinism ranks knowing above feeling and doing, doctrine over life, it is often assumed. Underscoring God's sovereignty, human sinfulness (even that of believers), justification by an imputed righteousness, and utter dependence on grace surely undermines personal responsibility. And if you stress God's sovereignty and grace too much, you'll not only stop evangelizing; you'll stop praying, praising, and pursuing holiness. It's a recipe for disaster.

But the actual history of Calvinism—including what Calvinists have consistently written, preached, prayed, sung, and witnessed—doesn't fit the stereotypes. Of course, one may encounter cold and joyless Calvinists. But is that a generally valid characteristic or is it a caricature? And when people run into Calvinists of this sort, is it a reflection of personal characteristics and conditions or of the doctrine itself? And if Calvinists have in fact been in the vanguard of evangelism and missions, as I'll point out later, then is it possible that critics have misunderstood the logic and implications that they ascribe to Calvinism?

Critics have frequently confused Calvinism with hyper-Calvinism, and sometimes contact with hyper-Calvinists proves the caricature. Often, bowled over by a sense of God's majesty and grace, new Calvinists enter what we call "the cage phase." Like any new convert, we can be hard to live with when we've just experienced a radical paradigm shift. Why weren't we taught this when it seems so evident in Scripture? How can our fellow Christians ignore these doctrines and even squelch any discussion? In this condition, enthusiasm can turn to frustration and even to arrogance and divisiveness. Only superficially acquainted with Reformed teaching at this stage, we swing from one extreme to the other, misunderstanding and misrepresenting these doctrines. This often proves the caricature. No doubt, many critics of Calvinism have encountered this, and it puts them off from taking a second look at the position.

However, mainstream Calvinism has been associated with personal renewal as well as doctrinal reformation. In fact, Reformed piety has resisted the false choice between head and heart, doctrine and life, church and individual. In the sixteenth and seventeenth centuries, both Lutheran and Reformed traditions reflected a concern for doctrine and life as one integrated pattern. Like the Reformers themselves, the evangelical movement was deeply impressed with the significance of Christian truth for daily living. That is why the Bible was translated into the common languages of the people and widely distributed to parishes and households, along with catechisms, prayer books, and psalters.

Grace was not just a doctrine but a person—namely, God himself, in Jesus Christ, clothed in the gospel. Hearts were filled with thanksgiving and joy in the presence of a holy God who had forgiven, justified, and renewed sinners—with the assurance of resurrection in the age to come. It was not just a collection of great ideas that turned Christendom upside down, but a radical experience of grace. It changed the way people related to God and to each other. And this is the experience of many Christians today as well.

In the United States, historians and sociologists have long observed the disintegration of the Reformation—and particularly, Calvinist—presuppositions that guided many Christians in colonial America. With the Second Great Awakening (1790–1845), especially under the influence of revivalist Charles Finney, these presuppositions were replaced with a characteristically modern (and *American*) confidence in the rugged individual. At the end of his teaching stint in the United States, before returning to Germany where he would eventually be executed under the Nazi regime, Lutheran theologian Dietrich Bonhoeffer described America as "Protestantism without the Reformation." As recently as the 1980s, veteran evangelical theologian Clark Pinnock claimed with some celebration that the defenders of Augustinian and Calvinistic distinctives were dwindling to the vanishing point.[1]

So it was surprising to many in 2009 when *Time* magazine named "The New Calvinism" as the third of ten trends shaping the world today. Clearly, the death of Calvinism has been somewhat exaggerated. In this book, I explore the biblical historic roots of the doctrinal beliefs commonly associated with Calvinism, offer some context on the renewal of interest in these "doctrines of grace"—those unique emphases of the tradition that shape life and thought—and finally, hope to encourage others to consider its rich resources for faith and practice in the twenty-first century.

Though it is a mistake to reduce the beliefs of Calvinism to five emphases, it is true that most of the objections and attacks on Calvinism focus on certain doctrinal distinctives, sometimes known as the "five points of Calvinism." The "five points" are as follows:

- *Total depravity*: Our bondage to sin in Adam is complete in its extensiveness, though not in its intensity. In other words, we're not as bad as we can possibly be, but original sin has thoroughly corrupted every aspect of our existence—including the will.
- *Unconditional election*: Out of his lavish grace, the Father chose out of the fallen race a people from every race to be redeemed through his Son and united to his Son by his Spirit. This determination was made in eternity, apart from anything foreseen in the believer.
- *Particular redemption*: Christ's death is sufficient for the whole world, but secured the redemption of the elect.
- *Effectual grace*: The Holy Spirit unites sinners to Christ through the gospel and faith is the effect, not the cause, of the new birth.
- *Perseverance of the saints*: All of those chosen, redeemed, and regenerated will be given the gift of persevering faith, so that not one will be lost.

Many people know these five points by the TULIP acronym. While intending no disrespect for the noble flower, I prefer (for reasons that I will defend) *particular redemption* and *effectual grace* to the terms *limited atonement* and *irresistible grace*. This book will focus on explaining, defending, and clarifying these five points as distinctive elements of the Calvinist doctrinal position. Instead of using the acronym TULIP, I'll simply refer to these doctrinal emphases as the "five points," the "Calvinist distinctives," or (my personal favorite) the "doctrines of grace."

WHAT'S AT STAKE?

A recent Pew study reported that atheists and agnostics know the Bible and Christian doctrine better than evangelicals. Mormons and Jews came in second. This simply corroborates other surveys that point up the urgency of basic instruction in our churches today. Christians need to know what they believe and why they believe it.

Of course, the deeper we wade into the reservoir of Christian faith and practice, the more we encounter debates that have not only brought clarity and unity, but also debate and division. The Calvinist-Arminian debate is one of those long-running conversations. Touching as it does on so many questions at the heart of our understanding of God, ourselves, and salvation, it is not surprising that this controversy continues to provoke interest and opposition.

All Christians have some assumptions about God's sovereignty and human freedom, sin and grace, election and free will, the nature and extent of Christ's saving work, God's faithfulness, and human faith and obedience. The question is whether we have tested these assumptions by Scripture, arriving at explicit convictions rather than vague sentiments. You are probably reading this book because you are interested in these questions. That means that regardless of the views you currently hold, you are not content to assume the "moralistic, therapeutic deism" that sociologists document as the default setting of most Americans today. But how can we say that the Bible clearly reveals saving truth if godly believers disagree so strongly in their conclusions? The Arminian-Calvinist debate especially presses that question.

This debate goes to the heart of the gospel itself. That does not mean that those with whom we differ don't really believe the gospel. We are justified through faith in Christ, not through doctrinal precision. However, are our doctrinal assumptions and convictions consistent with that profession of faith? Much of the debate comes down to one basic difference: Arminians affirm *synergism* (i.e., "working-together," or cooperation between God's grace and human willing and activity), while Calvinists affirm *monergism* (i.e., "one-working," or God's grace as the effectual source of election, redemption, faith, and perseverance).

Calvinists do not deny that there are commands in Scripture and that these reveal God's moral will. Nevertheless, as Calvin put the matter, "we must have this gospel daily repeated in the church." "For although faith believes every word of God, it rests solely on the word of grace or mercy, the promise of God's fatherly goodwill," which is only realized in and through Jesus Christ.[2] "For in God faith seeks life," he adds, "which is not to be found in commandments or the pronouncement of penalties, but in the promise of mercy—and only a free promise."[3] It may well be that Arminians will affirm this, but the question is whether Arminianism actually can square this with its other convictions.

DOES SCRIPTURE OFFER A CONSISTENT INTERPRETATION?

Many Christians assume that the questions at issue between Calvinists and Arminians are ultimately irresolvable. Calvinists have "their verses" and Arminians have theirs. Calvinism reminds us that we cannot save ourselves and Arminianism reminds us of our responsibility to trust and obey. Furthermore, there have been good people on both sides of this debate throughout the centuries; do we really think that we'll be able to come down on one side or the other? However, with all due respect to those who assume it, it must be said that this is a lazy position.

First, neither Calvinists nor Arminians have "their verses." All of Scripture is God-breathed and is therefore the common treasure of all Christians. No more than a theory in the sciences can theology accept an interpretation that fails to respect the whole counsel of God. There are many questions we cannot answer—even about these doctrines. There our reason must halt before God's majesty and leave his secrets to himself. However, where God has spoken, we must hear and respond. All of the relevant passages must be taken into consideration.

As a Calvinist, I believe that the doctrines of grace represent the best interpretation of the whole teaching of Scripture on these questions. Regardless of how successful we are in carrying it out in every case, we must resolve to teach what Scripture teaches and with the proportionate emphasis that Scripture gives to it. To say that there are "Calvinist" verses and "Arminian" verses is to conclude that the Bible itself is internally incoherent and self-contradictory. If Calvinism cannot do justice to the passages put forward by Arminians, then it is inadequate from the start.

Second, neither Calvinists nor Arminians would accept the framing of their position as I have represented them above. Arminians too believe that we cannot save ourselves and Calvinists affirm our responsibility to trust and obey. So the issues at stake are deeper than this easy solution. We cannot resolve it simply by adding a dash of Calvinist confidence in grace and a dash of Arminian emphasis on human willing and effort.

Third, there are indeed good people on both sides of this debate. However, this is beside the point. There are fine people on both sides of Christianity and Islam, Judaism, or Buddhism. I have friends who are atheists and they are terrific people. How much more should we cherish our fellowship with Arminian brothers and sisters with whom we differ!

I have never met an evangelical Arminian who would say, "I'm trusting in Christ and in my own effort for salvation." It is not only unhelpful but erroneous to suggest that Arminians do not take the Bible seriously or entrust their salvation to God's grace in Christ. So it's not a question of whether there are conscientious believers on both sides, but whether Arminianism as a system can affirm consistently that "salvation belongs to the Lord" (Jon. 2:9). This particular dismissal of the debate also exhibits an implicit faith in the "experts": if scholars and teachers of the Bible can be found on both sides, the Bible itself must be unclear.

However, the same could be said of a host of doctrines that Calvinists and Arminians agree are clearly taught in Scripture, such as the Trinity, the deity and humanity of Christ, and his atoning work and resurrection. There have been many controversies in church history over these doctrines, yet the Spirit has illumined the church to understand and to embrace clear biblical teaching over against these heretical departures. We cannot choose which parts of Scripture are important and what we can ignore, and this certainly holds true also for doctrines concerning the character of God, the condition of human beings before and after the fall, the nature and extent of God's saving grace in Jesus Christ, and the assurance of final salvation from our sins. These are not ivory-tower speculations, but some of the most practical and existential questions that we will ever face in our daily lives.

Calvinists and Arminians do not disagree at every point, to be sure, but they do disagree on important points. Whether we acknowledge it or not, all of us have at least a working theology. It may be explicit or implicit, but any believer who searches the Scriptures will have to face these questions that lie at the heart of this historic debate.

"CALVINISM" IS JUST A NICKNAME

I should begin by saying that I don't like the term "Calvinism" very much. In fact, I don't know many Calvinists who do. Like many today, I prefer to speak of *the doctrines of grace* rather than the five points of Calvinism. Before the Reformation, there were many respected theologians who defended these doctrines under the nickname "Augustinian." Besides Augustine himself, we think of Anselm, Gregory of Rimini, Archbishop Bradwardine, and Luther's own mentor, Johann von Staupitz, who led the Augustinian order in Germany and wrote a marvelous tract defending these truths even before Luther.

Luther wanted to be known simply as an *evangelical*—"of the gospel." He recoiled at hearing his Roman Catholic critics call evangelicals "Lutherans." Similarly, Calvin expressed disapproval when his Lutheran critics saddled Reformed evangelicals with the nickname "Calvinists." Neither Reformer objected out of a sense of false modesty, but out of their conviction that the doctrines that they taught were revealed in the Word of God and were not recent inventions. The Reformers did not believe that they were starting over from scratch or restoring the church after centuries of oblivion. Rather, they called the Catholic Church to reformation according to the Word of God.

Charles Spurgeon (1834–1892), a renowned Baptist pastor in London, wrote in his autobiography that the root of every heresy in history is adding something of our own to the work of Christ. "I have my own private opinion that there is no such thing as preaching Christ and Him crucified, unless we preach what nowadays is called Calvinism," he wrote. "It is a nickname to call it Calvinism; Calvinism is the gospel, and nothing else."[4]

At first blush, Spurgeon's comment sounds sectarian. Clearly, he did not mean that only Calvinists believe and proclaim the gospel—in fact, throughout his public ministry he expressed respect for evangelical Arminians like John Wesley. His point was that the doctrines of grace, which for better or worse are nicknamed "Calvinism," are not really Calvin's, but the teaching of the Scriptures, Augustine, and a trail of preachers, reformers, missionaries, and evangelists ever since.

Furthermore, Spurgeon did not accept the Calvinist system lock, stock, and barrel. He criticized the Reformed understanding of baptism (especially the baptism of infants). Nevertheless, he was convinced that the doctrines of grace—what have become known to us as "the five points of Calvinism"—are *the richest and most faithful exposition of the gospel.* He was happy to be called a "Calvinist" only if it was shorthand for someone who adhered to these biblical teachings. Although the Calvinist/Arminian divide cuts across many church traditions, from Anglican to Baptist, it also unites believers across the same spectrum. The Anglican Thirty-Nine Articles, the Savoy Declaration of Congregationalism, and the London/Philadelphia Baptist Confession embrace these truths, along with the Reformed and Presbyterian churches.

The "five points" themselves are a summary of the conclusions reached at the Synod of Dort (1618–1619), which was responding to the "five points" presented by the Remonstrant (Arminian) party. The closest thing to an ecumenical council in early Protestantism, this conference included delegates not only from Reformed churches throughout the continent, but from the Church of England. Today, its conclusions are confessed by churches on every continent. Though his reforms were later rejected, even the ecumenical Patriarch of Constantinople, Cyril Lucaris (1572–1638), embraced the canons of the Synod of Dort and incorporated them into his 1629 Confession.

It is remarkable that a set of doctrines so controversial even within denominations historically committed to them has nevertheless also brought together Christians from a spectrum that no other system has accomplished. For all of their crucial differences, a wide variety of Protestants—Anglicans, Reformed and Presbyterians, Congregationalists, and Baptists—have embraced these doctrines explicitly in their confessional documents, doctrinal texts, hymns, and preaching.

Of course, Arminianism also has enjoyed a long and wide pedigree. Although the early fathers reflect greater diversity (even ambiguity), with good reason have Arminians appealed to many of the later theologians of the East for support of synergism. It is certainly not difficult to find antecedents in the medieval West or among Renaissance humanists like Erasmus. Furthermore, Arminianism claims just as great a breadth of influence among Protestants. In fact, an implicit Arminianism seems more widely represented today than Calvinism, even in churches formally committed to Reformed convictions.

So it would seem that throughout history, division between monergism and synergism forms a massive divide across denominations even more than between them. Calvinism is not a sect. It is not a group within the church, seeking its own independent status. Rather, it is an affirmation of *sola gratia* in the history of the church of Jesus Christ. The nickname "Calvinism" is unfortunate, but the content is what we will be exploring in this book. These doctrines of grace may be vilified or celebrated, but they are never boring or trivial. Throughout the history of the church their recovery has provoked debate, reformation, renewal, and mission. My prayer is that the Spirit will yet again stir up Christ's body by these astonishing truths in his Word.

ONE

THE ESSENCE OF CALVINISM

If Calvinism is more than "five points," it is surely not less, and that is why the bulk of this book is devoted to these doctrines. Before embarking on that quest, though, it is valuable to offer a summary of what I consider the essence of Calvinism. This chapter will therefore be broader and wider than the others: a survey from thirty thousand feet.

HISTORICAL DEFINITIONS

The label "Calvinism" came into use around 1558 in Lutheran polemics against the Reformed view of the Lord's Supper articulated especially (but far from exclusively) by John Calvin (1509–1564). Although Luther's name became incorporated in Lutheran churches, "Calvinist" churches have been identified historically as "Reformed." Calvin has never occupied the unique and decisive role in the development of the Reformed tradition that Luther has had in Lutheranism. In spite of his obvious importance, none of Calvin's writings is subscribed in Presbyterian and Reformed churches, whereas the Lutheran Book of Concord includes several of Luther's writings and John's Wesley's sermons are included in the Methodist statement of faith.

There are many key leaders whose names Reformed Christians would have recognized in their day alongside Calvin. In fact, he was actually a second-generation Reformed leader. However, Geneva became one of the major centers for the international movement, and the leadership of its major Reformer grew quickly. Given his enormous output (the *Institutes*, sermons, commentaries, and treatises), it is not surprising that Calvin became so prominent in the tradition's history. From Scotland to Hungary, he became the most widely read pastor of his generation. However, he was dependent on elders and contemporaries in the development of his own insights as well as the refinements of those who followed—in many different cultural and historical contexts.

Another historical feature is that Reformed Christianity grew most rapidly in cities, spread out over Europe, while Lutheranism was established by princes in Germany and Scandinavia as the territorial faith. Furthermore, in many places where the Reformed movement was growing—especially in France and Spanish Netherlands—churches were living "under the cross." This diversity of experience, ranging from establishment to persecution, is a major reason why there were various confessions (e.g., French, Scottish, Belgic, Helvetic), though each one expressed the same substance. Reformed churches on the Continent embraced the Belgic Confession, the Heidelberg Catechism, and the Canons of the Synod of Dort. The Church of England sought to pattern itself on "the example of the best Reformed churches on the continent," but adopted its own national confession (The Thirty-Nine Articles of Religion).

Most Reformed churches came to embrace a presbyterian form of government, but some (especially in Hungary and England) retained episcopal government. The English parliament called the Westminster Assembly in order to create a new constitution for the Church of England on presbyterian principles, resulting in the Westminster Confession and Catechisms as well as the Directory of Worship. Further strains on the consensus appeared with the rise of Independency (congregational government). Eventually, some Independents rejected infant baptism, yet continued ardently to affirm the doctrines of grace. Wanting to distinguish themselves both from the established church and from Arminian (General) Baptists, they often identified themselves as Particular or Calvinistic Baptists.

Over the last few decades, the terminology has shifted quite a bit. The "New Calvinism" movement that has received publicity in recent years is identified as "Reformed," although much of the numerical strength of this resurgence is to be found in non-Reformed denominations (such as the Southern Baptist Convention). This shifting of definitions offers both opportunities and challenges. Reformed churches can only celebrate the revival of interest in doctrines they cherish and, all too often, take for granted. Indeed, most mainline churches in the Reformed and Presbyterian tradition today either ignore or reject their Calvinistic distinctives. One hopes that the "New Calvinism" trend will lead not only to more widespread enjoyment of God's grace but bring to Reformed churches a vitality and a renewed appreciation for these precious truths that are the common treasure of all Christians in God's Word. At the same time, Reformed Christianity is more than five points. There is a tendency in conservative American Protestantism toward reducing the richness of the faith to a few fundamentals.

CATHOLIC, EVANGELICAL, AND REFORMED

If the tendency of some in our day is to dilute the definition, the danger at the other extreme is toward isolation. It has become a habit to speak of "the Reformed faith," but properly speaking there is no such thing. There is only the *Christian* faith, which is founded on the teaching of the prophets and apostles, with Jesus Christ as its cornerstone. It is better, then, to speak of the Reformed confession of the Christian faith. Reformed churches do not add any new doctrines to the Christian faith, but claim that they are merely recovering the clear teachings of Scripture that had become obscured in the medieval church.

Not even the "five points" are believed to be doctrines that set us apart from other churches; rather, they are our confession of the articles that all Christians confess in the ecumenical creeds. In short, we believe that the Reformed confession most faithfully articulates what we mean by "God the Father Almighty," Jesus Christ and his saving work, the Spirit's person and work, the forgiveness of sins, "one holy, catholic, and apostolic church," and the last judgment, resurrection, and "life everlasting."

This point may be best explained with the following illustration:

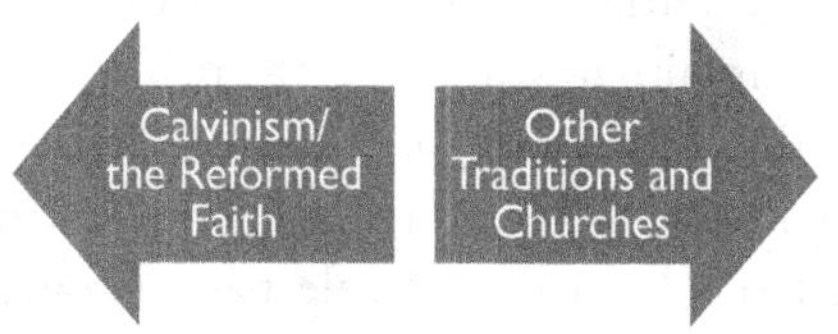

"Reformed" Defined by Distinctive Doctrines

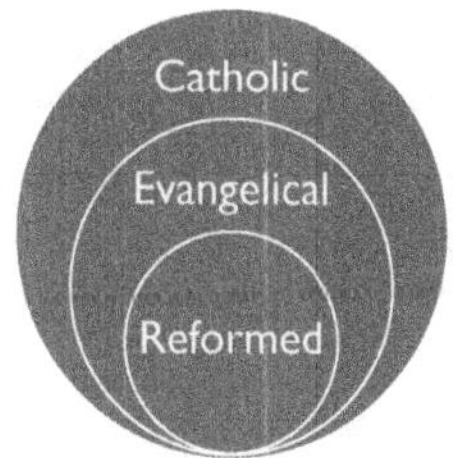

"Reformed" Defined by Distinctive Formulations

In the first model, we define what it means to be Reformed by what we believe and teach that others do not. This approach is encouraged by reducing Reformed theory to TULIP. As Kenneth Stewart has shown recently, there is no evidence of this acronym being used before the twentieth century.[1] The tendencies of this approach are obvious: pride and sectarian isolation. Of course, we do have to testify to what we believe the Scriptures do teach and also to reject errors. Especially in an eclectic age, when people pick and choose the components of their faith cafeteria-style, it's important to say not only, "This we believe," but also, "Therefore, this we deny." We can't just add sheets of paper to our three-ringed binder without realizing that when we add certain pages, others need to be pulled out. We need to think consistently about our faith and practice, in faithfulness to the self-consistent Lord who addresses us in Scripture. Nevertheless, we are not defined merely by what we are not, but by what we are eager to confess together on the basis of God's Word.

In the second model, Reformed convictions are *elaborations* of *Christian* faith and practice. We teach some doctrines that other Christians reject. However, even these distinctive teachings are intended to buttress convictions that are shared by the church at large. For example, total depravity represents a clear articulation of the doctrine of original sin. Particular redemption (or, traditionally, limited atonement), perhaps the most distinctive (and controversial) petal of the TULIP, is not an isolated dogma. Rather, it articulates a more precise understanding of what Scripture means when it teaches that Christ's work actually saves all for whom he died. When we confess our faith in Christ for "the remission of sins," we intend many of the same things that non-Reformed Christians affirm, but we are also confessing something more definite: namely, that Christ's death on the cross was intended to redeem all of the elect and accomplished this goal.

All Christians believe in the new birth, but Calvinists believe that it is a gift that God gives us so that we will believe, not because we believed. Calvinists not only confess with the whole church that we are saved and kept by God's grace, but that God's grace alone ensures that everyone who is redeemed and renewed will persevere to the end.

Reformed teaching, then, draws on its own specific interpretations while nevertheless aiming at doctrines that are embraced by the whole church. This means, on one hand, that we confess the same faith as the whole church and, on the other hand, that on virtually every point we affirm some things that are more controversial or distinctive. I would argue that this is true of every Christian tradition. In my view, this second model helps us to understand Reformed Christianity as a distinctive tradition that nevertheless aims at a common confession and interpretation of the faith.

First, to be Reformed is to be *catholic*—that is, a living expression of Christ's visible church that affirms the ecumenical creeds on the basis of Scripture. The formative English Puritan William Perkins was not speaking out of school when he titled one of his doctrinal summaries *The Reformed Catholic* (1597). Reformed Christians are not restorationists. That is, they do not believe that the Reformation was a break from catholic Christianity, or that the church had ceased to exist until the Reformers came along. Rather, they believe in "one holy, catholic, and apostolic church" that was reformed according to God's Word and stands in constant need of being reformed by that Word until Christ returns.

Unlike myriad sects, we do not regard our congregations or denominations as the only true church, but as part of the catholic church across all times and places. For example, Reformed theology is deeply trinitarian, and this is especially evident in the prominence it gives to the covenant of redemption: that eternal pact between the Father, the Son, and the Spirit for the salvation of the elect. Each person is engaged in our election, redemption, calling, and preservation in grace. However, this merely highlights a belief in the Trinity that all Christians profess.

Second, to be Reformed is to be *evangelical*, not in the sense of a party label or social movement, but as those who believe, confess, and spread the good news of God's saving work in Jesus Christ. Not all who regularly confess the Apostles' or Nicene Creed believe that "the remission of sins" requires at its heart belief in justification by grace alone through faith alone, but this is essential to an evangelical confession of that article. And not all who affirm that salvation is by grace alone share the Reformed conviction that this evangelical confession is inextricably linked to the scriptural teaching of unconditional election. Even when we are defending distinctly Reformed formulations, our goal is to confess the catholic and *evangelical* faith.

The key theses of the Reformation are often summarized by the "solas": Scripture alone (*sola scriptura*) is the source and norm of Christian faith and practice, and this Word proclaims a salvation that is by God's grace alone (*sola gratia*), in Christ alone (*solo Christo*), through faith alone (*sola fide*). Consequently, all of the glory goes to God alone (*soli Deo gloria*). Every distinctive feature of Reformed theology or Calvinism is aimed at clarifying and defending this evangelical core of Christianity, with the goal of reconciling sinners to God in Christ for true worship of the triune God.

DOES CALVINISM HAVE A CENTRAL DOGMA?

Impatient with complexity, we often try to reduce major systems and traditions to a central idea. If Calvinism can be reduced to "five points," why not just one? Some—both friends and foes (mostly the latter)—have argued that Calvinism is a orderly system deduced logically from the central dogma of predestination or the sovereignty of God. Happily, this thesis is coming to rack and ruin among scholars. However, it takes a while for the news to get out.

There are a few good reasons for challenging the popular assumption that predestination is Calvinism's central dogma.

First, Calvin was not the first Calvinist. The standard medieval view affirmed unconditional election and reprobation and held that Christ's redemptive work at the cross is "sufficient for the world, efficient for the elect alone." Furthermore, the new birth occurred by grace alone, apart from any human cooperation (although this was identified with baptismal regeneration), and none of the elect could finally be lost. On even the most controversial aspects of predestination, Calvin's view can scarcely be distinguished from that of Augustine, Bernard of Clairvaux, Archbishop Thomas Bradwardine, and Gregory of Rimini. If the "five points" are sufficient to define a Calvinist, Thomas Aquinas comes pretty close.

Yet these formal agreements hide deep differences over the meaning of grace, merit, and justification. The leader of the Augustinian Order in Germany, Johann von Staupitz, wrote a marvelous defense titled "On the Eternal Predestination of God," and his famous pupil, Martin Luther, defended it in *The Bondage of the Will* and his first edition of the commentary on Romans. Calvin introduces nothing novel in his treatments of the subject. In fact, some of Luther's strong comments in *The Bondage of the Will* make Calvin moderate by comparison.

By temperament and intent, the Genevan Reformer was conservative. His genius lay not in his creativity and innovative spirit. In fact, his arguments against the corruption in his day evidence a concern that the church had allowed relatively recent novelties to bury the simplicity of the apostolic faith and practice that continued into the early centuries of the church. Calvin also warned frequently against speculation—particularly on this subject.

The strength of Calvin's contribution was his ability to integrate the orthodox convictions of historic Christianity with the evangelical clarity of Luther, and to refine the insights of his fellow Reformers in a pastorally rich interpretation of Scripture. Like Luther, Calvin believed that the doctrine of unconditional election exalted God's glorious grace, providing a crucial support to the doctrine of justification. For the Genevan Reformer, predestination—when defined by Scripture alone—was a practical doctrine, affording tremendous assurance for all who are in Christ. It is the fodder for praise and thanksgiving, not for controversy and speculation.

Second, Calvin was not the only shaper of the Reformed tradition. Although his formative influence is justly recognized, he regarded himself as a student of Luther. The Strasbourg Reformer Martin Bucer also left a decisive imprint on Calvin, as on a whole generation, including Archbishop Thomas Cranmer. Calvin was also a friend of Luther's associate, Philip Melanchthon (although he, like the orthodox Lutherans, was alarmed by Philip's later turn to synergism). Heinrich Bullinger, John Knox, Jan Łaski (John à Lasco), Girolamo Zanchi, and Peter Martyr Vermigli were also among the many contemporaries of Calvin who shaped Reformed teaching, not to mention the following generations of leaders who refined and consolidated the gains of the sixteenth century. Reformed Christians who taught predestination did not rely on Calvin any more than on various other sources. Far more than Lutheranism, Reformed theology was a "team sport," whose faith and practice were shaped by international cooperation among many figures whose names are now largely forgotten.

Third, it is interesting that John Calvin never identified predestination or election as a central dogma. He spoke of the doctrine of justification as "the primary article of the Christian religion," "the main hinge on which religion turns," "the principal article of the whole doctrine of salvation and the foundation of all religion."[2] Obviously, he considered predestination an important doctrine. But he was not only unoriginal in his formulation; he did not raise it to the level of a central dogma. Predestination does not even appear in his Geneva Confession (1536), although the necessity of baptizing covenant children is explicitly mentioned, as well as the meaning of the Lord's Supper.

In fact, divine election is asserted more directly in the Thirty-Nine Articles of the Church of England than in the Heidelberg Catechism. In these statements, like many other Reformed confessions and catechisms of the period, the focus is on the essential articles of the Christian faith—

particularly where it differed from Roman Catholic and Anabaptist interpretations. Arminius was not even born.

However, Calvin was challenged directly in Geneva by outspoken opponents of the doctrine and engaged them in extended polemics. These debates reflect the greater attention Calvin gave the subject with each new edition of the *Institutes.* Yet even in the final 1559 edition, predestination is nothing like a central dogma and follows on the heels of a richly devotional treatment of prayer. As B. B. Warfield pointed out, Calvin's emphasis on God's fatherly love and benevolence in Christ is more pervasive than his emphasis on God's sovereign power and authority.

Subsequent disturbances in Reformed churches, especially the rise of Arminianism, provoked fresh controversies. As was true in the controversies over the Trinity, the deity of Christ, and the nature of grace in the ancient church, challenges always give rise to greater refinement. The Belgic Confession (1561) summarizes election in a few rich but sparse sentences. However, with rising challenges within Lutheran and Reformed circles over predestination, more had to be said. While rejecting reprobation, orthodox Lutherans raised unconditional election to confessional status in the Formula of Concord (1580), the Synod of Dort was called in 1618–1619 to settle the Arminian debate, and the Westminster Assembly incorporated the conclusions of Dort into its Confession (1646).

None of this is to diminish the obvious importance of election in Reformed theology, but it does serve to dissuade us from regarding it as a central dogma or as a uniquely Calvinistic tenet. No one began with predestination as the heart of Reformed theology; it gained importance to the extent that it was challenged from within.

The truth is, there isn't a central dogma in Calvinism, although it is certainly God-centered—and, more specifically, Christ-centered, since it is only in the Son that God's saving purposes and action in history are most clearly revealed. Yet even in this case, Christ does not serve as a central idea or thesis from which we deduce other doctrines. Rather, we are taught by Scripture itself to find Christ at its center from Genesis to Revelation.

With Melanchthon and Bullinger leading the way, covenant theology emerged as the very warp and woof of Reformed theology.[3] Even this is not a central dogma, however, but more like the architectural framework. As B. B. Warfield explains, "The architectonic principle of the Westminster Confession is its federal [covenant] theology, which had obtained by this time in Britain, as on the Continent, a dominant position as the most commodious mode of presenting the corpus of Reformed doctrine."[4] Although I am focusing on the "five points," it is my hope that readers, beginning with these marvelous doctrines of grace, will investigate the depths and breadth of Reformed teaching and practice.

A MAP OF THEOLOGICAL POSITIONS

Having offered a definition of Calvinism, it is worthwhile to draw a map of the different views that I will refer to from time to time throughout this book. Just as Calvinism has often been caricatured by its critics and distorted by extreme advocates, the same is true of Arminianism. Often, it is simply equated with Semi-Pelagianism or even Pelagianism, but a clearer picture will help us both to be more honest and to engage in real rather than imagined differences.

First, let's define *Pelagianism*. A monk living in Rome (possibly of British origin) between 354 and 440, Pelagius emphasized in his preaching the importance of free will and good works in determining final salvation. Pelagianism has been identified historically with a denial of original sin and the necessity of grace for salvation. Condemned by several popes and councils (Carthage in 418; Ephesus in 431), Pelagianism represented Adam as a bad example and Christ as a good example. God is gracious in that he sets before the human race the opportunity for life or death and has endowed everyone with the power of free choice for good or evil. Through constant exhortations and instructions, one may be brought to repentance and faith and continue in the life of good works that finally merits everlasting life.

Second, *Semi-Pelagianism* arose as a modification. Although it did not accept original sin, this view taught that the fall weakened the moral nature of human beings so that they required strengthening grace. The initial act of responding to God is due to free will, but grace assists the believer in a life of faith and good works. This view was condemned at the Council of Orange in 529. This council declared that grace is necessary at the beginning as well as throughout the Christian life. Given the popular views often held by evangelicals today, the following citation is worth quoting at length:

> If anyone says that the grace of God can be conferred as a result of human prayer, but that it is not grace itself which makes us pray to

> God, he contradicts the prophet Isaiah, or the Apostle who says the same thing, "I was found by them that did not seek Me; I appeared openly to them that asked not after Me." If anyone maintains that God awaits our will to be cleansed from sin, but does not confess that even our will to be cleansed comes to us through the infusion and working of the Holy Spirit, he opposeth the Holy Spirit Himself who says through Solomon, "The will is prepared by the Lord." If anyone says that not only the increase of faith but also its beginning and the very desire for faith, by which we believe—if anyone says that this belongs to us naturally and not by a gift of grace, that is, by the inspiration of the Holy Spirit amending our will and turning it from unbelief to faith and from godlessness to godliness, it is proof that he is opposed to the teaching of the Apostles.... For those who state that faith by which we believe in God is our own make all who are separated from the Church of Christ in some measure believers.... If anyone says that we can form any right opinion or make any right choice which relates to the salvation of eternal life, or that we can be saved, that is, assent to the preaching of the gospel through our own powers ... he is led away by a heretical spirit.... If anyone maintains that he comes through free will, it is proof that he has no place in the true faith.[5]

Pelagianism arose primarily as a reaction against *Augustinianism*. As the bishop of the North African city of Hippo, the mature Augustine (354–430) was profoundly drawn to the theology of grace. His controversy with Pelagius served to sharpen his insights as he, along with Jerome and other church fathers, refined the Western church's formulation of original sin, predestination, the atonement, and the perseverance of the saints in grace. Like most of us, Augustine did not start out confessing the doctrines of grace. Rather, he became more interested in searching the Scriptures on these points especially as he encountered challenges and wrestled with his own heart. From beginning to end, Augustine concluded, salvation is by grace alone. The fallen will, bound to sin, is unable even to seek God's grace apart from the grace that he gives to his elect. Augustinianism was virtually equivalent to orthodoxy in the West, although it always encountered fresh opposition.

With these coordinates in mind, we turn now to movements arising out of the Reformation. Luther's debate with Erasmus over the freedom of the will and divine election underscored the sovereignty of God's grace in election and reprobation.[6] The Lutheran confessions, however, affirm God's unconditional election of those on whom he will have mercy but deny his reprobation of the rest as an actual decree. While confessional Lutheran and Reformed theologies differ with respect to the decree of reprobation, the extent of the atonement, and the resistibility of God's grace, they are united in their defense of *monergism* (i.e., God alone working in salvation), grounded in his unconditional election of sinners in Jesus Christ.[7] Calvinists question the consistency of monergism in the Lutheran system, however, and I refer to some examples in the following chapters.

At last we arrive at *Arminianism*. A student of Calvin's successor Theodore Beza, Jacob (James) Arminius first attracted attention when he denied that Paul's description of the struggling person in Romans 7 could possibly refer to a genuine believer. Eventually, he came to reject a particular election, redemption, and effectual calling of the elect in favor of conditional election.

After his death, Arminius's followers offered their Articles of Remonstrance to the Reformed Church in the Netherlands. In it, they affirmed total depravity and the necessity of prevenient grace (that is, grace that "goes before" all of our actions). However, they held that this grace is given to everyone and that it is consequently in the power of every person either to accept or reject the gospel by their own free will. God has chosen those whom he foresaw would believe, Christ died to make salvation possible for every person, the Spirit's regenerating work may be resisted, and even believers may so resist the Spirit's sanctifying work that they are finally lost.[8]

Roger Olson points out that Arminius was still working within the covenantal paradigm of Reformed theology: "The difference between Arminius's federal theology and that of the continental Calvinists (and the British Puritans) is the former's conditionality and the latter's absoluteness."[9] This difference proved decisive, which is why many Calvinists saw (and see) Arminianism as synonymous with "neo-nomianism"—that is, turning the gospel into a new law.

In comparison with Calvinism, the Arminian system seems closer to Semi-Pelagianism. In fact, I would argue that it lists in that direction. Whenever Arminianism loses its evangelical way, it is always in a "Pelagianizing" direction. Nevertheless, it is important to state the actual views that people hold rather than the views that we think they should hold or will hold if their logic is followed consistently. The crucial difference between Arminianism and Semi-Pelagianism is that the former insists upon the necessity of grace prior to all human response. At least as Arminius taught it, Arminianism does not deny original sin or the inability of human beings to save themselves. Nevertheless, Arminians do hold that sufficient prevenient grace is given to all people to exercise their free will, and election is based on God's foreknowledge of those who will in fact cooperate with his grace in faith and good works. Final salvation is dependent to some extent on one's cooperation with God's grace.[10]

Arminians themselves affirm that "synergism" is the appropriate term for this system's view of salvation. However, Roger Olson distinguishes helpfully between "evangelical Arminians" (of the heart) and "liberal Arminians" (of the head). Representing the latter, Philip Limborch (1633–1712) taught that the fall perverted our mind but not our will.[11] Historically, liberal Arminianism usually merged into Socinianism (see below) or what we know as Unitarian Universalism. A more evangelical Arminianism is represented among Anglicans like Jeremy Taylor, William Law, and John Wesley and some non-Conformist Puritans like Richard Baxter and John Goodwin.

The Calvinist-Arminian divide is evident not only between Protestant denominations, but cuts across them as well: General Baptists, influenced by Mennonite communities, often in a more explicitly Semi-Pelagian direction, and Calvinistic Baptists (see the London/Philadelphia Confession of 1644); Wesleyan and Calvinistic Methodists (the latter following George Whitefield); Old School and New School Presbyterians (the latter following Nathaniel Taylor and Charles Finney).

Going well beyond Arminianism, radical Protestantism generated another position that is important to mention. Named after Laelius Socinus (d. 1562), *Socinianism* not only denied God's predestination, but also God's exhaustive foreknowledge of the free actions of creatures, which Arminians and Calvinists both affirmed.[12] As the fountainhead of Unitarianism, the Socinian movement also denied the Trinity and the deity and preexistence of the Son. Therefore, Socinianism represented a revival of Pelagian and Arian heresies. Through the energetic efforts of Laelius's nephew Faustus (d. 1604), the tenets of Socinianism became widely influential in the thinking of Newton, Locke, Voltaire, Lessing, Kant, and other Enlightenment figures.

Now that we have a broader view of Calvinism's contours and a map of rival positions, we are prepared to explore the scriptural arguments.

TWO

OF REGENTS AND REBELS: THE HUMAN CONDITION

Far from the caricature of a system whose logic dissolves mystery, Calvinism recognizes the paradox that lies at the heart of every great doctrine of the faith. It affirms simultaneously God's unity and trinity, Christ's divinity and humanity, God's sovereignty and human responsibility. Believers are urged with all seriousness to work out their own salvation, and yet this salvation is already assured as a gift from the Father, in the Son, through the Spirit. The kingdom of Christ is present now, inaugurated by Christ's resurrection, and yet not fully consummated until he returns. Ignoring these tensions (the irrationalist temptation) or resolving these tensions (the rationalistic temptation) are always easy options. Living in the tension is more difficult: listening where God has spoken, but restraining our curiosity beyond his Word.

Another paradox appears in Calvinism's view of human nature. In my reading, no theological system has been more affirming of this world and human nature as such while being so profoundly struck by the misery of fallen existence. In fact, this tragic character of our corrupt existence is measured by the height from which we have fallen and the glorious future that awaits us at Christ's return.

GOD'S GLORIOUS IMAGE-BEARER: HUMAN DIGNITY

Calvinism teaches that human beings are basically good in their intrinsic nature, endowed with free will, beauty of body and soul, reason, and moral excellence. In short, we are created in God's image. Now, that might not fit the stereotype, especially when the famous "TULIP" starts with Total Depravity. However, Reformed theology never starts with the fall, but with God's good creation. If we start with total depravity, we easily assume that human beings are just rotten from the beginning, without any goodness, integrity, or free will. However, Calvinists believe that this is a grave distortion of the matter and will lead inevitably to a misunderstanding of total depravity.

Calvin began his *Institutes of the Christian Religion* with the famous lines:

> Nearly all the wisdom we possess, that is to say, true and sound wisdom, consists of two parts: the knowledge of God and of ourselves. But, while joined by many bonds, which one precedes and brings forth the other is not easy to discern. In the first place, no one can look upon himself without immediately turning his thoughts to the contemplation of God, in whom he "lives and moves" [Acts 17:28]. For, quite clearly, the mighty gifts with which we are endowed are hardly from ourselves; indeed, our very being is nothing but subsistence in the one God. Then, by these benefits shed like dew from heaven upon us, we are led as by rivulets to the spring itself.[1]

How could it be otherwise, since human beings are created in the image and likeness of God (Gen. 1:26–27)? When we marvel at human intelligence, wisdom, intentional acts of kindness, and love of social relations, and when we examine the intricacies and abilities of the human body, we can only exclaim with the psalmist, "For you formed my inward parts; you knitted me together in my mother's womb. I praise you, for I am fearfully and wonderfully made. Wonderful are your works; my soul knows it very well" (Ps. 139:13–14).

In fact, Calvin and his heirs have criticized Roman Catholic theology for locating sin in an alleged weakness of human nature itself. According to this view, human beings are related to God and the angels by virtue of their "higher self"—the mind or soul—but are related to other animals by virtue of their "lower self"—the appetites associated with the body. This idea, influenced by Plato, gave rise to the notion of *concupiscence*: that is, the desires of the body for sensual pleasure. Concupiscence is not itself sin until it is acted upon, but it does suggest a weakness or defect in human nature as created by God.

Aquinas, following Augustine, spoke of this concupiscence as the "kindling wood" for the fire of passion that leads to actual sins. However, this inclination is not itself sinful, and free will—though weakened—is still able to cooperate with grace toward its healing.[2] The married life is not evil but lower than the contemplative life of the monk, and sexual relations within marriage are for procreative purposes alone, not for sensual pleasure. It is this sensual (animal) aspect of our constitution that drags us down from the heights of pure spiritual contemplation.

The most fundamental problem with this view, says Calvin, is that it attributes sin to human nature as God created it. Against those "who dare write God's name upon their faults," Calvin says, "they perversely search out God's handiwork in their own pollution, when they ought rather to have sought it in that unimpaired and uncorrupted nature of Adam." Not God, but we are guilty "solely because we have degenerated from our original condition." Our mortal wound comes not from nature itself, but from its corruption through the fall.[3] The depravity of human nature "did not flow from nature," he says. "Thus vanishes the foolish trifling of the Manichees [Gnostics], who, when they imagined wickedness of substance in man, dared fashion another creator for him in order that they might not seem to assign the cause and beginning of evil to the righteous God."[4]

Concerning Adam's fall, Calvin adds:

> For not only did a lower appetite seduce him, but unspeakable impiety occupied the very citadel of his mind, and pride penetrated to the depths of his heart. Thus it is pointless and foolish to restrict the corruption that arises thence only to what are called the impulses of the senses; or to call it the "kindling wood" that attracts, arouses, and drags into sin only that part which they term "sensuality." In this matter Peter Lombard has betrayed his complete ignorance. For, in seeking and searching out its seat, he says that it lies in the flesh, as Paul testifies; yet not intrinsically, but because it appears more in the flesh. As if Paul were indicating that only a part of the soul, and not its entire nature, is opposed to supernatural grace!

Rather, says Calvin, Paul teaches that the whole person is created in God's image and in that same wholeness is fallen as well as redeemed.[5]

So Calvin rejects the body-soul dualism that tends to identify sin with the former. Rather, the image of God pertains no less to the body than to the soul, and it consists primarily of "true righteousness and holiness" (Eph. 4:24; Col. 3:10). Though not yet confirmed in everlasting immortality and holiness, Adam and Eve were good creatures, reflecting the moral attributes of the triune God.[6] Just as the dignity of the image of

God settled on the body as well as the soul, after the fall, "no part is free from the infection of sin."[7] The mind is no less fallen than the affections or the body.

Furthermore, the image of God is not just an individualistic concept; it is the corporate identity of the human race as God's covenant partner. This means that each person must "freely embrace the other as his own flesh.... Any inequality which is contrary to this arrangement is nothing else than a corruption of nature which proceeds from sin."[8]

God's liberality is evident in the diversity of creation that he puts at the disposal of his human partner.[9] The ingratitude that Scripture imputes to fallen humanity is revealed in the fact that, like Adam and Eve, we do not want a liberal *provision* of gifts from a good God; we want to *be* God ourselves. So the fall was due not to natural failure (a weakness of created nature), but to moral failure. This high view of human dignity has always encouraged Calvinists to contribute to the defense of human rights and civic welfare.[10]

A SHATTERED IMAGE

Calvin believed that freedom of choice was an important gift of God to humans in creation. "In this integrity man by free will had the power, if he so willed, to attain eternal life. Here it would be out of place to raise the question of God's secret predestination because our present subject is not what can happen or not, but what man's nature was like. Therefore Adam could have stood if he wished, seeing that he fell solely by his own will." There was no inherent propensity toward sin in human nature as God created it, no dangerous lure of the lower self. Adam's faculties "were rightly composed to obedience, until in destroying himself he corrupted his own blessings."[11]

The problem comes when we extrapolate from this natural and original integrity a liberty of the will to choose the good after the fall:

> Hence the great obscurity faced by the philosophers, for they were seeking in a ruin for a building, and in scattered fragments for a well-knit structure. They held this principle, that man would not be a rational animal unless he possessed free choice of good and evil; also it entered their minds that the distinction between virtues and vices would be obliterated if man did not order his life by his own planning. Well reasoned so far—if there had been no change in man.

But since this was hidden from them, it is not wonder they mix up heaven and earth![12]

Calvin's point is crucial. When he (like Luther) speaks of the bondage of the will, it is in relation to *sin*, not to *God's sovereignty*. As created, human beings were completely free to choose good or evil, truth or error, God or idols. God's freedom is not a threat to human freedom, but the very presupposition of the latter's existence. However, after the fall, people are bent toward unbelief and sin. The heart chooses that which it approves and desires. A person who is dead in "trespasses and sins" (Eph. 2:1) and "does not accept the things of the Spirit of God, for they are folly to him, and he is not able to understand them because they are spiritually discerned" (1 Cor. 2:14) has lost this freedom for righteousness before God.

At the same time, the fall has not destroyed the will any more than it has destroyed the mind, the senses, or any other faculty. Rather, it has corrupted every faculty. Adam and Eve had the freedom to choose immortal life, but in breaking covenant with God, they and their posterity became a race of rebels: born in corruption, guilt, and death.

Reformed theology, therefore, focuses its attention squarely on the history that God's revelation interprets to us. Human nature is not determined by philosophical speculations about a higher or lower aspect, but by the historical events of the creation and the fall. It is the concrete act of covenant-breaking that marks the descent of humanity into guilt and corruption.

The Canons of the Synod of Dort begin with the dignity of creation: "Man was originally formed after the image of God. His understanding was adorned with a true and saving knowledge of his Creator, and of spiritual things; his heart and will were upright, all his affections pure, and the whole man was holy." Only after saying this did the divines assembled at Dort think it possible to add, "But, revolting from God by the instigation of the devil and *by his own free will*, he forfeited these excellent gifts; and in the place thereof became involved in blindness of mind, horrible darkness, vanity, and perverseness of judgment; became wicked, rebellious, and obdurate in heart and will, and impure in his affections."[13]

The same dual emphasis is found in the Belgic Confession, where, after commenting on the image of God, it is added, "But being in honor, he understood it not, neither knew his excellency, but willfully subjected himself to sin and consequently to death and the curse, giving ear to the words of the devil." Transgressing "the commandment of life," he "corrupted his whole nature" and "lost all his excellent gifts which he had received from God, and retained only small remains thereof, which, however, are sufficient to leave man without excuse."[14] The same affirmation of created dignity and total corruption appears in the Heidelberg Catechism (Q. 6) and in the Westminster Confession (Ch. IV.2) and its catechisms (Shorter, Q. 10, 15–19).

Therefore, "total depravity" is something that happens to human nature, not something that arises from it as created by God. "This is the inherited corruption," says Calvin, "which the church fathers termed 'original sin,' meaning by the word 'sin,' the depravation of a nature previously good and pure."[15] He appeals to the double imputation in Romans 5—i.e., the parallel between Adam and Christ. If human corruption is simply a matter of imitating Adam's trespass, then salvation comes by imitating Christ's good example.[16] Calvin refuses to become mired in the finer historical debates over the transmission of the soul from one generation to another, content to assert with Scripture that Adam stood as the covenantal representative for the human race.[17] Original sin includes both guilt and corruption.[18] This teaching is so clearly taught in Scripture that it is affirmed by Roman Catholics and historic Protestants alike.

Where Lutheran and Reformed teaching diverges from Rome concerns the depth and extent of this corruption. In addition to denying that concupiscence (the sinful inclination) is in any way due to a weakness of nature (i.e., the body and its desires), Reformation theology holds that the sinful inclination itself incurs God's judgment, and this inclination not only weakens but imprisons the whole person. No one can overcome this inclination through free will. Cooperation with grace will not heal the soul. From the sinful condition proceed sinful acts.

David, for example, realized that his grievous offenses against God, Bathsheba, and her husband, Uriah, were not just random acts but flowed from his heart: "In sin did my mother conceive me" (Ps. 51:5). Isaiah recognized that he was by nature "a rebel" from birth (Isa. 48:8). "Sin came into the world through one man," said Paul, "and death through sin, and so death spread to all men because all sinned ... many died through one man's trespass ... [and] the judgment following one trespass brought condemnation ... because of one man's trespass, death reigned through that one man." Therefore, he concludes, "one trespass led to condemnation for all men" (Rom. 5:12–18). Rome affirms that Adam's transgression is imputed to the whole race, leading to condemnation, but denies that this guilt includes the sinful inclination and that this inclination has so corrupted the mind and will that cooperation with grace is impossible prior to regeneration.

Our sober evaluation of the crisis has to account for the fact that "both Jews and Greeks are under sin, as it is written: 'None is righteous, no, not one; no one understands; no one seeks for God. All have turned aside; together they have become worthless; no one does good, not even one" (Rom. 3:9–12). We are "by nature children of wrath" (Eph. 2:3), "slave to sin" (John 8:34), and Jesus said, "No one can come to me unless the Father who sent me draws him" (John 6:44). We come into the world "dead in ... trespasses and sins" (Eph. 2:1). Though bound, we approve our slavery and try to justify it as freedom.

How Total Is Total Depravity?

"Total depravity" is often misunderstood. As understood in Reformation theology, it does not mean that each of us has committed every possible sin or that everyone is equally depraved in terms of outward actions. What it does mean is that everyone is equally guilty and condemned and that there is no aspect of our existence that is unscathed or open to God's grace. No less than our bodies and desires, our mind, heart, and will are under the command of sin and death. The "total" in total depravity refers to its extensiveness, not intensiveness: that is, to the all-encompassing scope of our fallenness. It does not mean that we are as bad as we can possibly be, but that we are all guilty and corrupt to such an extent that there is no hope of pulling ourselves together, brushing ourselves off, and striving (with the help of grace) to overcome God's judgment and our own rebellion.

The Reformers agreed the image of God pertained to the whole person and the whole person was corrupted by the fall. Yet they differed on the extent to which the original image itself was lost. For Lutherans, the fall so corrupted human nature that there is no vestige of the image of God; it has been entirely lost and can only be restored by redemption in Jesus Christ.[19] Again, Calvin's concern to uphold the integrity of God's creation is exhibited in his refusal to accept a total eradication of the divine image. In fact, particularly against the radical Anabaptists, Calvin offers a challenge that is worth quoting at length:

> Whenever we come upon these matters in secular writers, let that admirable light of truth shining in them teach us that the mind of man, though fallen and perverted from its wholeness, is nevertheless clothed and ornamented with God's excellent gifts. If we regard the Spirit of God as the sole fountain of truth, we shall neither reject the truth itself, nor despise it wherever it shall appear, unless we wish to dishonor the Spirit of God. For by holding the gifts of the Spirit in such slight esteem, we condemn and reproach the Spirit himself. What then? Shall we deny that the truth shone upon the ancient jurists who established civic order and discipline with such great equity? Shall we say that the philosophers were blind in their fine observation and artful description of nature? Shall we say that those men were devoid of understanding who conceived the art of disputation and taught us to speak reasonably? Shall we say that they are insane who developed medicine, devoting their labor to our benefit? What shall we say of all the mathematical sciences? Shall we consider them the ravings of madmen? No, we cannot read the writings of the ancients on these subjects without great admiration.... Those men whom Scripture calls "natural men" were, indeed, sharp and penetrating in their investigation of inferior things. Let us, accordingly, learn by their example how many gifts the Lord left to human nature even after it was despoiled of its true good.[20]

The Spirit is at work savingly in the elect, but also in common grace toward the reprobate.[21]

Luther too could speak of the potential for unregenerate humanity in "things earthly," but Calvin saw this as evidence not of the neutrality or indifference of earthly things in relation to God and his kingdom, but of the ineradicable and indelible imprint of God's image. Indeed, this is why humanity remains in some sense God's image-bearer and covenant partner, even though in their sinfulness they are filled with idolatry and sophisticated schemes of religious distortion. Fallen human beings are not irreligious but idolatrous. The image must be suppressed because it is still there. Like a mirror that reveals a reflection that we do not want to see, it must be distorted, covered over, and smeared with mud. Because it reflects the God whose existence stands over against us in judgment, the image of God is no longer redolent of high office, but is a burden to be cast off. Precisely because it cannot be eradicated, it is disfigured beyond recognition.

Again, this gives to Calvin's doctrine of sin an irreducibly ethical determination. In the fall, humanity lost nothing of its created nature. There is no missing "part"—no weak faculty—that could account for disobedience.

> Because of the bondage of sin by which the will is held bound, it cannot move toward good, much less apply itself thereto; for a movement of this sort is the beginning of conversion to God, which in Scripture is ascribed entirely to God's grace.... Nonetheless the will remains, with the most eager inclination disposed and hastening to sin. For man, when he gave himself over to this necessity, was not deprived of will, but of soundness of will.... Therefore simply to will is of man; to will ill, of a corrupt nature; to will well, of grace.[22]

This requires a distinction between *necessity* and *compulsion*. Freedom has reference to (a) compulsion, (b) sin, and (c) misery. We have freedom from compulsion, but not from sin and misery.[23]

According to Peter's sermon in Acts 2, Christ was delivered up according to God's predestined purpose. Therefore, it was necessary that Christ be crucified, since God had decreed it from all eternity. Nevertheless, Peter does not exonerate human beings from their culpability, since they were not compelled by any external force.

We are not free to choose whether or not we will be sinners, but in every sinful thought, desire, and action we are doing what we want to do. We are not compelled to sin. Just as God's immunity to sin derives from his own natural goodness rather than any external compulsion, so the reverse is true for sinners. Over against the medieval theologian Peter Lombard, Calvin appeals to Bernard of Clairvaux's argument that human beings are "oppressed by no other yoke than that of a kind of voluntary servitude." So, Calvin argues, fallen human beings are "not deprived of will, but of soundness of will."[24]

So do Calvinists believe that people have the ability to do what God commands? Do they at least have the ability to believe in Christ of their own free will? There are two distinctions that later Calvinists drew that are important for understanding what we mean by total depravity.

First, we need to distinguish between natural and moral ability. A libertarian view of human freedom insists on nothing less than the ability to choose anything. However, this means that the will is free not only from external compulsion but from the person who is exercising it! In other words, it assumes that the will is independent of the mind, preferences, character, and heart of persons. Yet not even God has this kind of freedom of will. God cannot choose to do evil or to tempt anyone to do evil. He can only choose that which is consistent with his nature. Nevertheless, we acknowledge God's freedom while recognizing that he is incapable of sin or error. God is free to be God; he cannot choose to be someone else.

Before the fall, humankind had the natural *and* moral ability to obey God with complete fidelity and freedom of will. After the fall, we still have the natural but no longer the moral liberty to do so. When it comes to our fallen condition, we all have the natural ability to think, will, feel, and do what we should. None of our faculties has been lost. We have all of the "equipment" necessary for loving God and our neighbors. Nevertheless, the fall has rendered us morally incapable of using these gifts in a way that could restore us to God's favor. I could choose to dedicate myself to becoming a marathon runner, but I cannot choose to dedicate myself to God apart from his grace.

Even in our rebellion, we are exercising the very faculties that God created good, yet we are employing them in a perverse way. We are not weak in our misuse of these gifts, but willful and energetic. The fall has not taken away our ability to will in the least, but only the moral ability to will that which is acceptable to God. It's not a question of *whether* we choose, but of *what* we choose. The Pharisees thought that they were free, but Jesus told them, "Truly, truly, I say to you, everyone who commits sin is a slave to sin" (John 8:34). Sounds kind of extreme, doesn't it? Yet it plumbs the depth of our condition. "Woe to you, scribes and Pharisees, hypocrites! For you clean the outside of the cup and the plate, but inside they are full of greed and self-indulgence" (Matt. 23:25).

"Well, at least her heart was in the right place," we often say of people. As we have seen, medieval theology tended to see the mind or soul as the unsoiled part of human nature. In our romantic and sentimentalized era, it is not the mind as much as the heart that is the locus of purity. The unbiblical idea is that the deeper you go, the better people are. They may be foul on the outside, but they're good inside. Jesus challenges this as hypocrisy. The Lord declared through Jeremiah, "The heart is deceitful above all things, and desperately sick; who can understand it?" (Jer. 17:9).

Our choices are determined by our nature; we choose what we desire and we desire what is most consistent with our nature. If we are bound by sin, then it is not a natural ability that we have lost but a moral ability. We can only choose sin and death—and we really do choose it (John 8:44)—until God liberates us from this bondage. "We admit that man's condition while he still remained upright was such that he could incline to either side. But inasmuch as he has made clear by his example how miserable free will is unless God both wills and is able to work in us, what will happen to us if he imparts his grace to us in this small measure?"[25] Again, it is not that the will is rendered inactive by sin, but that it is bound by sin until grace restores it in a one-sided, unilateral, and unassisted divine act.[26]

Calvin's distinction between necessity and compulsion was developed in Reformed theology in terms of natural versus moral ability. The point of both distinctions is that depravity is natural not in the sense that it belongs to our humanity as created, but in the sense that it is universally inherited. Even after the fall we retain the natural ability to contemplate God in his works because the image of God has not been completely lost, yet the moral ability to render gratitude, true worship, and obedience to God is entirely surrendered to the bondage of sin. Everyone still retains a *sensus divinitatis*: "a sense of divinity which can never be effaced is engraved upon men's minds."[27] In fact, superstition and idolatry are evidence both of this general revelation and its distortion in the fallen heart.[28]

This paradoxical view of the human condition—radiant with glory that is nevertheless smothered and actively effaced by us—is often overlooked by friends as well as critics. Calvin often speaks of remaining "embers," "shining lamps," and "remnants" of the image of God in all people. Total depravity never meant that human beings are as bad as they can be, as if they cannot do anything good, valuable, or praiseworthy in the eyes of fellow creatures. It does not mean that everything that we do apart from faith is equally sinful. It never meant that there is no difference between a serial murderer and a generous nurse.

Yet all of these differences are merely variations on a spectrum of guilt and corruption. Even the best works of the best Christians are still tainted by sin: pride, self-righteousness, a desire for appreciation, or even a good motive—such as love of neighbor—that is not yet good enough, since it does not aim at love of God. The problem goes deeper than this or that act; sin is a *condition* that yields the fruit of death. And this condition is total in its extent. It includes the whole person (body and soul:

thinking, willing, and doing), and it includes all persons (except for Jesus Christ).

Second, we need to distinguish between freedom in relation to God and freedom in relation to other fallen human beings. There is every reason for us to admire people—even non-Christians—who exhibit love and service to their neighbors. However, sin is not only a condition before it is an act; it is determined as *sin* in relation to God before it is an offense against other people. "Against you, you only, have I sinned and done what is evil in your sight," David confessed—even after having committed adultery against Bathsheba and indirectly murdering her husband (Ps. 51:4). Sin is therefore measured by its relation to God, however vicious or virtuous an act may be considered by us. In this light, even the attempt to appease God by our works is sinful, even though the work itself benefits someone else and deserves the approval of other sinners.

In fact, sin is never devoid of good and our best acts are never devoid of sin. Sin is parasitical on goodness. Like Augustine, Calvin thinks of evil not as a creative power of itself, but as a corruption of something that God made—as originally good. Satan cannot create, but can only corrupt. Death is the negation of life and ugliness is the marring of beauty. Stupidity and foolishness are the derangement of an original intelligence and wisdom; injustice, the undoing of justice; error, the distortion of the truth. Sin and evil cannot create, but only destroy. But not destroy *completely*. The rays of God's glory in creation still manage to penetrate through the mud that human beings have smeared onto the mirror, and God's gracious providence (what later Reformed theology would call common grace) enables humanity even in its perversity to arrive at some semblance of truth, goodness, and beauty in things earthly.

Humanity is therefore not as bad as it could possibly be, but as badly off as it could possibly be. We look for some hope of innocence in our intellect, blaming our bodies and senses for corruption, and yet we find that our mind has conceived sins that our hands have not carried out. Perhaps we think that our will is left sufficiently uncorrupted to choose God and that which is good, yet our desires are themselves corrupt. There is no residue of *obedient* piety in us, but only what Calvin called a *sensus divinitatis* (awareness of God) that we exploit for idolatry, self-justification, and superstition. Thus the same remnants of original righteousness that allow even pagans to create a reasonably equitable civic order in things earthly provoke them in their corruption to idolatry in things heavenly.

Perversely, false religion feeds off of God's general revelation, twisting, suppressing, and corrupting it.

Calvin took creation and the fall more seriously. He took issue with the popular notion that God simply holds out his hand in an offer of pardon to those who turn themselves toward him—and that this constitutes the grace of God in regeneration. God's revelation in creation renders us all inexcusable. In it God manifests his glory sufficiently for all people to be held accountable, but because of our blindness we do not see it.[29]

Only by the light of faith can we properly discern even the revelation of God even in creation, Calvin argues, appealing to Hebrews 11:3.[30] Creation is "a glorious theater"; indeed, "wherever you cast your eyes, there is no spot in the universe wherein you cannot discern at least some sparks of his glory."[31] In the theater of this world, "so many burning lamps shine for us in the workmanship of the universe to show forth the glory of its Author. Although they bathe us wholly in their radiance, yet they can of themselves in no way lead us into the right path. Surely they strike some sparks, but before their fuller light shines forth these are smothered."[32]

In general revelation, God's existence, power, wisdom, goodness, and justice are displayed. However, nature does not reveal the gospel, because this good news was only revealed to Adam and Eve after the fall. It's not surprising, then, that there is religion and morality in the world. However, there is no saving benefit in this revelation.

In his Romans commentary, Calvin follows Paul's logic closely: the consequence of human wickedness and suppression of the truth in unrighteousness is not atheism but idolatry, speculation, and the measuring of God's majesty according to human standards.[33] "He then intimates, that they, making a depraved choice, preferred their own vanities to the true God; and thus the error, by which they were deceived, was voluntary."[34] If "the Lord sings to the deaf as long as he does not touch inwardly their hearts," it is only because of our perversity.[35]

God continues to show general or common grace to the wicked. "For this reason, we are not afraid ... to call this man wellborn, that one depraved in nature. Yet we do not hesitate to include both under the universal condition of human depravity."[36] Therefore, in the court of human justice and opinion, there is great diversity. Some people are more vicious, others more virtuous; some more intelligent, artful, just, and generous than others. Yet before God's tribunal, all mouths are stopped. That is Paul's argument in the first three chapters of Romans.

Is God the Author of Sin?

As the quote earlier from the Canons of Dort attests, Calvinism in its official expressions attributes original sin to the transgression of Adam "by his own free will." It is not God's sovereignty that holds human freedom in bondage, but sin. Here, too, confessional Reformed theology is obliged to hold together two apparently conflicting theses: God has decreed whatever comes to pass, yet this in no way infringes on creaturely freedom. It would be easier, of course, for finite intellects to resolve this dilemma in the direction of either human autonomy or fatalism, but the Bible does not allow these options. It is a paradox for the human mind, and it will remain so even in glory.

God is not the author of sin, since he does not directly cause or bring it about. (In his treatment in the *Institutes*, Calvin, like Aquinas, employs the Aristotelian categories of primary and secondary causality.) That is, God does not make, create, or coerce creatures toward evil. This conclusion, in fact, Calvin regards as "blasphemy."[37] At the same time, the fall did not catch God by surprise. From all eternity, God had elected a people from the human race in Christ for eternal life.

The important thing for Calvin is simply to affirm simultaneously that God is neither the author nor the passive victim of creaturely aggression. He cautions:

> Let no one grumble here that God could have provided better for our salvation if he had forestalled Adam's fall. Pious minds ought to loathe this objection, because it manifests inordinate curiosity.... Let us accordingly remember to impute our ruin to depravity of nature, in order that we may not accuse God himself, the Author of nature.[38]

In fact, we only call this corruption "natural" "in order that no man may think that anyone obtains it through bad conduct, since it holds all men fast by hereditary right." Thus, it is not nature itself but its corruption that is in view in the idea of total depravity.[39]

Sin and Grace

We have seen that for Calvin human dignity rather than depravity must be the starting point for anthropology. And just as the dignity of created nature measured the depth to which we have fallen, the stark appraisal of sin was but a prelude to the gospel. Throughout Calvin's discussion of Romans 1–3, it is repeatedly observed that the apostle's grave commentary on human depravity is calculated to drive the sinner to God's mercy in Christ. The purpose was not simply to expose human perversity, but "Paul's object was to teach us where salvation is to be found"—namely, "in the grace of God alone"—in Christ rather than in us.[40]

The targets of Calvin's polemics are "the Pelagians of our own age."[41] At the heart of this heresy, even in its more moderate forms, was the failure to distinguish the nature of humanity as originally created from the state of humanity after the fall. The problem is sin, not nature. We are not saved from nature; rather, our nature is liberated from its bondage to sin and death. For this, though, we need the gospel. "In this ruin of mankind no one now experiences God either as Father or as Author of salvation or favorable in any way, until Christ the Mediator comes forward to reconcile him to us."[42]

> The natural order was that the frame of the universe should be the school in which we were to learn piety, and from it pass over to eternal life and perfect felicity. But after man's rebellion, our eyes—wherever they turn—encounter God's curse.... For even if God wills to manifest his fatherly favor to us in many ways, yet we cannot by contemplating the universe infer that he is Father. Rather, conscience presses us within and shows in our sin just cause for his disowning us and not regarding or recognizing us as his sons. Dullness and ingratitude follow, for our minds, as they have been blinded, do not perceive what is true.... Therefore, although the preaching of the cross does not agree with our human inclination, if we desire to return to God our Author and Maker, from whom we have been estranged, in order that he may again begin to be our Father, we ought nevertheless to embrace it humbly. Surely, after the fall of the first man no knowledge of God apart from the Mediator has had power unto salvation.[43]

It was this faith in Christ, directed by the shadows of the law and the prophetic promises, that kept a remnant in Israel looking toward the future in hope.[44] God can only be considered the object of faith with the qualification that "unless God confronts us in Christ, we cannot come to know that we are saved."

> In this sense Irenaeus [a second-century church father] writes that the Father, himself infinite, becomes finite in the Son, for he has accommodated himself to our little measure lest our minds be overwhelmed by the immensity of his glory.... Actually, it means nothing else than that God is comprehended in Christ alone.[45]

Apart from Christ, there can only be a "fleeting knowledge of God" that quickly turns to the vinegar of idolatry and superstition, however much unbelievers (Calvin refers to Moslems here) "proclaim at the top of their lungs that the Creator of heaven and earth is God."[46]

CONCLUSION

The Enlightenment had high hopes for humanity. Emancipated from the church, tradition, and Scripture, the self-made individual aspired to attain intellectual or at least (after Kant) moral perfection. Though humankind lost its way for a while, it was set on the right path again, ready to pass through the cherubim-guarded tree of life and claim its victory. For this realization of the moral kingdom, Christ was not absolutely necessary. Not only is there no such thing as original sin; the example or model of a life well-pleasing to God is already innate in our minds. Therefore, we may advance simply on the basis of "the moral law within," Kant and others argued.

Pelagianism—the religion of self-salvation—is not a modern innovation, but the default setting of the fallen heart ever since the fall. No one has to be taught Pelagianism; rather, we have to be taught out of it—constantly, since we gravitate toward it. We find it even in the nineteenth-century American evangelist Charles Finney, and it remains a potent theology in practice even in many places where it is denied in theory. Accordingly, the emphasis falls on human activity and striving, self-improvement and the moral progress of humanity. In many ways, modernity represents a theological and spiritual movement: a Christian heresy that could only arise as the negation of the faith that offended its moral sensibilities.

For a variety of reasons, John Calvin's treatment reminds us how powerfully Scripture still speaks to our condition. Wherever the realism of the biblical account of the human condition is taken seriously, the gospel is seen more clearly and embraced more deeply. Calvinism probes the tragic side of human existence deeply, and on different levels.

First, it affirms the biblical teaching that sin is a condition. Of course, it brings forth the fruit of actual sins, but we can all confess with the psalmist, "In sin did my mother conceive me" (Ps. 51:5). We aren't sinners because we sin; we sin because we are sinners. According to surveys, most professing evangelicals, along with the wider culture, deny original sin.[47] In his recent study, sociologist Christian Smith has characterized religion in America as "moralistic, therapeutic deism," with no distinction between those who have been raised in evangelical churches and those reared in liberal, Unitarian, or other unchurched backgrounds.[48] Having witnessed the baneful effects of Pelagianism on mainline Protestantism, the evangelical movement in North America seems increasingly to be reaping the whirlwind of the seeds sown by its revivalist legacy. Pragmatism, consumerism, self-help moralism, and narcissism are simply the symptoms of a disease that is, at its heart, theological: namely, the drift toward Pelagianism. Whatever the formal creed and regardless of whether it appears in the form of a rigorous legalism or a sentimental antinomianism, a seriously deficient appraisal of sin surely lies at the heart of the church's lack of confidence in the gospel to create and empower the church's life, worship, and witness.

If it is indeed accurate, or even partly accurate, then the condition of at least American Christianity may actually be worse than that of the medieval church. Arminian theologian Roger Olson is surely correct when he writes, "The gospel preached and the doctrine of salvation taught in most evangelical pulpits and lecterns, and believed in most evangelical pews, is not classical Arminianism but semi-Pelagianism if not outright Pelagianism."[49]

The fatal accommodation to the religion of self-help always begins with an unbiblical view of the sinful condition. Episcopal bishop C. Fitzsimons Allison has pointed to the link between a Pelagian view of the human condition and the various heresies that have come to dominate liberal Protestantism. If we are merely inhibited by Adam's poor example, then all that we need is a better example, not a divine-human Redeemer. A Pelagian analysis of the plight requires nothing more than an Arian and Socinian solution. When wedded to a therapeutic view of the self that dominates our modern era, the importance of Jesus Christ as anything more than a guide or model becomes questionable. "Justification is an understandably strange doctrine," he writes, "to those who have substituted self-realization for salvation."[50]

Second, Calvinism affirms that we are all bound together in covenantal solidarity—both as image-bearers and convicts, in dignity and in death. This is what Reformed theology means by the *covenant of works* (also known as the covenant of creation or law). Sin is not just something that individuals do, but a condition in which all of us share solidarity "in Adam." Just as all of us bear God's image, all of us are corrupt in mind, heart, will, soul, and body.

If sin were reduced to mere acts of sin, we could perhaps conclude that with enough education and moral reform, as well as good laws, we could eliminate injustice, immorality, and strife. If we could just identify the source of evil in some external social structure or group of people, perhaps there would be the hope that with proper prisons and therapy we could solve the problem. However, we are all both sinners and sinned against. This means that we cannot reduce sin to behaviors that one can just stop doing or to wrong actions and behaviors that have been committed against a person. The biblical view of sin is more complicated: we are both victims and victimizers. Caught up in the web of original and actual sin, blame is not easily placed simply on one person or on others or on social systems. We are violated and we violate.

Third, as they are "in Christ," the elect are not only accountable and therefore liable to condemnation, but are chosen, redeemed, called, justified, sanctified, and glorified. This is the *covenant of grace*. Visible members of this covenant belong to the church as beneficiaries of its baptism, catechesis, discipline, communion, and so forth. There is no abstract "self" hovering above these two networks of power relations. One is either a justified covenant-keeper in Christ or a condemned covenant-breaker in Adam.

Like Jesus' generation, which he compared to children who did not know either how to mourn or dance properly, we—even in the church—seem to regard the verdict of the law as too severe and the verdict of the gospel as too good to be true. Our age does not seem to know either the grandeur of creation, the tragedy of the fall, or the splendor of grace. However, the funeral game is just the warm-up for the wedding game, to which we now turn our attention.

THREE

LOVED BEFORE TIME (ELECTION)

The church of Christ was conceived by the triune God before the world was ever created. Out of the mass of our condemned race, a bride was chosen by the Father for his Son, united to the Son by the Spirit. So there was never a moment when God did not love us, even when he knew we would be (and in fact, while we actually were) his sworn enemies.

John Stott has written, "The doctrine of election is the product of divine revelation, not of human speculation. It was not invented by Calvin of Geneva or Augustine of Hippo. It is above all else a biblical doctrine and no biblical Christian can ignore it."[1] Far from being "irreverent, inquisitive, or trivial," as Erasmus thought, Martin Luther said that this doctrine is essential for the Christian. Otherwise, "I cannot worship, praise, thank, and serve God, since I do not know how much I ought to attribute to myself and how much to God. It therefore behooves us to be very certain about the distinction between God's power and our own, God's work and our own, if we want to live a godly life."[2]

Everyone who takes the Bible seriously must believe in election in some sense; it is a prominent theme throughout Scripture. The real difference (especially between Arminianism and Calvinism) emerges over whether the elect are chosen *unto* faith or *in view of* their faith. In other words, is election unconditional or conditional? Does God choose who will be saved, apart from their decision and effort, or does he choose those whom he knows will trust and obey? Another view, called *corporate election*, holds that God has chosen the church as a whole rather than electing individuals to belong to it. We will also examine that position in this chapter.

Calvinism is known for its stand in favor of unconditional election, but it is not unique to Calvin and his heirs. This doctrine is found in the writings of some of the church fathers, especially Augustine, and was held by some of the greatest writers of the medieval era, including Gregory the Great, Bonaventure, Albert the Great, and Thomas Aquinas. However, to the extent that the grace of God became obscured by a focus on human ability, this doctrine fell increasingly into eclipse. This is why all of the Reformers—Luther, Zwingli, Calvin, Knox, Cranmer, and others—emphasized unconditional election as an important aspect of the gospel.

DOES THE BIBLE TEACH ELECTION?

It is impossible to read the Bible without recognizing God's freedom to choose some and not others—and the fact that he does in fact exercise that right. God chose Israel from among the nations. No one can deny that God set his favor on the descendants of Abraham and that this sovereign choice distinguished the Jews from every other people: "The Lord your God has chosen you to be a people for his treasured possession, out of all the peoples who are on the face of the earth" (Deut. 7:6). Further, God's election depends on his own mercy, not on Israel's prestige: "It was not because you were more in number than any other people that the Lord set his love on you and chose you, for you were the fewest of all peoples, but it is because the Lord loves you and is keeping the oath that he swore to your fathers, that the Lord has brought you out with a mighty hand and redeemed you from the house of slavery" (vv. 7–8).

In fact, God's election is made not only without respect to Israel's merits, but in spite of its sin:

> Do not say in your heart, after the Lord your God has thrust [the nations] out before you, "It is because of my righteousness that the Lord has brought me in to possess this land," whereas it is because of the wickedness of these nations that the Lord is driving them out before you. Not because of your righteousness or the uprightness of your heart are you going in to possess their land, but because of the wickedness of these nations....
>
> Know, therefore, that the Lord your God is not giving you this good land to possess because of your righteousness, for you are a stubborn people.... From the day you came out of the land of Egypt until you came to this place, you have been rebellious against the Lord. (Deut. 9:4–5, 6–7)

Not only did God not base his election on foreseen faith and obedience; he made this choice in the full knowledge of Israel's disobedience.

It will be widely admitted that God chose Israel as his special nation, but does this mean that he also chose who would be saved before the creation of the world? And does not such a view mean that the church displaces Israel? We are not the first to ask that question. In fact, it was evidently a big question among the early Jewish Christians. Had God failed to keep his promise to Israel? Had he revoked his election? And if so, how can we trust him now to save all who call on his name?

God's sovereign election of people from every nation to form his church in no way supplants Israel. Rather, it is an enlarging of Israel's tent, which was announced by Israel's prophets. As Paul argues in Romans 9–11, God has broken off branches that did not bear fruit in order to graft in wild branches—and he will return to ethnic Israel when the fullness of the Gentiles is complete. Calvin observes, "The fellowship of the Gentiles did not take from the Jews the right of the first begotten ... they were always the chief in the Church of God."[3] "Christ has assigned to the Jews the first rank."[4]

Yet not all Jews are saved. If they are God's chosen people and yet many do not trust in Christ, then why should we be comforted by this teaching? Have God's purposes failed? Has God shifted from "Plan A" to "Plan B"? These are the questions Paul takes up in Romans 9–11.

As Paul reminds us in his defense of God's sovereign mercy in Romans 9, God has always exercised his freedom even within the covenant family. He chose Isaac and rejected Ishmael, and then Jacob rather than Esau. In fact, "when Rebekah had conceived children by one man, our forefather Isaac, though they were not yet born and had done nothing either good or bad—in order that God's purpose of election might continue, not because of works but because of him who calls—she was told, 'The older will serve the younger.' As it is written, 'Jacob I loved, but Esau I hated'" (Rom. 9:10–13).

This provokes the charge of injustice, but Paul reminds us that mercy is something that God shows to those who are at fault. By definition, no one deserves it. If God gave us what we deserved, the whole "lump" of sinful humanity would be condemned (Rom. 9:19–23). As it is, God's election saves not only a remnant of Jews but a remnant of Gentiles as well from all the nations—people who would never have chosen him (vv. 24–29). "So too at the present time there is a remnant, chosen by grace. But if it is by grace, it is no longer on the basis of works; otherwise grace would no longer be grace" (11:5–6).

This extended argument leads Paul to worship:

> Oh, the depths of the riches and wisdom and knowledge of God! How unsearchable are his judgments and how inscrutable his ways!
>
> "For who has known the mind of the Lord,
> or who has been his counselor?
> "Or who has given a gift to him
> that he might be repaid?"
>
> For from him and through him and to him are all things. To him be glory forever. Amen. (11:33–36)

"Amen" indeed!

Election reminds us that God is always on the giving end and sinners are always on the receiving end of grace. "Salvation belongs to the LORD!" (Jon. 2:9). Given the condition of humanity described in the previous chapter, what would God have foreseen apart from his own election and grace? Looking down through the corridors of time, would God have seen people turning to him in repentance and faith, obeying him, and persevering to the end? If we answer yes, then we are not "dead in … trespasses and sins" and salvation is not of the Lord. Salvation may be *provided* by the Lord, but it is up to us to choose ourselves for this gift and to make Christ's redeeming work effective by our decision. It is impossible to believe that God chose us based on foreseen faith and obedience if no one is in fact morally able to trust and obey. The only thing that God could foresee is our spiritual death and his own gift-giving: granting faith to embrace Christ and all of his benefits.

In Ephesians 1, Paul again exults,

> Blessed be the God and Father of our Lord Jesus Christ, who has blessed us in Christ with every spiritual blessing in the heavenly places, even as he chose us in him before the foundation of the world, that we should be holy and blameless before him. In love he predestined us for adoption as sons through Jesus Christ, according to the purpose of his will, to the praise of his glorious grace, with which he has blessed us in the Beloved. In him we have redemption through his blood, the forgiveness of our trespasses, according to the riches of his grace, which he lavished upon us.…

> In him we have obtained an inheritance, having been predestined according to the purpose of him who works all things according to the counsel of his will. (Eph. 1:3–8, 11)

The other side of election is reprobation: God's decision *not* to save some. In passages already cited, especially Romans 9, God is said to be free to choose and to reject, to save and to harden, "to make out of the same lump one vessel for honorable use and another for dishonorable use" (Rom. 9:21). However, the "whole lump" is guilty and corrupt. It is not a neutral lump of clay, but a condemned mass. God is not arbitrarily choosing some and rejecting others. Rather, he is choosing some of his enemies for salvation and leaving the rest to the destiny that all of us would have chosen for ourselves.

All Calvinists agree that the fall was included in God's plan, that this decree in relation to the fall was permissive rather than active, and that reprobation (the rejection of the nonelect) was not capricious or arbitrary but took account of sin.[5] Often, when the term "Calvinism" is mentioned, people think of an arbitrary God who drags some people into heaven kicking and screaming, while telling others who want to be saved that they're simply not on the list. Sometimes this caricature is actually given life by hyper-Calvinists. However, it has never had any place in the Calvinist system.

In strong terms, the Canons of the Synod of Dort (1618–1619) declared, "Reformed Churches ... detest with their whole soul" the view "that in the same manner in which the election is the fountain and cause of faith and good works, reprobation is the cause of unbelief and impiety."[6] God takes no pleasure in the death of the wicked (Ezek. 18:32) but delights in the salvation of the elect (Eph. 1:5–6). No one is saved by divine coercion and no one is rejected apart from his or her own will.

God is not active in hardening hearts in the same way that he is active in softening hearts. Scripture does speak of God hardening hearts, not only in Exodus 7:3 and Romans 9:18 but also in Joshua 11:20; John 12:40; Romans 11:7; 2 Corinthians 3:14. Yet it also speaks of sinners hardening their own hearts (Ex. 8:15; Ps. 95:8; Isa. 63:17; Matt. 19:8; Heb. 3:8, 13). However, no passage speaks of sinners softening their own hearts and regenerating themselves. Human beings are alone responsible for their hardness of heart, but God alone softens and in fact re-creates the hearts of his elect (1 Kings 8:58; Ps. 51:10; Isa. 57:15; Jer. 31:31–34; Ezek.

11:19; 36:26; 2 Cor. 3:3; 4:6; Heb. 10:16). In short, God only has to leave us to our own devices in the case of reprobation, but it requires the greatest works of the triune God to save the elect, including the death of the Father's only begotten Son.

IS ELECTION UNCONDITIONAL?

The just-mentioned passages teach that the motive of election is in God, not in us. God's own love, mercy, and freedom determined that we would belong to him in his Son. Jesus told his disciples, "You did not choose me, but I chose you and appointed you that you should go and bear fruit and that your fruit should abide" (John 15:16). God chose Jacob and rejected of Esau, before they were born "and had done nothing either good or bad—in order that God's purpose of election might continue" (Rom. 9:11). Indeed, "in this the love of God was made manifest among us ... not that we have loved God but that he loved us and sent his Son to be the propitiation for our sins.... We love because he first loved us" (1 Jn 4:9–10, 19).

What then of Romans 8:29, where we read, "For those whom he foreknew he also predestined"? Doesn't this teach that God predestined those whom he foreknew would choose him? "Foreknow" in Scripture means more than "to know something beforehand." Adam "knew" Eve (Gen. 4:1); God "knew" Jeremiah while he was still in his mother's womb (Jer. 1:5). In Amos 3:2, God tells Israel, "You only have I known of all the families of the earth," and in 1 Peter 1:20 Jesus is said to have been "foreknown before the foundation of the world."

Clearly, the kind of knowledge is not merely informational; it is personal. God knew—that is, set his loving affection upon—all whom he predestined. Paul says, "*those whom* he foreknew," not "*that which* he foreknew." It is not that God foreknew our decision, but that he foreknew those whom he predestined. Furthermore, the question arises again as to what God would have foreseen apart from his own merciful decision and action. If no one can believe apart from God's regenerating grace, then God could never have foreseen someone believing apart from his prior decision to give that person saving faith.

Many find conditional election (based on foreseen faith) attractive out of a concern to protect God from the charge of injustice. However, mere foreknowledge does not resolve the problem of evil or the final judgment of the lost. Let's say that God knows from all eternity that I will gossip about my neighbor and this will lead to his or her being fired at work. Can God be wrong in his knowledge? Given God's perfection, this is impossible. Whatever God knows, he knows truly. God is incapable of error. Therefore, if God knows perfectly from all eternity that I will commit this sin, then it is just as certain as it would be if he predestined it.

While rejecting God's foreordination of the fall, Arminian theologian Richard Watson said that "God could have prevented it but decided to allow it."[7] Thus, Watson acknowledges that there was a divine decision from all eternity concerning the fall: God "decided to allow it." This is precisely what Reformed theologians say, but they are satisfied to call it foreordination, since it is after all a determination. Realizing the fact that such foreknowledge is a kind of determination, a recent movement in evangelical circles (known as "open theism") has moved beyond the Arminian view toward the Socinian position. Advocates of this view hold that God does not have exhaustive foreknowledge of the acts performed by free creatures.[8]

The Calvinist says that everything that happens is not only foreknown but determined by God, yet in some cases through his own action (such as working all things together for our good) and in other cases through his permission (such as allowing creatures to commit a particular sin). In either case, God remains sovereign over history. Given the terrible evils that creatures commit each day, it is comforting news that we are not the ones who are ultimately in charge of how things turn out. The one who is ultimately in charge of the universe is good, kind, wise, merciful, just, and righteous.

Mere foreknowledge without foreordination means that God does not have any larger purpose, that every natural disaster or human aggression is meaningless and random. If God foreknows these tragedies in advance but does not determine that he will allow them as part of a greater purpose that terminates in his glory and our good, then why pray? Why would we imagine that God either cares or has the ability to make our intercession a means through which he fulfills his purposes? And if God's realization of his purposes in history depends ultimately on us, how can we be confident that our future will end in blessing rather than disaster? Do we think we are any better than others?

Again and again, the point is made—especially in the prophets—that the only hope God's people have is that there is an everlasting covenant, absolute and unconditional, that no human disobedience can void.

God will work all things together—even sin—for his glory and our salvation (Rom. 8:28). Scripture teaches us to trust God not only in those situations where his goodness is obvious, but also when sin and evil seem to be gaining the upper hand. While God never causes sin, he is Lord over it, and it can progress no further than his wisdom and goodness will allow. In short, with conditional election you get foreknowledge without purpose: salvation is finally of us, not of the Lord.

IS ELECTION INDIVIDUAL OR CORPORATE?

Given the obvious evidence of election in Scripture, many Arminians today are attracted to the view that God chose the church as a corporate entity in Christ from all eternity, but not particular individuals to belong to it.[9] Although there are of course individuals chosen for certain tasks (such as David and Cyrus) and others are rejected (such as Pharaoh and Saul), these contexts do not have anything to do with salvation, argues Ben Witherington.

> Election for Paul is a corporate thing. It was in ethnic Israel; it is now "in Christ." From Paul's viewpoint, which is simply an adaptation of the view found in early Judaism, "election" does not guarantee the final salvation of individual Christian converts any more than it guaranteed the final salvation of individual Israelites in the past.[10]

This view is to be faulted not for what it affirms but for what it denies. Calvinists agree that the church, as known to God, is the corporate body of the elect. They also emphasize that election is "in Christ," the Mediator who is both the electing God and the elect head in whom his people are chosen. We also agree that some people are chosen and rejected for certain temporal tasks rather than with reference to salvation.

However, there is simply too much biblical evidence for the election of individuals in Christ to leave the matter there. Paul's point in Romans 9 is the opposite of Witherington's claim. In fact, the apostle bases his argument for God's freedom to elect and reject today on the fact that he has always exercised this freedom in Israel's history. That individuals are in view is indisputable: they have names (Ishmael and Isaac, Jacob and Esau, Moses and Pharaoh). Furthermore, Paul's application is clearly soteriological (i.e., concerning salvation). "This means that it is not the children of the flesh who are the children of God, but the children of the promise are counted as offspring" (Rom. 9:8).

The question has to do with being "heirs of the promise"—that is, heirs of the saving grace of God in history. Because it is based on "God's purpose of election ... not because of works but because of him who calls," salvation is all of grace (Rom. 9:11). It is not a question of whom God will use in his service for specific tasks, but of whether people are saved by "human will or exertion" or by "God, who has mercy" (v. 16). Some are "vessels of wrath" not merely in a temporal sense, but as those "prepared for destruction," in contrast to the "vessels of mercy, which he has prepared beforehand for glory—even us whom he has called, not from the Jews only but also from the Gentiles" (vv. 22–24).

Ephesians 1 is also clearly soteriological in context and includes individuals ("the saints who are in Ephesus"). Both points are evident in the passage:

> He chose us in [Christ] before the foundation of the world, that we should be holy and blameless before him. In love he predestined us for adoption as sons through Jesus Christ.... In him we have redemption through his blood, the forgiveness of our trespasses....
>
> In him we have obtained an inheritance, having been predestined according to the purpose of him who works all things according to the counsel of his will" (Eph. 1:4–5, 7, 11).

Surely no one would say that individuals are not adopted or that Christ redeemed by his blood the church corporately but not individuals, or that the church but not the individuals who compose it are forgiven.

Furthermore, Paul adds, "In him you also, when you heard the word of truth, the gospel of your salvation, and believed in him, were sealed with the promised Holy Spirit" (Eph. 1:13). Surely he is addressing individual believers as well as the church corporately. The apostle tells the Thessalonians that "God chose you as the firstfruits to be saved, through sanctification by the Spirit and belief in the truth" (2 Thess. 2:13). Here, it is not just the church that is chosen but the Thessalonian believers who were chosen to believe the gospel. It is not only the church, but individual believers who are saved, "not because of our works but because of his own purpose and grace, which he gave us in Christ Jesus before the ages began" (2 Tim. 1:9).

Corporate election is merely another way of expressing the traditional Arminian view of election based on foreseen faith: God elects believers, but he does not elect sinners to believe. All who accept Christ are saved (and therefore elect), but God does not elect anyone to salvation.

However, Scripture teaches that God has elected his church in Christ because he has chosen who will belong to it from all eternity.

IS ELECTION FAIR?

How would you feel if you had been a loyal employee in the same company for thirty years and some kid fresh out of college was given the same pay, title, and retirement? Or what if your younger brother or sister wasted the family's inheritance on wine, women, and song and your father welcomed him home with a party—and the same status in the house as you? By now you're probably realizing that I am paraphrasing two of our Lord's parables: the laborers in the vineyard and the prodigal son. In the first, Jesus makes the point: "'Am I not allowed to do what I choose with what belongs to me? Or do you begrudge my generosity?' So the last will be first, and the first last" (Matt. 20:15–16). The Pharisees were the laborers who had worked all day and were scandalized by the owner's decision to pay the same wage to those (i.e., Gentiles) who showed up a little while ago. They are the elder brother, jealous of the Father's love for the dissolute sibling. The same point is made in the parable of the wedding feast: "For many are called, but few are chosen" (Matt. 22:14).

When it comes to salvation, there are no wages. In fact, "the wages of sin is death" (Rom. 6:23). So if we want to talk about getting what we deserve, we're in for a rough ride. Salvation is a gift, not a reward (Rom. 4:4–5). Is election fair? Hardly. But who wants fairness in this matter? After all, if God were to give everybody what is deserved, nobody would be saved. He could leave every one of us in our spiritual death and the condemnation that we have chosen for ourselves.

When we talk about what is fair, then, we need to start with the baseline that each and every one of us deserves: eternal death. The amazing thing is that God chooses to save anybody, especially when he knows that the people he has chosen would not choose him apart from his grace. In his healing ministry, Jesus healed some but not others. When we come to such passages, do we question his generosity? Not at all; we praise Christ's mercy. This is Paul's point in Romans 9: "What shall we say then? Is there injustice on God's part? By no means! For he says to Moses, 'I will have mercy on whom I have mercy, and I will have compassion on whom I have compassion.' So then it depends not on human will or exertion, but on God who has mercy" (Rom. 9:14–16).

In 2 Timothy 1:9, Paul makes God's purpose, not our decision or effort, the source of election: God "saved us and called us to a holy calling, not because of our works but because of his own purpose and grace, which he gave us in Christ Jesus before the ages began." He gives thanks to God for the faith of the Thessalonian believers "because God chose you as the firstfruits to be saved" (2 Thess. 2:13). Since "no one can come" to Christ "unless the Father who sent me draws him" (John 6:44), what would God have foreseen in us prior to his own decision?

This is of enormous comfort. We are familiar with returning a favor. Someone does something nice for us, and we feel obligated to do something in return. When we lavish someone with a gift and he or she becomes a friend, it's hard to know whether the friendship will outlast their sense of being in our debt. Many people live like this in relation to God. However, election teaches us that God set his love on us before we ever existed, and he foresaw nothing but our hostility toward him and his grace toward us. So it's not quite accurate to say that God chose us without respect to anything that he foresaw in us. Yet what he foresaw was a mass of rebels who would never have chosen him unless he had first chosen us. This election is unchangeable and unconditional; it cannot be altered by what we do or fail to do (Heb. 6:17–18). God does not react to what we do; he "works all things according to the counsel of his will" (Eph 1:11).

It's also important to point out that classic Arminianism and Calvinism actually agree that God chose not to save everyone. God could have decided to save every human being, regardless of his or her response to the gospel. However, Arminians hold that it is more important to God to give people free will to decide their own destiny than it is to save everyone. Calvinists hold that God chose to have mercy on many and leave the rest to their own choice.

Nor does it help for Arminians to say that the issue is not fairness but God's love. After all, in this case, it is not God's love (ostensibly universal) that wins out, but God's concern for our free will. If we can still love God freely in heaven even without the possibility of sinning, surely God could have decided to glorify every person at Calvary, without anyone being finally condemned.[11]

The important point is that Calvinism and Arminianism both affirm that God has chosen not to save everyone; the paths diverge over whether God's electing grace or our free will is the deciding factor in salvation. In the Calvinist account, though, God's love is finally greater than the fallen heart's rebellion and resistance. God will not let those whom he has chosen to have the last word in this matter, but redeems them, renews them, and keeps them until glory. In the case of neither the elect nor the reprobate does God coerce the human will. Rather, in the former case he frees sinners from their bondage to sin and death, and in the latter case he leaves sinners to go their own way.

ELECTION AND HUMAN RESPONSIBILITY

Election is a subset of predestination. While predestination refers to God's foreordaining "whatsoever comes to pass" (Westminster Confession 3.1), election refers specifically to his decision to save sinners. In either case, the question arises concerning the compatibility of God's sovereignty and human responsibility.

In addition to being stated explicitly, predestination is demonstrated in the biblical narratives, including sinful actions (Gen. 50:20). Nebuchadnezzar eventually learned the lesson of God's sovereignty over all things, including his own kingdom (Dan. 4:34–37). The times and places of every person's life are included in God's decree (Acts 17:26). Even the falling of a bird and the number of hairs on each person's head are encompassed by God's sovereign wisdom (Matt. 10:29–30). Although humans are held responsible for their wicked acts in Jesus' crucifixion, he was "delivered up according to the definite plan [*boulē*] and foreknowledge of God" (Acts 2:23). Using the same term (*boulē*), and adding the phrase "predestined to take place," the believers later praised God by saying, "for truly in this city there were gathered together against thy holy servant Jesus, whom thou didst anoint, both Herod and Pontius Pilate, with the Gentiles and the peoples of Israel, to do whatever thy hand and thy plan had predestined to take place" (Acts 4:27–28 RSV). Once more, this passage does not tell us *how* God can decree their sin while holding them responsible; it simply states that this is the case.[12]

In theological terms, this is called "double agency," because two agents—God and human beings—are involved. From the examples we have of double agency (e.g., Gen. 50:20; Acts 4:28), God is said to have decreed the event and human beings are said to have executed it so freely that they are blameworthy of the act. Pilate was under no natural or moral necessity to surrender Jesus to death, yet he did freely what God had foreordained. God not only determines the end but the means, and the means are contingent. God not only chooses a person for eternal life in his Son, but he determines how that person will come to faith through the ordinary creaturely means of prayer, preaching, conversations with a believer, and so forth. Each of these acts undertaken by creatures (both believers and unbelievers) is free, precisely because God has included their free acts in his decree. We cannot resolve the mystery of divine and human agency, but we can—indeed, must—affirm whatever Scripture teaches us in this matter.

First, the Calvinist-Arminian debate reflects deeper differences concerning the God-world relationship, especially the relation between divine and human agency. Ironically, Arminians and hyper-Calvinists typically view divine and human activity as a single pie, divided unevenly between both parties. Both would give God a larger piece, but disagree over the precise size of the portions. Arminians speak of God's limiting himself, making room in the cosmos for free human beings: giving a piece of his "freedom pie." According to Clark Pinnock, we worship either a God who does not want to "control everything, but to give the creature room to exist and freedom to love," or "an all-controlling despot who can tolerate no resistance (Calvin)."[13] The choice is stark: either a "solitary monad" who is "immobile" or the "Living God," who is dependent on the creation for his happiness.[14]

Pinnock acknowledges his debt to modern philosophy at this point (especially Hegel, Teilhard, Whitehead, and other process thinkers).[15] "Just as Augustine came to terms with ancient Greek thinking, so we are making peace with the culture of modernity."[16] This is entirely justified since "modern culture ... is closer to the biblical view than classical theism."[17] Pinnock stacks the deck with terms like "omnicausality," as if Calvinism teaches that God directly causes everything that happens, never acknowledging that Reformed theologians have always explicitly rejected this view (though hyper-Calvinists lend support to that caricature).

Classic Reformed theology follows the best of the ancient and medieval theologians in starting with the incomprehensible majesty and transcendence of God—his absolute difference from creation. The world is not an emanation of God, like the rays of the sun. There is no part of creation, including angels or souls, that is semidivine. There is the triune God—and then there is everything and everyone else.

This means that the difference between God and creatures is not just quantitative but qualitative. We are made in God's image and likeness, as analogies rather than "a chip off the old block." God does not share his glory or other attributes—including his freedom—with creatures. We depend on other people and myriad circumstances for our well-being. Yet, "our God is in the heavens; he does all that he pleases" (Ps. 115:3). "Behold, the nations are like a drop from a bucket, and are accounted as the dust on the scales.... To whom then will you liken God, or what likeness compare with him?" (Isa. 40:15, 18). No creature can thwart God's ultimate designs (Dan 4:34–37).

God's being, knowledge, and power are original and unique. God is transcendent. Yet he is also immanent, freely bringing the world into existence, sustaining it by his power, and entering into covenantal relationships with his creatures. "In him we live and move and have our being" (Acts 17:28). Therefore, we shouldn't think in terms of a single pie that is divided between God and us, but of God's own way of being free (as sovereign Creator) and the creaturely freedom that God has given to us as his image-bearers.

This view of the God-world relationship shapes our understanding of "double agency." God wills and works and we will and work, but at no point do we trip over each other. God's agency operates over, in, and with creaturely agency, because God is the Father, the Son, and the Holy Spirit. In every external work of the Trinity, the Father is the source, the Son is the mediator, and the Spirit is at work within creation to bring about the appropriate effect. Yet in all of these works, the triune God and his agency transcend us.

Therefore, God cannot limit his freedom any more than he can limit his love, knowledge, holiness, or any other attribute. "The earth is the Lord's and the fullness thereof" (Ps. 24:1). Yet this in no way implies that God deprives us of the kind of freedom that he deemed appropriate for creatures. On the contrary, God is generous and liberal in his gifts. Tyrants stalk the earth, consuming the freedom of others in order to amass their own oppressive dominion, but God already possesses all authority in heaven and on earth and can create beings who have their own way of existing, thinking, willing, and acting.

Hyper-Calvinism begins with the central dogma of divine liberty (what Pinnock calls "omnicausalism"), while Arminians begin with the central dogma of human liberty. However, the consistent teaching of Reformed theologians has affirmed God's sovereign decree concerning "whatsoever comes to pass," yet without coercion or directly causing every event (Westminster Confession 3.1). *How* both can be true remains a mystery to us, but *that* both are true is clearly revealed in Scripture. It would only be a contradiction if God's freedom and ours belonged to the same register.

The caricature of Calvinism as advocating "omnicausalism" is refuted by our confessions, as we have seen. Some late medieval theologians had argued that God's will was so absolute that he could even condemn the elect if he chose. However, Calvin called this "a diabolical blasphemy," an example of the kind of speculation that avoids the revealed God and forges its own path to the hidden God. This emphasis on the absolute freedom of God, Calvin warned, would make us little more than balls that God juggles in the air.[18] Calvin explicitly rejected "omnicausality."[19] The truth of God's eternal decree (both in providence and election) is clearly revealed in Scripture and is comforting to believers in their trials. "Yet his wonderful method of governing the universe is rightly called an abyss, because while it is hidden from us, we ought reverently to adore it."[20] "Meanwhile, nevertheless, a godly man will not overlook the secondary causes."[21]

As a result of these distinctions, covenant theology focuses on the dynamic outworking of God's redemptive plan in concrete history, taking seriously the twists and turns in the road—including God's responses to human beings. But it does so without denying the clear biblical witness to the fact that God transcends these historical relationships.

Second, God cannot will or do anything inconsistent with his whole nature. He cannot love at the expense of his justice or decree something contrary to his wisdom or righteousness. God's eternal decree is said to be founded on his wisdom (Ps. 33:11; 104:24; Prov. 3:19; 19:21; Jer. 10:12; 51:15; Eph. 3:10–11). Because he is loving, righteous, good, and just, God cannot will any ultimate evil. That is, he cannot determine that any of his purposes will end in evil or sin. His purposes are to work even human sin and rebellion together for good (Rom. 8:28).

That is not to say either that everything is good or that sinful actions of human beings are beyond his knowledge or permissive decree. Rather, it is to say that it is inconsistent with God's nature and, in fact, unthinkable that God—who cannot do evil or be tempted by evil (Jas. 1:13)—should ever determine that any purpose that he plans will terminate in evil. Thus, God only permissively decrees evil in such a way that the same decree simultaneously determines the triumph of God's just and gracious purposes in Jesus Christ.

Someone might counter that, according to Calvinism, God does in fact limit his love by choosing some and not others. However, this rests on a confusion of categories. God is free in his love to create what he wills. God's love would not have been diminished in the slightest if he had not chosen to create this world. In fact, love is free, so to say that God's love was somehow dependent on his creation of the world is to empty love of any meaning. How much more would God's love remain undiminished if he did not save those who raise their hand against him every day? God is not free to surrender or diminish his attribute of love, but he is free to "show mercy on whom [he] will show mercy" (Ex. 33:19; Rom. 9:15).

Third, Reformed theology distinguishes between God's positive determination to fulfill his purposes and his permission to allow sin. God does not cause people to sin. "This means," says Louis Berkhof, "that God does not positively work in man 'both to will and to do' when man goes contrary to his revealed will."[22] When Paul says that God works in us "to will and to work for his good pleasure" (Phil. 2:13), he is talking about sanctification. Even if one believes that God only knows the future sinful acts of creatures and yet allows them to happen, predestination is acknowledged. After all, if God chooses to allow something to happen, it does not occur apart from his decree. As Berkhof observes, this is referred to in Reformed theology as God's "permissive decree," as he determines that certain acts will come to pass through "the free agency of his rational creatures."[23]

As the seventeenth-century theologian Francis Turretin summarized, God decrees all things, but in the case of sin and evil, he decrees what he will permit free agents to do and so directs the events that they can never terminate in evil. In sanctification, God "works in [us,] both to will and to work for his good pleasure" (Phil 2:13), but of the wicked we read, "I gave them over to their stubborn hearts, to follow their own counsels" (Ps. 81:12). "Therefore God gave them up in the lusts of their hearts to impurity" (Rom. 1:24). God does not cause creatures to sin: Turretin cites all of the Reformed confessions on this point.[24] In fact, Turretin charges the Counter-Reformation theologian Robert Bellarmine with "impiety and blasphemy" for asserting that God actually "twists and turns [the wicked] by his invisible operation," determining their wills to do evil.[25] He even says that Luther's *Bondage of the Will* speaks of God's activity in hardening the hearts of sinners "in far stronger terms than our divines."[26]

On one hand, the hyper-Calvinist will say that God directly and immediately hardened Pharaoh's heart. The Egyptian ruler simply had no say in the matter but was putty in God's hands. On the other hand, the Arminian will deny that God hardened Pharaoh's heart, emphasizing the passages in the narrative that speak of Pharaoh hardening his own heart. What are we to do here? First, it is instructive that the passages in which God says he will harden Pharaoh's heart come at the beginning of the narrative (Ex. 4:21; 7:3). It is a prophecy that God gives to Moses about what he will do. Therefore, as divine prophecy, it cannot fail to come to pass. Pharaoh's resistance is foreordained. Yet as the prophecy is fulfilled, the voice moves back and forth—as does the subject of the action in hardening.

After some of the plagues Pharaoh is said to have hardened his heart (Ex. 8:15, 32; 9:34). After others, it is said simply that "his heart was hardened" (7:13, 22; 8:19; 9:7, 35), and in still others it is said that "the LORD hardened Pharaoh's heart" (9:12; 10:20, 27; 11:10). From these verses, we cannot draw a false choice between God and Pharaoh as the subject of this heart-hardening action. On one hand, God is clearly hardening Pharaoh's heart, and on the other hand Pharaoh is hardening his own heart; the only way of resolving this is by recognizing that God uses means in his judging as well as saving work. The same signs that created faith in Israel hardened Pharaoh and his lieutenants.

God told Moses that these signs are to be told to the covenant children in coming generations so that they will know "what signs I have done among them, that you may know that I am the LORD'" (Ex 10:1–2). Even Pharaoh's own magicians had to confess, after the third plague, "'This is the finger of God.' But Pharaoh's heart was hardened, and he would not listen to them, as the LORD had said" (Ex. 8:19). In none of these instances was Pharaoh's heart immediately hardened by God. Rather, God hardened his heart indirectly and mediately, through his signs and wonders that confirmed his word of judgment for Pharaoh and deliverance for his people. Pharaoh grew more resolute in his hostility to the Lord precisely to the extent that God spoke his word and confirmed it by signs.

Pharaoh was hardly passive in all of this; he was hardening his own heart in response to God's word, even though in doing so God was bringing to pass what he had already told Moses would happen. Pharaoh's heart was not neutral; it was already hard enough to reject God's claim from the beginning. None of us is born any more neutral in relation to God than Pharaoh. The same word that is faith-producing and life-generating for some is for others an occasion to become more resolute in unbelief. God does not create unbelief; this is the natural state of fallen humanity. But he does need to create faith in the hearts of his elect. Because God uses means—both in salvation and in condemnation—we are accountable for our own response.

Fourth, we must distinguish carefully the decree in eternity from its execution in history. For example, some hyper-Calvinists have held the view that the elect are justified from all eternity. Yet this position collapses the execution of the decree (*ordo salutis*) into the decree itself. Scripture teaches that we are justified through faith, yet even this act of faith was graciously determined by the triune God before the creation of the world.

Purposes are different from their fulfillment; determinations are different from their accomplishment. God has not only determined the ends but the means by which he will achieve them. God may have determined our life span and where we would live (Acts 17:26), but these hidden purposes are fulfilled through our prayer, planning and investigation, real estate agents, moving companies, employers, and so forth. Even in our salvation, God fulfills his electing decree through myriad means—the prayers of friends and relatives, a neighbor who brings us to church or shares the gospel with us after work, and many other influences and events of which we are not even aware. Far from being opposed to our free action, God's secret predestination is the basis for it.

Teaching that God has decreed "whatsoever comes to pass," the Westminster Confession 3.1 adds immediately, "yet so, as thereby neither is God the author of sin, nor is violence offered to the will of the creatures; nor is the liberty or contingency of second causes taken away, but rather established." "Second causes" here refers to the actions of creatures. As A. A. Hodge points out, human agency is actually included in and therefore made possible by God's decree that "in the case of every free act of a moral agent ... the act shall be perfectly spontaneous and free on the part of the agent."[27] God's decree not only determines that the act will occur (Ps. 33:11; Prov. 19:21; Isa. 46:10), but that it will be freely done by the agent.

Like Mary at the annunciation, we may wonder how this is possible, but we too are simply told, "Nothing will be impossible with God" (Luke 1:37). So far is God's predestination from fatalism that Martin Luther can write, "And if God be robbed of His power to elect, what will there be remaining but that idol, Fortune, under the name of which all things take place at random!"[28] We are not at the mercy of a merciless universe, of meaningless chance, of the overwhelming forces of nature, or of powerful tyrants. The one who holds the whole world in his hands "so loved the world that he gave his only Son" (John 3:16).

Fifth, we must distinguish between natural and moral ability, which I introduced in the previous chapter. Much of the confusion regarding the Calvinist position can be attributed to overlooking this crucial distinction. As William Twisse, moderator of the Westminster Assembly, put it, God's promise to save "whoever believes in Jesus Christ" is given to the elect and reprobate alike. No one who trusts in Christ can be condemned.[29] But don't Calvinists teach that the reprobate cannot believe in Christ anyway? This is where the distinction comes into play: every human being, created in God's image, has the natural ability to respond affirmatively to God's promise. There is no sovereign necessity imposed by God that makes it impossible for a person to believe in Christ. It is not because they are bound by God's sovereignty to reject Christ, but because they—like all of us—are bound by sin in their intellect, will, and emotions. If God gives the elect the gift of faith, he is not to be reproached for leaving the rest to their own decision.

As Twisse points out (and the Westminster Confession 3.1 confirms), it is one thing to say that once God decrees something it becomes necessary, and quite another to say that the manner in which it comes to pass is coerced.[30] God's decree is the source, not the obstacle, since it includes the decision that his purposes will be realized through the free action of creatures.

Finally, God's sovereignty is not only demonstrated in narratives and described in doctrines; it is celebrated in praise. For example, in each of the arguments for God's predestining purposes in Christ, Paul moves from narratively grounded doctrinal arguments to scenic vistas, where he pauses to adore. Immediately after teaching, "Those whom he predestined he also called, and those whom he called he also justified, and those whom he justified he also glorified" (Rom. 8:30), he exclaims: "What then shall we say to these things? If God is for us, who can be against us?... Who shall bring any charge against God's elect? It is God who justifies" (8:31, 33). Then in chapter 11, after treating the same topic in the context of Israel's unfolding narrative, again he is left in wonder at the riches of God's unfathomable knowledge and grace (Rom. 11:33–36). Only when we are led to praise have we truly understood that part of the mystery of God's decree that he has revealed.

Interpreted properly, then, predestination in general and election in particular cannot lead us to fatalism or complacency. There is no basis for shrugging off our responsibility, as if to say, "What will be will be, and there's nothing I can do to change it." God will fulfill his purposes, but they are secret to us, and he holds us responsible for what he has revealed. Scripture nowhere imposes on us the responsibility to discover God's hidden will, but only his revealed will.

ELECTION AND ASSURANCE

God's revealed will is disclosed in Jesus Christ who declares, "Come to me, all who labor and are heavy laden, and I will give you rest" (Matt. 11:28). For some, predestination disturbs assurance, directing people to find signs of election within themselves. To others, such as Roman Catholics and Anabaptists, confidence in one's election yields "false assurance of salvation" to believers.[31] The assumption here is that a conviction of one's unconditional election will undermine the pursuit of holiness. We may be assured by our works that we are in a state of grace today, but a wariness of falling out of God's favor keeps us from false security.

There is indeed a danger of false security. Often, new converts are told that they are eternally secure because they have made a decision for Christ, even though they may not understand the call to repentance and faith. However, this can be a false security because it too lodges our confidence in our decision.

However, believers are entitled to that genuine security that is announced in Scripture, which is grounded in God's decision and effort and for that reason will always yield the results of repentance, faith, and perseverance. It is God's commitment to us, not our commitment to him, that brings us to faith and keeps us in faith to the very end. "When we come to election," Calvin observed, "we see nothing but mercy on every side."[32]

Scripture itself teaches us to draw assurance from God's unconditional election. Believers are not taught to doubt or question their election, but to "make [their] calling and election sure" (2 Peter 1:10). Jesus promised that he will gather his elect from the whole earth and deliver them from the wrath to come (Mark 13:27). He cares for his elect and answers their cries (Luke 18:7) and assures his own that they are chosen not only to be saved but to be preserved in that grace (John 13:18; 15:16). Who can charge against God's elect, since Christ has died for their sins and even now intercedes for them at the Father's right hand (Rom. 8:33)?

Sometimes storming out of the room, my father used to react viscerally whenever, as a teenager, I was debating election with my mother. On one occasion, I followed him outside and apologized for raising the subject when he made it clear that it offended him. Turning to me with tears, he asked, "What if your dad's not one of the elect?" It is so easy for us to turn gospel into law, faith-creating good news into anxiety-generating questions. It is true that in some circles election is not understood as a comforting and assurance-producing doctrine, but the very opposite. In some pietistic circles, a Christian can refrain from receiving communion for years—even over a lifetime—out of a lack of assurance concerning his or her election.

However, this is not how we find election taught in Scripture. In response to my dad's question, I quoted Jesus' words in John 10:27: "My sheep hear my voice, and I know them, and they follow me." "Have you heard his voice and followed him?" I asked.

"Yes," he replied.

"Then this is Jesus' answer to you in the next verse: 'I give them eternal life, and they will never perish, and no one will snatch them out of my hand.'" Everything changed, even in his countenance. Once he understood that point, election became the opposite of what it had been before to him; it was now a marvelous comfort. He would always say thereafter that this was a life-changing moment.

We do not discover our election in God's secret chambers but in his revealed will; not in ourselves but in Christ. Paul repeatedly refers to our election "in Christ," "in him," "in the Beloved." There is a real danger in talking about the sovereignty of God and election in an abstract way. I have come across some defenses of God's sovereignty that could have been written as they were even if there were no Trinity and no entrance of the eternal Son into our existence to bear our sins and be raised as the object of saving faith. Many struggle to find their election in themselves, by inspecting the quality of their repentance and faith. Yet this is a perversion of Calvinism.

Calvin borrowed Luther's expression "seeking outside the way" as a way of talking about this attempt to find God's secret designs apart from his revelation in Christ. Observe the remarks of Calvin on this point:

> Satan has no more grievous or dangerous temptation to dishearten believers than when he unsettles them with doubt about their election,

> while at the same time he arouses them with a wicked desire to seek it outside the way. I call it "seeking outside the way" when mere man attempts to break into the inner recesses of divine wisdom, and tries to penetrate even to highest eternity, in order to find out what decision has been made concerning himself at God's judgment seat. For then he casts himself into the depths of a bottomless whirlpool to be swallowed up.[33]

The only way to steer away from this whirlpool and find "safe and calm" waters is to look to Christ. We were not chosen in ourselves, but in Christ. "But if we have been chosen in him, we shall not find assurance of our election in ourselves; and not even in God the Father, if we conceive him as severed from his Son. Christ, then, is the mirror wherein we must, and without self-deception may, contemplate our own election." From Scripture "we have a sufficiently clear and firm testimony that we have been inscribed in the book of life [Rev. 21:27] if we are in communion with Christ." Election has no higher or greater blessing than our inheritance in Christ through faith alone. This faith is given to us by the Spirit through his Word alone. Therefore, we must cling to God's clear promise in the gospel and find our election in Christ.[34]

We cannot obtain certainty of our election by attempting "to penetrate to the eternal decree of God," for "we shall be ingulfed in the profound abyss." We must not seek to "soar above the clouds," but must be "satisfied with the testimony of God in his external word.... For as those who, in order to gain assurance of their election, examine into the eternal counsel of God without the word, plunge themselves into a fatal abyss, so they who investigate it in a regular and orderly manner, as it is contained in the word, derive from such inquiry the benefit of peculiar consolation."[35] Calvin always treated election as a comforting truth that highlighted the Father's gracious will toward us in Christ. Since we were chosen in Christ, it is only in Christ—not in our speculations, experiences, or works—that we discover our election:

> In the first place, if we seek the fatherly liberality and propitious heart of God, our eyes must be directed to Christ, in whom alone the Father is well pleased.... Consider and investigate it as much as you please, you will not find its ultimate scope extend beyond this.... If we are chosen in Christ, we shall find no assurance of election in ourselves; nor even in God the Father, considered alone, abstractly

from the Son. Christ, therefore, is the mirror, in which it behooves us to contemplate our election; and here we may do it with safety.[36]

We do not search for the elect in our proclamation of the gospel: "The gospel is preached indiscriminately to the elect and the reprobate; but the elect alone come to Christ, because they have been 'taught by God.'"[37]

All who trust in Christ are chosen in Christ. So the apostle can tell the Thessalonian believers, "For we know, brothers [and sisters] loved by God, that he has chosen you, because our gospel came to you not only in word, but also in power and in the Holy Spirit and with full conviction" (1 Thess. 1:4–5).

We may be encouraged by the fruit of the faith that we see in our lives, but the only basis for our assurance is the gospel itself. In fact, in Calvin's view, faith and assurance are one and the same thing. To believe in Christ is to be assured objectively that everything that belongs to him now belongs to us. Our experience of assurance may be weaker or stronger at different moments, but we do not place our confidence in what we see or feel within ourselves. As John reminds us, our love for our brothers and sisters may "reassure our heart before [God]." Nevertheless, he adds, "whenever our heart condemns us, God is greater than our heart" (1 John 3:19–20).

This is why the apostle Paul calls us to "put on Christ" as our full armor to withstand Satan's schemes. To be sure, Satan tries to distract us from Christ through obvious sins, but he knows that he can undermine our faith by causing us to look away from the gospel. All of the pieces of armor that Paul mentions are external to us: the belt of truth, the breastplate of righteousness, gospel shoes, the shield of faith, the helmet of salvation, and the sword of the Spirit, "which is the Word of God" (Eph. 6:10–17). Each of these pieces is a synonym for the others. The only sure confidence we have in the face of temptation and doubt is God's objective promise in Jesus Christ.

In addition, election comforts believers when their children are taken in death or have disabilities that deprive the parents of that joy in seeing their children exercise repentance and faith. The Canons of Dort confess:

> Since we are to judge of the will of God from His Word, which testifies that the children of believers are holy, not by nature, but in virtue of the covenant of grace, in which they together with the parents are comprehended, godly parents ought not to doubt the election and

> salvation of their children whom it pleases God to call out of this life in their infancy (Gen. 17:7; Acts 2:39; 1 Cor. 7:14).[38]

Similarly, the Westminster Confession 10.3 declares, "Elect infants, dying in infancy, are regenerated, and saved by Christ, through the Spirit, who worketh when and where and how he pleaseth: so also are all other elect persons who are incapable of being outwardly called by the ministry of the Word." Conversion—explicit repentance and faith—are the ordinary effects of the new birth, but the Spirit can raise from spiritual death in an extraordinary way anyone whom the Father has chosen in the Son.

On this scriptural basis, the Anglican Thirty-Nine Articles affirm that for believers "the doctrine of election is full of sweet, pleasant and unspeakable comfort."[39] Luther recognized:

> If therefore we are taught, and if we believe, that we do not need to know these things, Christian faith is utterly destroyed and the promises of God and the whole Gospel entirely fall to the ground; for the greatest and only consolation and assurance for Christians in their adversity is that ... God does all things immutably and that His will cannot be resisted, changed, or hindered.[40]

Although "the doctrine of this high mystery of predestination is to be handled with special prudence and care, attending the will of God revealed in his Word," all who are effectually called to Christ are "assured of their eternal election."[41]

Unconditional election is an *evangelical* doctrine. It is taught in the Reformed and Presbyterian churches, but also in the Thirty-Nine Articles of the Anglican communion, the Savoy Declaration of the Congregationalists, and the London Baptist Confession.

It is no less insisted upon in the Lutheran confession. An entire article is given to it in the eleventh of the Solid Declarations in the Book of Concord, where Lutherans confess that when unconditional election is taught from God's Word, it "neither can nor should be regarded as useless or unnecessary, much less as offensive or injurious, because the Holy Scriptures not only in but one place and incidentally, but in many places, thoroughly treat and urge [explain] the same."[42] Only on this firm foundation can we be assured of our salvation and indeed the salvation of the church.[43] Furthermore, adds the Lutheran confession, knowledge of this doctrine leads to godliness and true worship.[44]

It is therefore "a very useful, salutary, consolatory doctrine; for it establishes very effectually the article that we are justified and saved without all works and merits of ours, purely out of grace alone, for Christ's sake."[45] Thus, far from being a trivial matter, this doctrine is crucial for providing the comfort that the gospel intends for all believers in daily struggles. "Thus the doctrine concerning this article can be employed profitably, comfortingly, and savingly and can be transferred in many ways to our use."[46] The article concludes with the salutary reminder that we are to restrict our study of this doctrine to that which is revealed in Scripture, finding our election in Christ, and leave God's secret councils to himself.[47]

So for all of the differences in churches today over election, it has enjoyed a remarkably ecumenical consensus across many times and places. If we are to see our churches reformed and renewed again according to God's Word, it will require nothing less than a radical re-orientation of our focus, away from ourselves—our decisions, plans, accomplishments, experience, and activity—to the Father, who gives us his Son and unites us to him by his Spirit. If God grants us such a new reformation, the faithful exposition of his electing grace will surely be an indispensable feature—as it has always been in the history of renewal in his church.

CONCLUSION: ELECTION IS A MYSTERY

It is often said that election/predestination is a mystery. When said in the spirit of humble submission to the Word of God, refusing to speculate beyond what is written, that is a salutary reminder. There is a lot we do not know about God's electing purposes: *who* the elect are, *how* election is consistent with human responsibility, and other questions. But we do know *that there is* an election, a remnant "chosen by grace," from Jews and Gentiles (Rom. 11:5, 9, 24–26). God has clearly revealed that he has chosen some to be saved, leaving the rest to the destiny that we all would have chosen for ourselves apart from God's grace. God has also clearly revealed that we were chosen in Christ, and therefore anyone who is in Christ is to regard himself or herself as chosen by God. We are told that the motive for God's election is his own mercy and grace, not anything in or foreseen in us, and that the elect will believe, bear fruit, and persevere to the end by this same grace.

There is a lot that we are told about the *fact* of election, though not its *mechanics*. We err on one side by speaking where God has not spoken and on the other side by being silent where God has spoken. Both reflect a kind of arrogance in the face of God's gracious act of condescending revelation. Election is a mystery, but it is not a mystery as to whether the Bible teaches it.

All of the great truths of God's Word are mysteries in this sense. They elude our ability to capture their essence. They do not contradict reason, but transcend it. The Trinity, the hypostatic union of human and divine natures in Christ, God's love and wrath: these are too marvelous for the human mind to grasp. Yet they are clearly revealed. "The secret things belong to the LORD our God, but the things that are revealed belong to us and to our children forever, that we may do all the words of this law" (Deut. 29:29).

In neither Calvin's writings nor the Reformed confessions does predestination occupy a central place, and especially on this topic warnings abound against speculation. Francis Turretin spoke for Reformed scholastics generally when he warned against trying to seek out God and his purposes apart from Christ and the gospel.[48] "Therefore," he adds, "it becomes us to dismiss the curious and useless questions of the [medieval] Scholastics, who by a rash presumption undertake to define the incomprehensible secrets of God's majesty."[49]

According to Calvin, consideration of God's predestination is of inestimable benefit if we find our election in Christ as he is offered to all people in the gospel, but a dangerous labyrinth if we presume to investigate God's secret councils.[50] He offers wise pastoral counsel:

> We shall never be clearly convinced as we ought to be, that our salvation flows from the fountain of God's free mercy, till we are acquainted with his eternal election.... The discussion of predestination—a subject of itself rather intricate—is made very perplexed, and therefore dangerous, by human curiosity, which no barriers can restrain from wandering into forbidden labyrinths, and soaring beyond its sphere, as if determined to leave none of the Divine secrets unscrutinized or unexplored.... [The curious] will obtain no satisfaction to his curiosity, but will enter a labyrinth from which he will find no way to depart. For it is unreasonable that man should scrutinize with impunity those things which the Lord has determined to be hidden in himself.... As soon as the Lord closes his sacred mouth, [we] shall also desist from further inquiry.[51]

In one of his sermons Calvin offers a fitting prayer to close this chapter:

> Grant, Almighty God . . . that having cast away and renounced all confidence in our own virtue, we may be led to Christ only as the fountain of thy election, in whom also is set before us the certainty of our salvation through thy gospel, until we shall at length be gathered into that eternal glory which He has procured for us by his own blood. Amen.[52]

FOUR

MISSION ACCOMPLISHED (ATONEMENT)

For whom did Christ die?

Far from speculative, this question is clearly addressed in Scripture and carries enormous theological and practical implications. In fact, the *extent* of Christ's work is connected inextricably with its *nature.*

Limited atonement (the "L" in TULIP) is an unfortunate label, found in no Reformed confession. It is better to speak of the work of Christ as specific or definite in its intention and scope. Alternative terms such as "definite atonement" or "particular redemption" seem more useful in clarifying this position. All orthodox Christians maintain that the atonement is limited either in its extent or in its nature. Calvinists believe that it is limited (or definite) in its extent, but unlimited in its nature or efficacy: Christ's death actually saved the elect. Arminians believe that it is unlimited in its extent, but limited in its nature or effiacy: Christ's death makes possible the salvation of everyone, but does not actually save any. Only universal salvation teaches that Christ's work is unlimited in both its extent and efficacy: Christ died for every person and every person is therefore saved. However, Arminians and Calvinists reject universal salvation on exegetical grounds.

In my view, one of the strongest arguments in favor of particular redemption is consideration of the nature of Christ's work. So even before we examine the passages dealing with the extent, I will focus on the efficacy of the cross.

THE NATURE AND EFFECTS OF CHRIST'S WORK ON THE CROSS

Contrary to caricatures, Reformed theology has never reduced Christ's redeeming work to the subsitutionary motif. It has recognized the various consequences of the cross, integrating these different emphases into its atonement doctrine. It may therefore be worthwhile to mention some of these other prominent motifs.

Atonement Theories

Sin is not merely on the surface of things, following Adam's negative example. Sin is not merely negative behaviors that need to be reformed; it is a condition from which we cannot extricate ourselves, and it incurs a penalty that a just and righteous God must execute. Death results from sin, and sin is defined by the law. It is the law's sentence that must be reversed if we are to share in everlasting life. The legal issue must be resolved if the symptoms of the curse are to be lifted. Therefore, the doctrine of penal substitution has always been at the heart of Reformed (as other) accounts of Christ's redemptive work.

Penal Substitution

Briefly defined, this work is *penal* not chiefly as punishment for God's offended dignity, but because God's holy justice requires payment of the debt incurred against his covenant law. It is *substitutionary* because someone else, namely, the God-Man, Jesus Christ, bears the sanctions (curses) of this law in our place.

Thus, reconciliation is not first of all subjective but objective. Because God can now legally forgive and justify the ungodly—in other words, he is objectively reconciled to the world—he can simultaneously reconcile the world to himself (Rom. 5:10; 2 Cor. 5:19–20). Other terms employed for this sacrifice (*lytron* and *antilytron*) as well as the prepositions *peri*, *hyper*, and *anti* (in the place of) underscore the substitutionary, vicarious nature of this sacrifice.

The sacrificial system of the old covenant gives us the typology for the priestly work of Christ as both mediator and victim. If our understanding of Christ's work does not correspond to—even better, is not grounded in—the sacrificial typology of Israel, it is not adequately Christian. Christ's saving work at Golgotha must be seen as the fulfillment of the elaborate ceremonies that turned on the imputation of guilt to a substitute who bears it away in its death. Jesus is "the Lamb of God, who takes away the sin of the world" (John 1:29).

This is precisely how the early Christians understood Christ's death. As Martin Hengel observes, "dying for" is a Pauline formula rooted in the earliest Jerusalem community (cf. Acts 6:13). The Jewish council accused Jesus, Stephen, and Paul of attacking the temple, which suggests, according to Hengel, that the heart of the church's earliest proclamation was "the death of the crucified Messiah, who had vicariously taken upon himself the curse of the Law, had made the Temple obsolete as a place of everlasting atonement for the sins of Israel." "Therefore the ritual Law had lost its significance as a necessary institution for salvation."[1] Apart from the notion of appeasement of God's wrath, the joyful announcement, "Behold, the Lamb of God, who takes away the sin of the world" (John 1:29) is inconceivable. It is the sinless substitute for the sinful people that is of central importance in the biblical doctrine of the atonement (Matt. 26:28; 2 Cor. 5:21; Gal. 3:13; Heb. 9:28; 1 Peter 2:24; 3:18; etc.).

It is not only the love of the Father but of the Son that secures this substitution. In Isaiah 53, Yahweh is the one who offers up the Suffering Servant on behalf of the people. And the good Shepherd himself says that *he* lays down *his own life* for the sheep, even adding, "No one takes it from me, but I lay it down of my own accord. I have authority to lay it down, and I have authority to take it up again" (John 10:18).

While those involved in carrying out the execution, both Jews and Gentiles, can be blamed in one sense, ultimately they did "whatever [God's] hand and [God's] plan had predestined to take place" (Acts 4:28). As "a lamb without blemish or spot," Peter declares, "he was foreknown before the foundation of the world but was made manifest in the last times for the sake of you" (1 Peter 1:19–20). That God's wrath required punishment underscores his justice, but the fact that he himself gave what was required in the place of our punishment underscores his merciful love. In both cases it is God who gives up his Son to the cross and the Son who gives himself up in the Spirit.

Recapitulation

Especially in the second-century theologian Irenaeus (Book 5 of *Against Heresies*), we encounter the prominent motif of Christ's saving work as involving a *recapitulation* (lit., "re-headshiping"). In this view, Christ—not only by his death and resurrection, but also by his incarnation and obedient life—undoes the work of the first Adam and fulfills his commission representatively on our behalf. From Adam, we receive death, but from Christ we receive life. This view finds clear parallels in the Reformed emphasis on covenantal headship, including the saving significance of Christ's life as well as death, which we underscore in the doctrine of Christ's active obedience.

Christ's Victory over the Powers (Christus Victor)

A more general way of speaking about Christ's death as a conquest over Satan is identified as the *Christus Victor* (Christ the Victor) model. Christ indeed "disarmed the rulers and authorities and put them to open shame, by triumphing over them in him" (Col. 2:15). This aspect of Christ's work received special emphasis in the writings of the church fathers as well as Martin Luther, who regarded the cross not only as the climax of Christ's humiliation for us but as the beginning of his exaltation.

Strictly speaking, it is not simply the forgiveness of transgressions and satisfaction of divine justice or dignity that is envisioned, but the beauty before God of a life that truly conforms to his covenantal will revealed in creation and in Israel (Ps. 24; 51:7). Christ not only brings forgiveness, but fulfillment of God's design for an obedient humanity. He crushes the serpent's head, foreshadowed in his victory over the demons, sickness, and death during his earthly ministry. Neither Satan nor Caesar is Lord, and eventually what is true in this one human representative, Jesus Christ, will be true of the new humanity taken from every nation. As our head is now glorified in heaven, completely righteous and beyond the reach of sin and death, so will we be as his body. God will finally have the obedient humanity he designed for his glory, with Christ as the firstborn of many brothers and sisters. Christ's death is the ground not only of forgiveness and justification, but of sanctification and glorification as well.

Human "principalities and powers" on earth are often witting or unwitting emissaries of the evil powers in heavenly places that seek to thwart God's redemptive plan. The "rulers of this age" who are "doomed to pass away" do not understand God's unfolding redemptive mystery, "which God decreed before the ages for our glory ... for if they had, they would not have crucified the Lord of glory" (1 Cor. 2:6–8). The powers here are not limited to spiritual beings (Satan and demons); these principalities and powers in heavenly realms are visible to us on earth in the regimes of oppression and violence, just as the church is that part of Christ's kingdom that is now visible in grace and suffers for his name.

The kingdoms that rise up against Yahweh and his Anointed are exposed as a sham, childish play-acting gone terribly wrong, something no longer in any way determining the obligations, loyalties, and destinies of those who are in Christ. Because of Christ's triumph, believers are no longer bound by the "elemental spirits of the world" (Col. 2:8). However, Christ's victory does not inaugurate a kingdom of glory here and now. It is not a power alongside other powers, vying for control through socio-political action.

Since Gustav Aulen's important work, *Christus Victor* (1931), the West has enjoyed a renewed appreciation for the often neglected model of conquest over the powers.[2] However, this view is often defended as an *alternative* to the emphasis on vicarious substitution.[3] While this model explores the richness of the church's participation in Christ's victory over sin and death, the tendency in contemporary defenses of this model is (1) to downplay the wrath of God in favor of the evil powers as the problem solved by Christ's work, and (2) to erase the qualitative distinction between Christ's unique work ("once and for all") and the church's conquering labors.

However, the important aspect of Christ's work as victory over the powers cannot be regarded as an alternative to the concept of vicarious substitution. Although it has emphasized Christus Victor, the East has always affirmed the curse-bearing substitution as central in its liturgical and doctrinal sources. More importantly, there are exegetical reasons why Christ's victory over the powers (*Christus Victor*) cannot be treated as an alternative to vicarious substitution. The love and the righteousness of God are equally revealed in the triumph of grace at the cross. After all, Satan and his demonic forces, including death, hold sway only as long as there is a legal basis for God's own case against us.

Colossians 2:13–15 is generally regarded as a prime text for the *Christus Victor* view. Here we read that Christ triumphed over the powers of darkness and made a public spectacle of them at the cross. However, this passage also says that he did this by nailing to the cross the list of legal violations with which we were charged according to God's law. Clearly, then, far from being an alternative, Christ's victory over the powers is based on its character as penal substitution. Christ bore our curse, and in so doing, he triumphed over Satan and his hosts. Similarly, in 1 Corinthians 15:53–57 the gift of immortality is attributed to Christ's having taken away the legal basis for death's dominion: "The sting of death is sin, and the power of sin is the law. But thanks be to God, who gives us the victory through our Lord Jesus Christ."[4]

Satisfaction of Divine Honor (Anselm)

The doctrine of penal substitution is often identified with the formulation of the eleventh-century Anselm of Canterbury. However, Anselm's view differs from penal substitution enough to justify its own treatment. According to Anselm, Christ's self-offering is received by the Father as a fitting satisfaction for the offense to his royal dignity that sin incurs.[5] This view has come to be identified as the *satisfaction theory*. Like a monarch slighted by the demeaning act of a subject, God must have a suitable tribute to outweigh the affront to his honor. Given the infinity of God's majesty, the penalty must be infinite, and only an infinite substitute can satisfy it.

There is an important truth in this theory, but it should not be equated with the Reformed understanding of the nature of Christ's redemptive work. Anselm's formulation properly directs our attention to the objective character of the atonement: *God's* problem with sin. It is God who has been offended. We need to know something about the distinctive character of this God who has been offended by our sin and the covenantal relationship in which he created us as image bearers. Sin reaches every nook and cranny of human relationships, but it is treated throughout Scripture as primarily a transgression of God's command. Sin's character is not sufficiently appreciated when it is reduced simply to broken lives and relationships between human beings or even to the individual's subjective sense of anxiety, guilt, and alienation from God. Apart from Christ's saving work, we are objectively enemies of God and subject to his just condemnation.

Nevertheless, the Anselmian interpretation has certain exegetical and doctrinal weaknesses. Louis Berkhof explains, "The theory of Anselm is sometimes identified with that of the Reformers, which is also known as the satisfaction theory, but the two are not identical."[6] While Anselm grounds the atonement in the need to satisfy God's offended *dignity*, Reformation theology recognized that it was God's *justice* that was at stake. There is no room in Anselm's theory for Christ's meriting life for us by his active obedience or for his suffering the penalty for our sin; only the offer of a tribute that more than compensated for human offense—"and this is really the Roman Catholic doctrine of penance applied to the work of Christ."[7] Furthermore, Reformed theology has faulted the theory for reducing atonement to a commercial transaction between God and Jesus Christ without any treatment of its communication to sinners.[8]

Moral Influence

Reacting against Anselm's theory, Abelard (1079–1142) defended what has come to be known as the *moral influence* theory. In this view, Christ died to offer a moving example of God's love for sinners, sufficient to induce them to repentance. Although Abelard included other aspects (particularly in his *Exposition of the Epistle to the Romans*), this model has been attractive especially in the trajectory that leads from Socinianism (forerunners of the Unitarian-Universalists) through the Enlightenment to liberal Protestantism.

This model is rooted in a Pelagian understanding of human nature after the fall. The only grace that we need, in this view, is the law, the opportunity to fulfill it, and a good model to imitate to that end. Semi-Pelagianism conceded that God's grace was necessary: we believe by our own free will, but grace is needed for perfection in sanctification. Both views fell under repeated condemnations by church councils, as we have seen. In a Pelagian/Semi-Pelagian view, Adam and Christ function as moral examples (cautionary and inspiring, respectively). It is not surprising that this movement tends toward an Arian or adoptionist Christology that denies Christ's eternal divinity.

In the sixteenth century, these heresies, combined in the movement known as Socinianism, led to Protestant liberalism. These assumptions were especially evident in the Enlightenment. Especially in Immanuel Kant, Christ's death can only offer a motive for repentance, but it is our own repentance that finally effects our redemption.[9] Since one does not need a radical salvation, one does not need a divine Savior.

Governmental Theory

Mediating between Socinian (moral influence theory) and Reformation perspectives, the great Arminian scholar Hugo Grotius (1583–1645) advanced the *governmental theory*.[10] According to this view, God's nature does not demand absolute justice and the satisfaction of his righteous purposes. Rather, Christ's death makes it possible for God to offer salvation on easier terms than those required by the law. Thus Christ's death is not a real payment of a debt, but is merely the basis on which God's just rule is exhibited.[11] The basis of salvation is therefore not Christ's perfect fulfillment of the law and curse-bearing in the place of sinners, but the imperfect obedience of believers to a relaxed law.[12]

Contemporary Preference for Subjective Atonement Theories

The moral influence and governmental views are basically subjective theories of atonement. That is, they focus on the change that the cross effects *in us*, which moves us to faith and repentance. Our faith and repentance then become the basis of God's acceptance. The bad news is not as bad (since God's justice does not require perfect fulfillment of his law) but the good news is not as good. Instead of the announcement that Christ has fulfilled all righteousness and has borne our judgment, the message is that we can be saved by less strenuous obedience. The objective character of Christ's work as creating a new state of affairs in God's relation to sinners is diminished to the vanishing point.

Liberal Protestants like Friedrich Schleiermacher and Albrecht Ritschl broke entirely from any judicial (legal or courtroom) understanding of the atonement. "With them and with modern liberal theology in general atonement becomes merely at-one-ment or reconciliation effected by changing the moral condition of the sinner. Some speak of a moral necessity, but refuse to recognize any legal necessity."[13]

Closer to home, the nineteenth-century American revivalist Charles G. Finney made the same arguments regarding Christ's work, although he did not deny Christ's divinity. Finney's scheme was essentially Pelagian, beginning with a rejection of original sin.[14] Reflected throughout his *Systematic Theology* is a commitment to a combination of the moral influence and moral government theories. It is legally impossible for one person—even Jesus Christ—to fulfill the law and bear the sanctions of violating that law in the place of others, Finney insisted. "If he had obeyed the law as our substitute, then why should our own return to personal obedience be insisted upon as a sine qua non of our salvation?"[15] The atonement is simply "an incentive to virtue."[16]

Rejecting the view that "the atonement was a literal payment of a debt," Finney can only concede, "It is true, that the atonement, of itself, does not secure the salvation of anyone."[17] Going beyond most advocates of the subjective theories, Finney insisted that our own perfect obedience to God's law is "the sine qua non" of our justification.

Yet even the softer versions fail to recognize that God's law is not merely a reflection of his will but of his moral nature. God *cannot* relax his holy will or righteous demands. Death is not merely an example of his displeasure or an arbitrary punishment. Rather, it is the legal sentence for violating his covenant (Ezek. 18:4; Rom. 6:23). God is as incapable of being unrighteous in his judgments as he is of being untruthful in his speech.

Especially in recent years, mainline theologians have pointed out the basically Pelagian and Socinian assumptions in modern theories of the atonement. Yale theologian George Lindbeck says that at least in practice, Abelard's view of salvation by following Christ's example (and the cross as the demonstration of God's love that motivates our repentance) now seems to have edged out any notion of an objective, substitutionary atonement. "The atonement is not high on the contemporary agendas of either Catholics or Protestants," Lindbeck surmises. "More specifically, the penal-substitutionary versions ... that have been dominant on the popular level for hundreds of years are disappearing."[18]

This situation is as true for evangelicals as for liberal Protestants, Lindbeck observes. This is because justification through faith alone (*sola fide*) makes little sense in a system that makes central our subjective conversion (understood in synergistic terms as cooperation with grace), rather than the objective work of Christ.[19] "Our increasingly feel-good therapeutic culture is antithetical to talk of the cross," and our "consumerist society" has made the doctrine a pariah.[20]

In our day, the influences are varied, but there is a widespread revulsion among many Protestant theologians against any notion of penal substitution—that is, the belief that Christ suffered in the place of sinners, bearing God's just wrath. In much of evangelicalism today, the emphasis falls on the question "What Would Jesus Do?" rather than "What Has Jesus Done?" Jesus provides the model for us to imitate for personal or social transformation. Especially in some contemporary Anabaptist and feminist theologies, the theme of God's wrath against sinners is regarded as a form of violence that legitimizes human revenge. Rather than see Christ's work as *bearing a sentence* that we deserved, it should be seen as *moral empowerment* for our just praxis (good works) in transforming the world.[21]

At least implicitly combining various subjective theories already mentioned, this trajectory is especially represented in the work of Jürgen Moltmann and liberation theology, but also in much of the popular preaching and teaching in contemporary evangelicalism.[22]

Like some Arminian theologians in the past, Clark Pinnock dismisses the penal substitution doctrine as if it were simply a curious and dangerous holdover from Calvinism.[23] Even in evangelical circles where substitutionary atonement is held in theory, the popular message seems to be that the principal purpose of Christ's death was simply to display God's love, which should provoke us to love him in return. However, as Roman Catholic scholar John Knox observes, "The concept of the cross as sacrifice belongs to the very warp and woof of the New Testament, while there is no evidence whatever that the early Church entertained the view that the purpose of Christ's death was to disclose the love of God."[24] Of course, it does disclose God's love, but only because, beyond expressing good intentions, it actually secures our salvation. In fact, if Christ's death is merely an object lesson rather than necessary for the satisfaction of God's justice, it exhibits divine cruelty rather than love.

An Integrated View of Christ's Work

Calvinists have always affirmed that the nature and effects of Christ's saving work cannot be reduced to a substitutionary sacrifice that brings forgiveness of sins. Recognizing the vastness of sin's effects, Reformed theology interprets Christ's saving work as including the recapitulation of Adam's disobedience, fulfilling all righteousness in our place as our federal head. "In short," noted Calvin, "from the time when he took on the form of a servant, he began to pay the price of liberation in order to redeem us."[25] Atonement cancels debts, but justification raises us upright in God's presence, with Christ's righteousness credited to our account. Atonement bears away our guilt, but justification gives us that positive standing in God's court so that we are not only forgiven but wholly acceptable, righteous, holy, and pleasing to God for Christ's sake.

Therefore, rather than accept a false choice between a substitutionary death and a saving life, there is much in the Irenaean theory of recapitulation that belongs to the warp and woof of vicarious substitution itself. Christ's penal substitution is not the whole of Christ's work, but without it nothing else matters. Therefore, his incarnation and obedient life are as necessary as his voluntary death.

Furthermore, Christ's death conquers the powers of Satan, evil, and death that hold this present age in bondage, and his saving work encompasses the resurrection and ascension, and his return to make all things new. Christ not only redeems souls but bodies as well, and not only bodies but the whole creation. Reformed theology has always encouraged a richer and more integrated understanding of Christ's saving work that encompasses his incarnation, obedient life, sacrificial death, and triumphant resurrection. Christ's sacrificial love is also an example for us to imitate (Matt. 20:25–28) and establishes God's moral government (Rom. 3:25).

However, Calvinism also points out that *none of these other aspects can actually be realized unless Christ's work is first of all a vicarious substitution, addressing the objective problem of guilt before a holy God.*

- Does Christ's work undo Adam's trespass, recapitulating a new humanity under Christ's life, death, and resurrection? Certainly it does, but we are still left in our sins unless Christ's death actually cancelled our debt.
- Does Christ's work conquer the powers of death and hell? Surely, but only because it first of all has satisfied justice so that the sentence of death may be lifted and Satan be deprived of his claims against us.
- Does the cross display God's love? Indeed it does, but only if it actually satisfies God's righteous demands and absolves us of our debt. Otherwise, it is a cruel object lesson. If the death of Christ was not *necessary* for the satisfaction of God's justice, it then reveals God's injustice rather than his love.
- Does Christ's saving work uphold God's just government and moral order in the world? Yes, but only if it actually satisfies the demands of justice to the full rather than serving merely as a moral deterrent.

THE EXTENT OF CHRIST'S WORK

From all that we have seen concerning the nature of Christ's work, it is apparent that Christ's death actually restores what was lost in Adam. More than that, it brings those for whom Christ died into a state that human beings have never entered, namely, the everlasting Sabbath—the consummated glory of the new creation. The powers of death and sin are vanquished. Christ's headship cancels Adam's. Our debts become Christ's and his righteousness becomes ours.

Yet what conclusions can we draw from this concerning the extent of Christ's saving work?

Option 1: Christ's Death Redeemed Every Person

One answer is that Christ's death objectively redeemed every person. The Scriptures unmistakably teach that God loves the world and that Christ died for the world (John 1:29; 3:16; 6:33, 51; Rom. 11:12, 15; 2 Cor. 5:19; 1 John 2:2). Therefore, advocates of this first view conclude that it was Christ's purpose to save each and every person who has ever or will ever live. Officially condemned in the sixth century, Origen's theory of universal restoration (*apokatastasis*) held that all spirits (though not bodies), including Lucifer, would be reunited in heavenly bliss.[26]

Refusing to bind God's freedom, Barth stopped short of a formal doctrine of universal salvation although his doctrines of election and reconciliation suggest it.[27] Confessional Lutheranism also teaches a universal and objective atonement, although (unlike Barth) it also holds to a limited and unconditional election. Only the elect will be finally saved, but some receive the saving benefits of Christ's work only for a time and then lose these benefits through mortal sin or unbelief. In this view, then, not all of those for whom Christ died will be saved, in spite of its universal intention.

Option 2: Christ's Death Made the Salvation of Every Person Possible

A second option is that Christ died to make salvation of every person possible. The intent of Christ's death, according to the Dutch Remonstrants (Arminians), was to make it possible for God to offer salvation by grace-enabled cooperation: namely, faith and evangelical obedience. It is generally recognized by Arminian theologians that if Christ actually accomplished the salvation of sinners at the cross (beyond making their salvation possible), then all for whom Christ died are actually saved. John Wiley therefore observes:

> The penal substitutionary theory leads of necessity either to universalism on the one hand, or unconditional election on the other. Dr. Miley makes the charge that "such an atonement, by its very nature, and by immediate result forever frees them from all guilt as a liability to the penalty of sin."[28]

These Arminian theologians recognized that if Christ's death itself actually *accomplished* salvation for everyone for whom it was intended, then the only options are Calvinism and universalism.

There is another version of this second view. A mediating position between the orthodox Calvinism defined by the Synod of Dort in 1618–1619 and Arminianism became known as "hypothetical universalism" (also "Amyraldianism," after its architect Moises Amyraut). Christ bore the sins of every person without exception, but since God knew that no one would embrace Christ apart from the gift of faith, he elected some to receive the benefits of Christ's work. Many evangelical Protestants hold to either an Arminian or Amyraldian view, in either case agreeing with the position expressed by Lewis Sperry Chafer: "Christ's death does not save either actually or potentially; rather it makes all men savable."[29] Similarly, Robert Lightner says that he rejects the Calvinist view "that the work of Christ on the cross was effective in and of itself."[30]

Option 3: Christ Redeemed All of the Elect

A third view is that Christ died for all of the sins of the elect, thereby redeeming them at the cross. According to this view, expressed by the Canons of Dort (chap. II, art. 3), Christ's death is "of infinite worth and value, abundantly sufficient to expiate the sins of the whole world," although Christ objectively and effectively bore the sins of the elect alone. Dort was repeating a common formula, "sufficient for the whole world but efficient for the elect alone." This formula is found in various medieval systems, including the writings of Aquinas, Gregory of Rimini, and Luther's mentor, Johann von Staupitz. As the formula indicates, this view does not limit the sufficiency or availability of Christ's saving work. Rather, it holds that the specific intention of Christ as he went to the cross was to save his elect.

As the seventeenth-century Puritan John Owen observed, every position that recognizes that some will finally be lost places a limit on the atonement at some point—either it is limited in its extent or in its effect. Owen summarizes the options: Christ died for (1) all of the sins of all people; (2) some of the sins of all people, or (3) all of the sins of some people.[31] If unbelief is a sin and some people are finally condemned, there is at least one sin for which Christ did not make adequate satisfaction.

PARTICULAR REDEMPTION

Among the arguments in favor of particular redemption (the third view) are the following. *First, this view maintains that Christ's death actually saves.* Scripture nowhere teaches that Christ came into the world to make salvation possible, much less that it becomes actual because of faith in Christ. This would be to make the *instrument* of receiving salvation (viz., faith) the *basis* of redemption.

The good news everywhere announced in the Scriptures is that God has reconciled us to himself through Christ's death, that this happened at the cross with Christ's blood-shedding, and that it has secured an objective forgiveness of sins (Isa. 53:10–11; Matt. 26:28; John 1:29; 3:17; 4:42; 1 Tim. 1:15; etc.). "Now that we are reconciled [by his death], shall we be saved by his life" (Rom. 5:10). All for whom Christ died have been redeemed, reconciled, and saved from the wrath of God. Through faith we receive this salvation that was accomplished at Golgotha. The "once and for all" accomplishment of Christ in his saving work at the cross leaves nothing for sinners to complete by their own actions, whether their decision or effort (Rom. 9:12–16).

This is why the evangelistic appeals in the New Testament are unhesitatingly joyful and full of comfort. All who embrace this gift are assured that Christ's work has already secured their salvation, the benefits of which they now receive through the gracious work of the Spirit that was included in Christ's purchase of his people.

Second, this view emphasizes the relationship between the Trinity and redemption. In the eternal councils of the Trinity (the covenant of redemption), the Father elected a certain number of the human race and gave them to his Son as their guardian and mediator, with the Spirit pledging to bring them to Christ in order receive all of the benefits of his mediation.

Jesus said that he came not to make salvation possible but to actually save "all that the Father gives me." He adds, "And this is the will of him who sent me, that I should lose nothing of all that he has given me, but raise it up on the last day.... This is why I told you that no one can come to me unless it is granted him by the Father" (John 6:37–39, 65). In John 10, Jesus said, "The good shepherd lays down his life for the sheep.... I am the good shepherd. I know my own and my own know me, just as the Father knows me and I know the Father; and I lay down my life for the sheep" (John 10:11, 14–15), which includes Gentiles as well as Jews (v. 16).

With Golgotha heavy on his heart, Jesus prays to the Father:

> Father, the hour has come; glorify your Son that the Son may glorify you, since you have given him authority over all flesh, to give eternal life to all whom you have given him.... Yours they were, and you gave them to me, and they have kept your word.... I am praying for them.

> I am not praying for the world but for those whom you have given me, for they are yours. (John 17:1–2, 6, 9)

Once more Jesus includes all "who will believe in me through their word, that they may all be one" (John 17:20–21). Throughout John's gospel, then, there is an unmistakable thread, testifying to an eternal covenant of redemption between the persons of the Trinity, with the Father giving a people to his Son: "all that the Father gives me."

In the New Testament letters as well, there is the correspondence between the will and the work of the Father, the Son, and the Spirit in election, redemption, and calling, which creates an unshakable ground of comfort. From the mass of fallen humanity, the Father has elected individuals "in Christ" (Rom. 8:30–34; Eph. 1:4–13).[32]

Scripture clearly teaches that the Father chose many, but not all, to eternal life and entrusted their salvation to the Son (John 6:38–39; 15:16; 17:9; Rom. 8:29; Eph. 1:4–5, 7, 15). Scripture also teaches that the Spirit effectually calls the elect and unites them to Christ. Although they do indeed believe in Christ, it is because of God's sovereign grace rather than their own free will: the Spirit brings the elect to Christ, giving them faith (John 1:12–13; 6:44; 15:16; Rom. 8:30; 9:6–24; Eph. 2:8; 2 Thess. 2:13). Chosen in Christ "before the foundation of the world," the elect are redeemed by Christ and united to Christ by the Spirit (Eph. 1:3–14). Luke reports that when a group of Gentiles heard the gospel, "as many as were appointed to eternal life believed" (Acts 13:48). Our entire salvation is credited not to the cooperation of sinners with God, but to the cooperation of the persons of the Trinity. In unity with the Father and the Spirit, the Son's purpose was to save the elect.

No charge can be brought against "God's elect," since Christ has redeemed them and intercedes for them in heaven (Rom. 8:33–34). Therefore, Christ's death is referred to as "the blood of the eternal covenant" (Heb. 13:20). Peter wrote to believers as those who are chosen "for obedience to Jesus Christ and for sprinkling with his blood" (1 Peter 1:2). The rest are "vessels of wrath prepared for destruction" (Rom. 9:22). Prior to their decision—indeed their existence—God elected Jacob and rejected Esau, exhibiting God's prerogative to show mercy on whomever he chooses (Rom. 9:1–21).

Jesus actually redeemed his elect (Rom. 8:32–35), his sheep (John 10:11, 15), his church (Acts 20:28; Eph. 5:25–27), and his people (Matt.

1:21). He gave "his life as a ransom for many" (Matt. 20:28; 26:28; cf. Isa. 53:12; Heb. 9:28). Sent to fulfill the Father's purpose, Jesus was confident that "nothing of all that he has given me" will be lost but will be raised on the last day (John 6:38–39). The Savior entered Paradise as conqueror with the triumphant announcement, "Behold, I and the children God has given me" (Heb. 2:13).

All of this shows "the heirs of the promise the unchangeable character of his purpose," which was "guaranteed ... with an oath, so that by two unchangeable things, in which it is impossible for God to lie, we who have fled for refuge might have strong encouragement to hold fast to the hope set before us" (Heb. 6:17–18). "He has ... *accomplished* redemption *for his people*" (Luke 1:68 NASB, emphasis added).

Third, this view places the focus entirely on Christ rather than on the believer. How do I know if I am one for whom Christ died? The only answer given in Scripture is that we look to Christ, in whom we were chosen and whose death is sufficient every human being—indeed, for a thousand worlds.

However, short of affirming universal salvation, the alternative views hold that in spite of Christ's objective work, many for whom he died will be finally lost, bearing their own judgment. But what then of Christ's promise above that he will not lose any of those whom the Father had given him?

Karl Barth's position illustrates this problem. We saw above that in his view, everyone is elect in Christ and redeemed by Christ—objectively saved and justified. However, he leaves open the possibility that some may be finally lost. However, if *one person* for whom Christ died is lost—even potentially or hypothetically, then his death did not actually save *anyone*. The only way to maintain the objectivity of Christ's saving work on the cross as well as a universal atonement is to deny the possibility that any person will be finally condemned. If the notion of universal election is exegetically untenable, however, the concept of universal salvation is all the more so.

Calvinists proclaim Christ as the all-sufficient Savior for all people everywhere, and when people do believe, we assure them that there is not a single sin—past, present, or future—that can separate them from the love of God in Jesus Christ. We do not look for our election or redemption within ourselves, but outside of ourselves. Yet we can only do so because the objective judgment of God against us has been dealt with decisively, fully, and finally, at the cross rather than in our subjective experience.

If Christ's sin-bearing does not actually bear away God's wrath for every person for whom he died, then, as Herman Bavinck concludes, "The center of gravity has been shifted from Christ and located in the Christian." Instead of Christ's objective work, "faith is the true reconciliation with God."[33] In this view, then, faith not only receives this reconciliation but accomplishes it, and faith becomes a saving work—the basis of, rather than the instrument of receiving, God's forgiving and renewing grace.

RESPONDING TO OBJECTIONS

1. *The New Testament teaches clearly that Christ died for the world.*

That Scripture explicitly teaches Christ's death for the world has never been in doubt among Calvinists; in fact, it has been celebrated as wonderful "glad tidings." We often take for granted that Gentiles are made joint-heirs with Christ, spiritual children of Abraham along with believing Jews. However, this was a radical message for first-century Jews and Gentiles. It lay at the heart of "the mystery of Christ" unfolded by Paul, the apostle to the Gentiles (Eph. 2:11–3:13), and his opposition from some Jewish Christians. This mystery of Jews and Gentiles united in Christ prompted the controversy that was resolved at the Jerusalem Council in Acts 15.

Yet all along, God purposed to save the world through Israel. This was anticipated as early as the announcement of the gospel in Genesis 3:15, was more clearly propounded in God's covenant with Abraham as "the father of many nations" (Rom. 4:17), is repeatedly promised in the prophets, and was to be proclaimed to the world by the risen Christ. Jesus did not come to restore the Mosaic covenant (a geo-political theocracy), but to bring to fruition the worldwide blessing of the Abrahamic covenant. He is the seed in whom all families of the earth are blessed (Gal. 3:11–18, 28).

However, throughout redemptive history, "salvation" always came through a remnant. The world was saved from the judgment of the flood, even though it was only through Noah and his family—eight people in all (1 Peter 3:20; 2 Peter 2:5). He saved Israel and Judah through a remnant. And he saved the whole world in the same way, having "ransomed people for God from every tribe and language and people and nation" as "a kingdom and priests to our God" (Rev. 5:9–10). "For God so loved the world, that he gave his only Son, that whoever believes in him should not perish but have eternal life" (John 3:16). God's love for the world moved him to choose an innumerable company of enemies, to give his Son even "while we were enemies" (Rom. 5:10), and to unite these sinners to Christ by his Spirit as a massive choir celebrating his mercy and grace into all of eternity. In this way, the world is indeed saved.[34]

Calvinists proclaim as confidently as any Christian that Christ is "the Lamb of God, who takes away the sin of the world" (John 1:29). We declare not only generally to all but particularly to each person that Christ's death is sufficient to save him or her. In the words of the Canons of Dort, "The death of the Son of God is the only and most perfect sacrifice and satisfaction for sin, and is of infinite worth and value, abundantly sufficient to expiate the sins of the whole world."[35] No one can say, "I came to Christ, but there was no redemption left for me." There is sufficient redemption in Christ's cross for every person in this world and in a thousand worlds besides. So there is no place in this view for thinking of the work of Christ as a limited reservoir of forgiveness with just enough for the elect. The question is never the sufficiency of Christ's work but the purpose of the triune God.

2. *It's a sin issue, not a Son issue.*

Some argue that Christ did accomplish objective forgiveness for every person, so that unbelievers are condemned not for their sins but for their unbelief in Christ. However, John tells us that the unbeliever "is condemned already" (John 3:18). Born into the world guilty in Adam, we add to our debts each day. One does not become condemned the moment he or she hears and rejects the gospel. Paul says that God's wrath is being stored up for the ungodly because of their sins (Rom. 1:18), and he even lists examples of the sins for which God's wrath will be poured out on the last day (Col. 3:5–6). Many other passages could be cited to prove the point that unbelief is simply one of the sins for which people will be condemned on the last day.

3. *Isn't this "unfair"? How could God justly condemn people if Christ didn't die for them?*

If we accept the full force of the passages cited above, the Father did not choose to save everyone and the Spirit will not draw everyone effectually to the Savior. Therefore, this understandable objection is directed as much to election and the application of redemption as it is to its achievement. In Romans 9, the apostle Paul answers the "fairness" objection in relation to election simply by pointing to God's sovereign freedom to choose whom he will out of a mass of condemned humanity.

And that is the point. Christ did not die for neutral creatures, but for sinners—enemies, hostile rebels. God's great love for humanity is manifest in the fact that even before Adam freely disobeyed God and enslaved himself and us to sin, the Father gave a people to the Son and gave his Son for his people. God was under no obligation to save any of his enemies, but even while we raged against him, he loved us and sent his Son for our salvation. Grace is not grace if it is compelled—even by an inner necessity of God's being. God could have justly condemned us all: that is the presupposition of grace and mercy.

Furthermore, the depths of God's love are revealed in the fact that he sent his Son to accomplish everything necessary for our salvation, not merely to make humanity "savable." He did not come halfway, as if to say, "I did my part, and now you need to do yours." Rather, he has carried his loving purposes all the way, accomplishing and applying redemption to those who were "dead in ... trespasses and sins" (Eph. 2:1).

Finally, because the death of Christ is sufficient for everyone, no one is left out except those who refuse this gift. Of course, we would all have refused this gift apart from grace, but God is not held responsible for this sinful condition. On the day of judgment, human beings will have no one to thank for salvation but God and no one to blame for condemnation but themselves. To all who do not yet trust in Christ, we announce God's reconciliation through the all-sufficient work of the Savior, with the solemn warning that outside of Christ there is no hope of salvation, either potentially or actually. To all who trust in Christ, we declare with Scripture that they are already now saved from God's wrath, death, and hell. Their salvation is not potential, but actual. They are not savable, but saved. It is not something that they are to complete or to make effective by their decision or effort, but is to be received as a free gift.

FIVE

CALLED AND KEPT (EFFECTUAL CALLING AND PERSEVERANCE)

"And those whom he predestined he also called, and those whom he called he also justified, and those whom he justified he also glorified" (Rom. 8:30). It is not without reason that the great Elizabethan Puritan William Perkins called Romans 8:30 the "golden chain" of salvation. Each link is forged by God's love in Christ and bound to the other links by God's immutable purpose in grace. If any one of these links depended ultimately on us, the whole chain would fall apart.

Chosen in Christ from all eternity, we are called effectually to Christ in time. Through faith, which itself is God's gracious gift, we receive Christ and all of his benefits. Already in the prophets there is the anticipation of a "new covenant" with his people, "not like the covenant that I made with their fathers" at Mount Sinai. "But this is the covenant that I will make with the house of Israel after those days, declares the LORD: I will put my law within them, and I will write it on their hearts. And I will be their God, and they shall be my people" and "they shall all know me.... For I will forgive their iniquity, and I will remember their sin no more" (Jer. 31:33–34).

Likewise, the Lord gave Ezekiel a vision of a valley of dry bones. Commanding him to preach life into them, the Lord raised to life a vast host through the word of Ezekiel (Ezek. 37:1–14). "My servant David shall be king over them, and they shall all have one shepherd.... I will make a covenant of peace with them. It shall be an everlasting covenant with them" (vv 24, 26).

God calls the prophets to announce the curses for transgressing the covenant that Israel swore at Mount Sinai, saying, "All the words that the

LORD has spoken we will do" (Ex. 24:3). On the basis of this covenant, there is no hope. Exile from God's holy land is the only righteous judgment. Yet God never allows this to be the final word. The law's judgment is always followed with the gospel—not on the basis of the oath that Israel swore at Sinai, but on the basis of the oath that God swore to Abraham, Isaac, and Jacob. That oath in Genesis 15, signified and sealed in the vision of God passing through the carcasses as a way of assuming the curses upon his own head, was God's unilateral pledge to give Abraham an inheritance and through his seed to bless the nations of the earth. It was reiterated in the oath to Jacob as he saw the vision of a stairway from heaven to earth and angels descending and ascending on it. Again God issues his unilateral pledge. It is to this vision that Jesus refers when he tells Nathaniel, "Truly, truly, I say to you, you will see heaven opened, and the angels of God ascending and descending on the Son of Man" (John 1:51).

The Sinai covenant required the personal performance of all the stipulations of the law as the condition for remaining in the land of Canaan. However, God's saving promise of a messianic seed is announced to Adam and Eve after the fall, to Abraham, and to David as a unilateral oath. In these instances, God swears to accomplish what never could have been achieved by us. "For God has done what the law, weakened by the flesh, could not do. By sending his own Son in the likeness of sinful flesh and for sin, he condemned sin in the flesh, in order that the righteousness requirement of the law might be fulfilled in us, who walk not according to the flesh but according to the Spirit" (Rom. 8:3–4).

Earlier Paul states, "For the promise to Abraham and his offspring that he would be heir of the world did not come through the law but through the righteousness of faith." Otherwise, "the promise is void," since "the law brings wrath" (Rom. 4:13–15). When it comes to the principle of inheriting everlasting life, law and promise are antithetical; this is the recurring motif in Paul's letters, especially Romans and Galatians.

That is why the good news of coming deliverance is always "for the sake of the promise I swore to your fathers." On the basis of the Sinai covenant, Israel stands condemned along with the rest of the human family "in Adam." This is the recurring argument in the prophets that is carried over into the New Testament (see, e.g., Rom. 1–3, summarized in 3:9, 20, as well as in chap. 5). This is why in Jeremiah 31 the new and everlasting covenant is distinguished from the covenant at Sinai. No longer is Israel commanded to circumcise its own heart (Deut. 10:16); God will circumcise the hearts of his people. "For I will forgive their iniquity, and I will remember their sin no more" (Jer. 31:34).

All that Christ has won for us, outside of us in history, is given to us when the Holy Spirit unites us to him through faith. In Reformed theology, this is called "effectual calling," and it yields the treasures of our union with Christ: justification, adoption, sanctification, and glorification. The distinction is drawn between the general call, which is universal, and the effectual call, through which the Spirit draws the elect to Christ. In both cases, the means is the Word of God, but some hear it and resist the message while the Spirit melts the hard hearts of his elect and causes what was once an offense to become marvelously sweet and delightful.

According to the Westminster Confession 10.1:

> All those whom God hath predestined unto life, and those only, he is pleased, in his appointed and accepted time, effectually to call, by his Word and Spirit, out of that state of sin and death, in which they are by nature, to grace and salvation, by Jesus Christ; enlightening their minds spiritually and savingly to understand the things of God, taking away their heart of stone, and giving unto them a heart of flesh; renewing their wills, and, by his almighty power, determining them to that which is good, and effectually drawing them to Jesus Christ; yet so, as they come most freely, being made willing by his grace.

The Spirit's renovating work, which is nothing less than a "new creation," is not restricted to the hearts of individual believers. One day it will encompass our bodies—and not only human beings, but the whole creation in all of its breadth and diversity. Yet, as Calvin commented, for now "the principal work of the Spirit is faith."[1] The triune God is gathering a people, united to Christ, for the end-time festival.

ELECTION AND EFFECTUAL CALLING

As we see in Romans 8:30, Scripture itself draws the connection between election and effectual calling. Jesus said, "You did not choose me, but I chose you and appointed you that you should go and bear fruit and that your fruit should abide" (John 15:16). In the New Testament, the new birth and the presence of the Spirit in our hearts are harbingers of the age to come. In some remarkable sense, the future consummation has already penetrated this evil age, so that even now it is beginning to make all things new from the inside out. This is God's work.

Chosen in Christ before the creation of the world, redeemed by Christ in history, receiving an inheritance in Christ, and being sealed in Christ by the gospel, we receive our salvation from start to finish as the work of the Father, in the Son, by the Spirit (Eph. 1:3–14). In fact, in Romans 8 it is this realization of God's gracious election, calling, justification, and glorification (8:29–30) that leads Paul to the summit of doxology, first in verses 31–39, and then again finally in 11:33–36.

All of this means that the gospel is not an experience we have, much less one that we can bring about. It is an announcement that creates faith in the Redeemer who makes it. It comes to us from the outside. It *creates* new experiences and inner transformation that yields good works, but the gospel itself—and the Spirit's effectual calling through that gospel—remain distinct from anything done by us or within us. The gospel is God's life-giving word, creating a new world out of nothing (Rom. 4:16–17; 1 Peter 1:23, 25).

Those whom God chose before the creation of the world, he also calls in due time by his Spirit (Eph. 1:4–15). The connection between election and calling is well-attested, both within the Pauline corpus (Rom. 9:6–24; Eph. 1:4–13; 2 Thess. 2:13–15; 2 Tim. 1:9) and elsewhere (John 6:29, 37, 44, 63–64; 15:16, 19; Acts 13:48; 1 Peter 1:2; 2 Peter 1:10), and it proceeds as the execution of an eternal covenant of redemption within the context of a historical covenant of grace. In effectual calling, the Spirit unites us here and now to the Christ who redeemed us in the past.

We see Jeremiah's prophecy fulfilled throughout the book of Acts: as Christ was proclaimed, people responded in repentance and faith. When the businesswoman Lydia heard Paul's message, "the Lord opened her heart to pay attention to what was said by Paul," and she and her household were baptized (Acts 16:14–15). The accused became the justified and then witnesses in the courtroom. When the Gentiles in Antioch heard the gospel, "they began rejoicing and glorifying the word of the Lord, and as many as were appointed to eternal life believed" (Acts 13:48). Far from inhibiting evangelism, God's electing and regenerating grace ensured that "the word of the Lord was spreading throughout the whole region" (v. 49). Left to ourselves, none of us would receive this Word. God's sovereign grace guarantees the success of evangelism and missions.

EFFECTUAL CALLING AND THE BONDAGE OF THE WILL

The Spirit's effectual calling of sinners is not only predestined by the Father, in the Son; it is necessitated by our fallen condition. Years ago, a famous evangelist wrote a book titled *How to Be Born Again*, and many of us are familiar with sermons that have offered similar directions for attaining the new birth. However, this assumes a semi-Pelagian view of our condition as children of Adam.

Our will can only choose that in which our nature delights. If our nature is in bondage to unbelief, then our will is not free with respect to God. Jesus knew why some did not believe: "No one can come to me unless the Father who sent me draws him. And I will raise him up on the last day.... This is why I told you that no one can come to me unless it is granted him by the Father" (John 6:44, 65).

Note too what Jesus told Nicodemus, that one cannot even "see the kingdom of God" without being "born again [from above]" (John 3:3). As the conversation unfolds, it becomes clear that Jesus is not telling Nicodemus how he can bring about his new birth but how the Spirit accomplishes it. Jesus explains, "The wind blows where it wishes, and you hear its sound, but you do not know where it comes from or where it goes. So it is with everyone who is born of the Spirit" (v. 8). The new birth is a mysterious work of the Spirit in his sovereign freedom, not an event that we ourselves can bring about any more than our natural birth.[2] Two chapters earlier, we read, "But to all who did receive him, who believed in his name, he gave the right to become children of God, who were born, not of blood nor of the will of the flesh nor of the will of man, but of God" (John 1:12–13).

By nature, we "suppress the truth" in unrighteousness (Rom. 1:18). It is not that we are ignorant, but that we willfully reject, distort, and deny even that which we know about God from creation (vv. 20–32). Paul asks his fellow Jews, "Are we Jews any better off? No, not at all. For we have already charged that all, both Jews and Greeks, are under sin, as it is written: 'None is righteous, no, not one; no one understands; no one seeks for God'" (Rom. 3:9–11).

The fallen mind is darkened to the gospel apart from the Spirit's gift of faith (1 Cor. 2:14). Believers "were dead in the trespasses and sins in which [they] once walked.... But God, being rich in mercy, because of the great love with which he loved us, *even when we were dead* in our trespasses, *made us alive* together with Christ" (Eph. 2:1–2, 4–5, emphasis added). Even faith belongs to the gift that is freely given to us by God's grace (vv. 5–9). We are saved *for* works, not *by* works (v. 10). Therefore, salvation "depends not on human will or exertion, but on God, who has mercy" (Rom. 9:16).

In our fallen condition, we try to justify ourselves by assuming that while we may commit sins from time to time, we are basically good "deep down." At least our hearts are right. However, Scripture challenges this perspective. Jeremiah lamented, "The heart is deceitful above all things, and desperately sick; who can understand it?" (Jer. 17:9).

The Sinai covenant required Israel to circumcise its own heart (Deut. 10:16), but the command could not effect any change. Even in this constitution of the Sinai covenant itself God anticipates Israel's disobedience and the new covenant in which he will circumcise their heart and the heart of their children (Deut. 30:1–10).

This is more clearly prophesied in Jeremiah 31, where God's circumcision of the hearts of his people will be based on his forgiveness and grace alone. God's commands—even the command to repent and believe—cannot change hearts so that people can obey them. Through the law the Spirit inwardly convicts, but only the gospel—the announcement of Christ's saving person and work—can absolve us and give us a new heart. Jesus, too, emphasized that wickedness is not first of all perverse actions, but that these acts themselves have their fountainhead in a perverse heart (Matt. 12:34). We cannot change our own heart by an act of will or by changing our behavior.

Most Arminians will agree that we cannot make the slightest move toward God apart from his grace. We have already pointed out that classic Arminianism at least affirms original sin and the natural bondage to sin apart from grace. Nevertheless, many who have identified themselves with this Arminian stream have in fact made this Pelagian move.[3] Yet even in evangelical Arminianism, the Spirit's work is always conditioned on human cooperation. According to H. Orton Wiley, "the Holy Spirit exerts His regenerating power only on certain conditions, that is, on the conditions of repentance and faith."[4]

To Calvinist ears, this sounds like demanding that a blind person see before he or she has been healed of blindness. The glory of the new covenant is that God gives in the gospel what he demands in his law: both justification and the renewal of heart and life. Only because of God's one-sided act of regeneration does anyone repent and believe. So even though Arminianism should not be equated with semi-Pelagianism, it does in fact deny that the new birth is a unilateral act of God's grace. Every person is graciously enabled to believe, and the new birth is the consequence rather than the source of that decision.

EFFECTUAL CALLING OR IRRESISTIBLE GRACE?

Why do some who hear the gospel believe while others do not? This is a question that confronts every Christian, especially as we long for the conversion of loved ones. Caricatures abound on both sides of this issue. On one hand, it is sometimes assumed that Arminians believe that the fall has left the will unaffected; though weakened by sin, we are still free to choose or reject the gospel apart from any gracious assistance. I pointed out in chapter 1 that this is a misunderstanding, since at least Arminius and classical (evangelical) Arminians usually hold that no one can believe in Christ apart from grace.

At the other end is the caricature of Calvinism as teaching that God drags people into heaven kicking and screaming against their will, while denying grace to others who seek him but are not elect. As I argue below, the infelicitous term "irresistible grace"—popularized in the I of "TULIP"—contributes to that caricature. Traditionally, Reformed theology has referred to this inward work of the Spirit through the gospel as *effectual calling*, not as *irresistible grace*. "Irresistible" suggests coercion, the sort of causal impact that is exercised when force is applied to someone or something. As we will see, Calvinism denies in explicit terms that God coerces people against their will, either toward belief or unbelief.

In treating election I have demonstrated that *in relation to God*, our choices are free. It is *in relation to our sinful condition* that our will is bound, with our whole nature, to unbelief and idolatry. Calvinism also denies that God is as active in the condemnation of the nonelect as he is in the salvation of the elect. Not only *can* God's grace be resisted; it is *always* resisted by the fallen heart, until the Spirit opens our eyes to behold the glory of God in the face of Christ. There is no neutral moment where God would need to actively cause our unbelief; we are all born in a condition of spiritual death.

The external call and the inward or effectual call are not actually two different events. It is the same Word that is proclaimed, and through it saving faith is granted by the Holy Spirit. Yet one person believes and another does not. This is because the Word that is externally proclaimed by the lips of the preacher is made effectual in the hearts of the elect whenever the Spirit chooses.[5] Everyone is called to Christ, but only the sheep hear his voice. The Spirit delivers the gift of faith through the preaching of the gospel and confirms and strengthens it through the sacraments.[6] Yet some are attracted to the light, others repelled by it. Those who do come to trust in Christ are represented as "dead in sins" (Eph. 2:1–5), unable to respond until God graciously grants them the gift of faith to freely embrace what they would otherwise reject (Isa. 65:1; John 1:13; 3:7; 6:44; Acts 13:48; 16:14; 18:10; Rom. 9:15–16; 1 Cor. 2:14; Eph. 2:1–5; 2 Tim. 1:9–10; 2:10, 19).

Once more we see the value of that distinction we have already encountered between natural and moral ability. In Adam, we freely choose our alliance with sin and death. The fall has not destroyed our natural ability to reason, observe, experience, and judge, but rather our moral ability to reason, observe, experience, and judge our way to God as Lord and Redeemer. It is our moral blindness to God's Word that keeps us from raising our eyes to heaven to say, "Lord, be merciful to me, a sinner!" (Luke 18:13). The problem is not the *power* to will and to do, but the *moral* determination of that willing and doing by slavery to sinful autonomy. The will is moved by the mind and affections; it cannot act in isolation. "For the word of the cross is folly to those who are perishing, but to us who are being saved it is the power of God" (1 Cor. 1:18).

The Second Helvetic Confession teaches, "Therefore, in regard to evil or sin, man is not forced by God or by the devil but does evil by his own free will, and in this respect he has a most free will." In "heavenly things," he is bound in sin. "Yet in regard to earthly things, fallen man is not entirely lacking in understanding." While passive in this initial regeneration, those who are regenerated work actively in good works. "For they are moved by God that they may do themselves what they do.... The Manichaeans robbed man of all activity and made him like a stone or a block of wood.... Moreover, no one denies that in external things both the regenerate and the unregenerate enjoy free will," as in deciding whether to leave the house or remain at home. However, with respect to salvation, their will is bound by sin until God graciously acts.[7]

More precisely, the Westminster Confession (chap. 11) states: "God hath endued the will of man with that natural liberty that it is neither forced, nor by any absolute necessity of nature determined to good or evil."

Before the fall, the will was entirely free to choose good or evil, but after the fall, humanity "has wholly lost all ability of will to any spiritual good accompanying salvation," rendering every person "dead in sin ... not able, by his own strength, to convert himself, or to prepare himself thereunto."

> When God converts a sinner and translates him into the state of grace, he frees him from his natural bondage under sin and, by his grace alone, enables him freely to will and to do that which is spiritually good; yet so as that, by reason of his remaining corruption, he does not perfectly or only will that which is good, but does also that which is evil. The will of man is made perfectly and immutably free to good alone in the state of glory only.[8]

Such statements reflect a basic Augustinian consensus, filtered through the Reformation. The Westminster divines add that God is pleased "in his appointed and accepted time, effectually to call, by his Word and Spirit," all of the elect "out of that state of sin and death in which they are by nature, to grace and salvation by Jesus Christ." He accomplishes this by "enlightening their minds ... taking away their heart of stone ... renewing their wills ... and effectually drawing them to Jesus Christ; *yet so as they come most freely, being made willing by his grace*" (emphasis added).[9]

The Synod of Dort affirmed that God's inward calling always meets with success. However, just as the fall "did not abolish the nature of the human race" but "distorted" it and led to spiritual death, "so also this divine grace of regeneration does not act in people as if they were blocks and stones; nor does it abolish the will and its properties or coerce a reluctant will by force, but spiritually revives, heals, reforms, and—*in a manner at once pleasing and powerful*—bends it back" (emphasis added).[10] The will is liberated, not violated. "If it be compelled," says John Owen, "it is destroyed."[11]

While "irresistible grace" conjures the image of a physical cause-and-effect (i.e., coercion), "effectual calling" suggests an act of communicating. If I yell, "Fire!" in a crowded theater, the effect may certainly be powerful (namely, clearing the room), but it is not the same as forcing people to leave against their will. On one hand, Calvinists rightly insist that the Spirit's regenerating work is more than moral persuasion, a gentle wooing that can be yielded to or resisted. On the other hand, they deny that this work is coercive.

Here we may be aided by a formulation by some of the ancient fathers, especially Basil, picked up by Calvin: "To the Father is attributed the effective principle of what is done, and the fountain and wellspring of all things; to the Son, wisdom, counsel, and the ordered arrangement of what is done; but to the Spirit is assigned the power and efficacy of the action."[12] So in effectual calling, it is not an impersonal force acting on an object, but the Father, communicating the life-giving message concerning his Son, and the effect (namely, trusting in Christ) is brought about *within us* by the mysterious power of the Spirit. Therefore, we are responding to the Father, understanding who Christ is and what he has done for us, and yielding free assent to and confidence in that saving news. When God says, "Let there be light!" there is light. However, like that original act of creating, the new creation occurs through the Word and Spirit. When the Father talks about his Son, things happen!

In the conversion of Lydia in Acts 16:14, we read, "The Lord opened her heart to pay attention to what was said by Paul." Apart from the Spirit's work, not even the Father as the speaker or the Son as the content could melt her heart. We cannot be persuaded into the kingdom by the greatest of rhetoricians or subject matter; we need to be liberated from within to embrace the gospel from without. This is why "irresistible grace" is simply the wrong term for the work that our Reformed confessions identify as effectual calling. In the words of Canons of Dort, the Spirit "pervades the inmost recesses of man; he opens the closed and softens the hardened heart, and circumcises that which was uncircumcised" and "quickens the dead."[13]

This is the language of Jeremiah 31. This is not mere "moral persuasion," as if, "after God has performed His part, it still remains in the power of man to be regenerated or not." Yet neither is it coercive. Rather, it is "a supernatural work, most powerful, and at the same time most delightful, astonishing, mysterious and ineffable; not inferior in efficacy to creation or the resurrection of the dead."[14] It is not without reason that the New Testament compares regeneration to these miraculous events.

God's Word is not, therefore, only the speech of the Father concerning the Son, which we then make effective by our own decision, but the instrumental action through which the Spirit brings about within us the corresponding response. It is a *performative* Word. In effectual calling, the Spirit draws us into the world that the Word not only *describes* but *brings into existence*. Through this Word, the Spirit works not only to propose, lure, invite, and attract, but actually kills and makes alive, sweeping sinners from their identity "in Adam" to the riches of their inheritance in Christ. Spectators become participants in the unfolding drama. When *God* is the dramatist, in command of both the plot (redemption) and the casting (effectual calling), we can conclude that in this case at least, the "new creation" is simultaneously effective and uncoerced.[15]

Effectual calling, therefore, does not occur apart from means. God brings us to faith through the proclamation of the gospel. Such proclamation cannot be confused with moral exhortation. It is a powerful announcement. Nor is it mere doctrinal instruction, but through it the Spirit creates the world of which the Father speaks through the lips of his ministers. "The word of God is living and active" (Heb. 4:12). We are reminded in Isaiah 55:10–11:

> For as the rain and the snow come down from heaven
> and do not return there but water the earth,
> making it bring forth and sprout,
> giving seed to the sower and bread to the eater,
> so shall my word be that goes out from my mouth;
> it shall not return to me empty,
> but it shall accomplish that which I purpose,
> and shall succeed in the thing for which I sent it.

In the gospel, Christ is not only promised; he *is* the promise. "For all the promises of God find their Yes in him. That is why it is through him that we utter our Amen to God for his glory" (2 Cor. 1:20). In this way, we who were accustomed to singing Walt Whitman's "Song of Myself" find ourselves humming a different tune. Once those who "by their unrighteousness suppress the truth" (Rom. 1:18) are swept into the story that God is telling the world, they find themselves "born again, not of perishable seed but of imperishable, through the living and abiding word of God.... And this word is the good news that was preached to you" (1 Peter 1:23, 25b). Peter adds:

> In his great mercy he has given us new birth into a living hope through the resurrection of Jesus Christ from the dead, and into an inheritance that can never perish, spoil or fade. This inheritance is kept in heaven for you, who through faith are shielded by God's power until the coming of the salvation that is ready to be revealed in the last time. (1 Peter 1:3–5 NIV)

The Father objectively reveals the Son and the Spirit inwardly illumines the understanding to behold the glory of God in the face of Christ (2 Cor. 4:6; cf. John 1:5; 3:5; 17:3; 1 Cor. 2:14), liberating the will not only to assent to the truth but to trust in Christ (Jer. 32:39–40; Ezek. 36:26; Eph. 2:1–9; Heb. 8:10). Regeneration or effectual calling is something that happens to those who do not have the moral capacity to convert themselves, yet it not only happens *to* them; it happens *within* them, winning their consent. The God who says, "Let there be.... And there was ..." also says, "Let the earth bring forth...." Because the Word of God is not mere information or exhortation but the "living and active" energies of the triune God, it is far more than a wooing, luring, persuasive influence that might fail to achieve the mission on which it was sent. In both instances, it is the work of the Father, in the Son, by the Spirit.

CONVERSION

It is vital to distinguish the new birth (or effectual calling) from conversion. In the former, we are passive: acted upon and within by the triune God through the gospel. In the latter we are active (having been "activated" by grace), since we are raised from spiritual death to everlasting life. If we fail to distinguish these "moments," we easily fall into the Arminian error of thinking that repentance and faith cause the new birth, or the hyper-Calvinist error of thinking that because the new birth precedes our response, there is no place for the latter.

The new birth yields the fruit of repentance and faith, not the other way around. We hear the gospel and the Spirit creates faith in our hearts to embrace it. However, in conversion we are active. "In the covenant of grace, that is, in the gospel," notes Bavinck, "there are actually no demands and no conditions. For God supplies what he demands. Christ has accomplished everything, and though he did not accomplish rebirth, faith, and repentance in our place, he did acquire them for us, and the Holy Spirit therefore applies them." At the same time, there are still commands in the Bible, including the command to repent and believe. Yet even these come to us not as conditions that we must fulfill, but as gifts that God promises to give.

> The covenant of grace, accordingly, is indeed unilateral: it proceeds from God; he has designed and defined it. He maintains and implements it. It is a work of the triune God and is totally completed

> among the three Persons themselves. *But it is destined to become bilateral*, to be consciously and voluntarily accepted and kept by humans in the power of God. (emphasis added)[16]

We are passive receivers of our justification and renewal, but the goal is not to leave us silent and inert; it is to give us our voice back, so that we can join the choir of praise to God's glorious grace, to give us a heart of gratitude, legs that walk, hands that give to those in need.

In conversion (unlike regeneration), we are told, "work out your own salvation with fear and trembling, for it is God who works in you, both to will and to work for his good pleasure" (Phil. 2:12–13). This does not mean that in conversion our salvation shifts from God's sovereign grace in Christ to our activity and cooperation, but that the salvation that has been given is worked out by that same Spirit, through the same gospel, in a genuine relationship in which we become covenant partners who are now alive to God in Christ. Apart from our repentance and faith, there is no justification or union with Christ. Yet even this human response is a gift of the Spirit through the gospel.

Does this mean that we are monergists at the point of regeneration and justification, only to become synergists thereafter? Not at all. Our faith and grateful obedience are not only responses to God's gift, but are produced in us from beginning to end by the same grace of God. In the new birth, the Spirit gives us faith to cling to Christ, an act that involves the intellect but is more a matter of the heart. As Calvin says, "The knowledge of faith consists in assurance rather than in comprehension."[17] This gift of a new heart is even greater than a change of mind. The Spirit's work is to be praised especially in the heart's confirmation in the gospel, Calvin notes, since "the heart's distrust is greater than the mind's blindness."[18]

For the unbelieving world a kind of superficial happiness and general well being full of entertainments but lacking any real plot hides the fear of death. Apart from God's grace, we cannot come to terms sufficiently either with our mortal wound or enter into the genuine revelry and mirth of God's kingdom. Denying our sin (not just *sins*, but our sinful condition), we do not see the need for repentance—at least the deep change of mind that causes us to rethink everything in our relationship to God. Like the generation that Jesus compared to children playing the funeral game (John the Baptist's ministry of repentance) and the wedding game

(Christ's ministry of dancing and mirth), we do not know how to weep or to laugh.

Christ does not come to improve our lives—the "old self," to use Paul's vocabulary—but to crucify it and bury it with him so that we may be raised with him in newness of life (Rom. 6:1ff.). Repentance (*metanoia*) means "change of mind." It is treated in Scripture as first of all the knowledge of sin produced by the law (Rom. 3:20). In Jesus' Upper Room discourse, the Spirit is an attorney sent to convict us inwardly of God's righteousness and our unrighteousness (John 16:8–11). This knowledge, however, is not merely intellectual but emotional—it involves the whole person.

In David's confession in Psalm 51:1–9, we see the elements of repentance. First, he acknowledges the righteousness of God's judgment of his sin. What makes it more than a mistake or failing to live up to his potential or even engaging in antisocial behavior is the fact that his sin against Bathsheba and her husband is first and foremost a sin against *God*. Second, he does not wallow in guilt, but turns in faith to God's free forgiveness:

> Purge me with hyssop, and I shall be clean;
> wash me, and I shall be whiter than snow.
> Let me hear joy and gladness;
> let the bones that you have broken rejoice.
> Hide your face from my sins,
> and blot out all my iniquities. (Ps. 51:7–9)

As Paul observes, "godly grief produces a repentance that leads to salvation without regret, whereas worldly grief produces death" (2 Cor. 7:10). After all, "God's kindness is meant to lead you to repentance" (Rom 2:4). While the law produces a *legal repentance* (fear of judgment), the gospel engenders an *evangelical repentance* that bears the fruit of real change. David turns outside of himself to his merciful God. Here we see the closest possible link between repentance and faith. By itself repentance is merely the experience of damnation—until one looks by faith to Jesus Christ.

Although repentance itself is a decisive change of mind, it leads to what Scripture calls "fruit in keeping with repentance" (Matt. 3:8) or "deeds in keeping with their repentance" (Acts 26:20; cf. Matt. 7:16; Luke 3:9; 8:15; John 12:24; Rom. 7:4; Gal. 5:22; Col. 1:10). In this sense, of course, repentance is always partial, weak, and incomplete in this life. Nor is it a one-time act. As the first of Luther's Ninety-Five Theses states, "Our Lord and Master Jesus Christ, in saying 'Repent ye,'' intended that the whole life of believers should be penitence."

The Spirit brings us to repentance by convicting us of sin by the law, the gospel leads us to faith in Christ, and this faith produces within us a hatred of our sin and a craving for righteousness. Since our tendency even as believers is still to turn back toward ourselves and trust in our repentance, we must be driven again to despair of our righteousness as well as our sins by the law and to cling to Christ. Therefore, this is not a once-and-for-all transition from legal repentance to faith in Christ to evangelical repentance, but a perpetual cycle that defines the Christian life.

According to Scripture it is not our tears but Christ's blood that satisfies God judgment and establishes peace with God (Rom. 5:1, 8–11). In the words of the familiar hymn "Rock of Ages,"

> Not the labors of my hands can fulfill Thy law's demands;
> Could my zeal no respite know, could my tears forever flow,
> All for sin could not atone; Thou must save, and Thou alone.

God heals the bones that he crushes and raises up those whom he has cast down. "But he gives more grace. Therefore it says, 'God opposes the proud, but gives grace to the humble'" (Jas. 4:6). The law begins repentance by convicting us of sin, but only the gospel can lead us to boldly claim God's promise with David: "Let me hear joy and gladness; let the bones that you have broken rejoice. Hide your face from my sins, and blot out all my iniquities" (Ps. 51:8–9).

Conversion not only includes repentance but faith. Arrested, arraigned, and indicted, in repentance we turn away *from* ourselves—our untruths, our sins, and our fraudulent claim to righteousness—and in faith we look *to* Christ for salvation and for every spiritual gift. To put it differently, in repentance we confess (with David) that God is justified in his verdict against us, and in faith we receive God's justification. Dead to sin and alive to Christ once and for all in regeneration (Rom. 6:1–11), we are called to die daily to our old self and to live daily by "the free gift of God," which "is eternal life in Christ Jesus our Lord" (6:12–23).

Faith is not merely a subjective experience or positive attitude. It is not wishful thinking. Faith is only as good as its object. In Hebrew, it means to say "amen" to God's Word, or to take refuge in and lean on him. In the New Testament, faith is trusting in Christ through the testimony of his apostles (2 Cor. 4:13; Phil. 1:27; 2 Thess. 2:13; especially in John). More often still, it is specifically exhibited as faith in Jesus and his declarative Word (John 4:50; 5:47; Rom. 3:22, 25; 5:1–2; 9:30–32; Gal. 2:16; Eph. 2:8; 3:12), a trustful reliance in Jesus Christ (*en*: Mark 1:15; John 3:15; Eph. 1:13; *epi* plus dative: Isa. 28:16, quoted in Rom. 9:33; Luke 24:26; Rom. 10:11; 1 Tim. 1:16; 1 Peter 2:6; cf. Acts 16:34; Rom. 4:3; 2 Tim. 1:5, 12). The use of *epi* with the accusative or *eis* with the accusative ("into") emphasizes the transfer of trust from ourselves to God in Christ (John 2:11; 3:16, 18, 36; 14:1; Rom. 10:14; Gal. 2:16; Phil. 1:29, etc.). Such faith is described as looking to Christ (John 3:14–15, with Num. 21:9), hungering, thirsting, and drinking (Matt. 5:6; John 4:14; 6:50–58); coming and receiving (John 1:12; 5:40; 7:37–38; 6:44, 65). These instances (besides many others) underscore the role of faith *in the act of justification* as a passive receiving and resting in Christ. However, the faith of the justified is also active in good works (Jas. 2:26).

Faith is the same in both the Old and New Testaments, both in its act and object. In fact, Abel, Noah, David, and other Old Testament figures are treated in the New Testament as examples of those who had faith in Christ (esp. Heb. 11). Abraham is especially paradigmatic as the one who was justified by faith and is the father of all who have faith in Christ (Rom. 2:28–29; 4; Gal. 3; Heb. 11:8–19; Jas. 2:14–26). Throughout the New Testament this continuity is assumed (John 5:46; 12:38–39; Rom. 1:17; 10:16; Gal. 3:11; Heb. 10:38; cf. Hab. 2:4). As Berkhof reminds us, "The giving of the law did not effect a fundamental change in the religion of Israel, but merely introduced a change in its external form. The law was not substituted for the promise; neither was faith supplanted by works."[19]

Paul's legalists misunderstood the true nature of the law: to lead us to Christ, not to lead us to self-confidence. The demand for faith does not turn faith into a work. On the contrary, it is a command to cease our labors and enter God's rest (Heb. 4). Just as the grace of God has appeared" (Tit. 2:11), so Paul also speaks of faith as arriving: "Now before faith came, we were held captive under the law, imprisoned until the coming faith would be revealed." Because "Christ came," "faith has come" (Gal. 3:23–25). Again, this cannot mean that the Old Testament saints were not justified through faith—especially since this same chapter underscores continuity on this point. Rather, the contrast for Paul lies in the fact that the old covenant (Sinai) was an external form of government for the nation that established cultic and legal practices that clearly pointed to Jesus Christ (hence, the contrast between the "two covenants" in 4:21–31). Yet this Sinai covenant did not—and could not—replace the Abrahamic covenant of grace (Gal. 3:15–18).

While upholding the continuity of faith in Christ from Abraham (indeed, from Adam and Eve after the fall) to the present, the New Testament also announces that something new has dawned. The law itself could not create faith, hope, or love, but because of sin could only place the world in prison awaiting the Redeemer (Gal. 3:22–23) or under a guardian awaiting its maturity in order to receive the inheritance (v. 24). Throughout Acts, Christ is proclaimed and the appropriate response is repentance and faith. In Hebrews, the great fathers and mothers of Israel are commended for their faith in the promise even though they did not yet see its fulfillment (Heb. 11:1–12:2). Moses and his liberated followers, according to Paul, "drank from the spiritual Rock that followed them, and the Rock was Christ" (1 Cor. 10:4). In fact, the wilderness generation is said to have "put Christ to the test" when they rebelled (v. 9).

PERSEVERANCE OF THE SAINTS—OR GOD'S PERSEVERANCE WITH THE SAINTS

The final distinctive doctrine of Calvinism (though it is, in reality, no less important than justification, sanctification, and glorification) is the perseverance of the saints. In the words of Augustine, "This grace [God] placed 'in Christ in whom we have obtained a lot, being predestined according to the purpose of Him who worketh all things.' And thus as he worketh that we come to Him, so He worketh that we do not depart."[20]

Let us recall the golden chain with which we began this chapter: "And those whom he predestined he also called, and those whom he called he also justified, and those whom he justified he also glorified" (Rom. 8:30). Paul does not say merely that *some* of those whom he predestined, called, and justified will also be glorified. In fact, he even puts glorification in the past tense as well, stressing its certainty for all of the elect. The apostle immediately adds:

> What then shall we say to these things? If God is for us, who can be against us? He who did not spare his own Son but gave him up for us all, how will he not also with him graciously give us all things? Who shall bring any charge against God's elect? It is God who

> justifies. Who is to condemn? Christ Jesus is the one who died—more than that, who was raised—who is at the right hand of God, who indeed is interceding for us. Who shall separate us from the love of Christ? Shall tribulation, or distress, or persecution, or famine, or nakedness, or danger, or sword? As it is written,
>
> "For your sake we are being killed all the day long;
> we are regarded as sheep to be slaughtered."
>
> No, in all these things we are more than conquerors through him who loved us. For I am sure that neither death nor life, nor angels nor rulers, nor things present nor things to come, nor powers, nor height nor depth, nor anything else in all creation, will be able to separate us from the love of God in Christ Jesus our Lord. (Rom. 8:31–39)

Paul ransacks his mind for every possible threat to our security in Christ, whether heavenly or earthly opposition, whether external or internal opposition, and concludes with that gloriously absolute and unqualified assurance: nothing can separate us from God's love in Christ.

Baptized into Christ: The Triumphant Indicative That Yields Reasonable Imperatives

In the Greek language there are (among others) two distinct moods: the *indicative* mood, which is declarative, simply describing a certain state of affairs, and the *imperative* mood, setting forth commands. For example, in Romans Paul first explains who believers were in Adam and what is their new status in Christ (justification), and then he reasons from this indicative to the imperatives as a logical conclusion: "Do not present your members to sin as instruments for unrighteousness, but present yourselves to God as those who have been brought from death to life" (Rom. 6:13). He concludes with another imperative (command), but this time it is really an indicative: "For sin will have no dominion over you, since you are not under law but under grace" (v. 14). This seems just as contradictory to our moral reason as his earlier statement that God "justifies the ungodly" (Rom. 4:5). What judge declares the unjust to be just? And how can the apostle tell us that sin no longer has dominion over us because we are not under law but under grace? Isn't it the role of religion to give people moral instruction so that they will no longer be dominated by their sinful habits?

As counterintuitive as this may seem to our natural way of thinking, Paul says that the gospel is the answer not only to our guilt and condemnation but to our corruption and slavery to sin. In his hymn, "Rock of Ages," Augustus Toplady spoke of the gospel as "the double cure," saving us from both sin's guilt and power. In the act of justification, works and grace are totally opposed. However, once our persons are justified, so too our works can be "saved" in spite of their imperfections. *The faith that receives Christ apart from works for justification also receives Christ for works in sanctification.* Only as the fruit of grace-wrought faith are good works even possible. The tyranny of sin over your life has been toppled; therefore do not live as though this has not happened—this is the order of Pauline logic. In fact, presenting our bodies as a living sacrifice, according to Paul, is "your reasonable [*logikēn*] service" in the light of "the mercies of God" that have been explored to that point (Rom. 12:1 KJV). It is the good news that yields good works.

From all of the other elements of the *ordo salutis*, it should be obvious that not just some but all of those who are chosen in Christ, redeemed by Christ, and called into union with Christ receive every blessing, including glorification (Rom. 8:30). Jesus assured his disciples—and us—that all whom he has come to save, those who were given to him by the Father, will be raised to everlasting life on the last day—*without exception* (John 6:37–39; 10:27–30).

If there is "now no condemnation for those who are in Christ Jesus" (Rom. 8:1), on the sole basis of Christ's righteousness imputed, then a reversal of the court's verdict is impossible. That verdict has already set into motion the process of inward renewal, as the believer has been inserted by the Spirit into the powers of the age to come. "Therefore, if anyone is in Christ, he is a new creation. The old has passed away; behold, the new has come. All this is from God, who through Christ reconciled us to himself" (2 Cor. 5:17–18).

Even our sanctification is the result of "the power [of God] at work within us" (Eph. 3:20), and not only our justification but our walking in good works is predestined by God (Eph. 2:10). "As many as were appointed to eternal life believed" (Acts 13:48). God calls those whom he has chosen (John 15:16; Eph. 1:11–13; 2 Thess. 2:13, etc.). There is no indication in Scripture that God effectually calls (i.e., regenerates) those whom he has not chosen or that he draws into vital union with his Son those whom he allows finally to perish.

The believer's perseverance is guaranteed by God's perseverance, so that Paul can say, "I am sure of this, that he who began a good work in you will bring it to completion at the day of Jesus Christ" (Phil. 1:6). And to Timothy he writes, "But I am not ashamed, for I know whom I have believed, and I am convinced that he is able to guard until that Day what has been entrusted to me" (2 Tim. 1:12). God *does* what he *declares*. When he pronounces someone righteous in Christ, he immediately begins also to conform that person to Christ, to whom he has united them. The vine that has been chosen and grafted onto Christ cannot fail to bear fruit that will last (John 15:16). Justification, sanctification, and glorification are inseparable gifts of our union with Christ through the same act of faith.

If our regeneration is the consequence of God's election, redemption, and effectual calling (John 1:12–13; 3:3, 5; 15:16; Rom. 9:11–18; Eph. 1:4–13; 2 Thess. 2:12–13; 2 Tim. 1:9, etc.), rather than our decision and effort, then he is able to finish what he has started. Yes, there is opposition. "But the Lord is faithful. He will establish you and guard you against the evil one" (2 Thess. 3:3). Paul wrote:

> Therefore I endure everything for the sake of the elect, that they also may obtain the salvation that is in Christ Jesus with eternal glory. The saying is trustworthy, for:
>
> If we have died with him, we will also live with him;
> if we endure, we will also reign with him;
> if we deny him, he also will deny us;
> if we are faithless, he remains faithful—
> for he cannot deny himself. (2 Tim. 2:10–13)

Peter also adds that we have been given "an inheritance that is imperishable, undefiled, and unfading, kept in heaven for you, who by God's power are being guarded through faith for a salvation ready to be revealed in the last time" (1 Peter 1:4–5). For this reason, "your faith and hope are in God" (v. 21). "You have been born again, not of perishable seed but of imperishable, through the living and abiding word of God" (v. 23). Of course, left to ourselves, we not only could but would fall from grace, but God "is able to keep you from stumbling" (Jude 24).

The Danger of Apostasy

The image of vine and branches that serves Israel's relationship to Yahweh in the Old Testament is also invoked in the New Testament. Christ is the life-giving vine, and we are his fruit-bearing branches (John

15:1–11; cf. Matt. 13:24–30; 17:20; 20:1–6). Thus, the New Testament member of the covenant of grace is in the same position as a covenant member in the Old Testament: outwardly received by Christ as belonging to his people, each member must inwardly receive Christ as his Savior.

Just as John the Baptist and Jesus warned of the breaking off of unproductive branches and Pentecost initiated the fulfillment of the annual Jewish feast of harvest or ingathering, Paul can speak of Gentiles as wild branches grafted onto the living vine of Israel, which may also be broken off if they do not yield the fruit of faith (Rom. 11:16–24). Thus, there are dead and living branches: those who are related merely outwardly and visibly and those who are united to Christ inwardly and invisibly in the communion of the elect.

So apostasy is not only hypothetical; it actually happens. Even if we are unfaithful, "he remains faithful—for he cannot deny himself." Yet in the same breath Paul warns that "if we deny him, he also will deny us" (2 Tim. 2:11–13). Jesus warned that the Father "takes away" "every branch in me that does not bear fruit" (John 15:2); yet he tells his disciples, "Already you are clean because of the word that I have spoken to you.... You did not choose me, but I chose you and appointed you that you should go and bear fruit *and that your fruit should abide*" (15:3, 16, emphasis added). The gospel is proclaimed publicly to all people, but only the elect receive it, Jesus says (Matt. 22:14).

Similarly, in Romans 9 Paul addresses the question provoked by the unbelief of the majority of Jews by explaining, "It is not as though the word of God has failed. For not all who are descended from Israel belong to Israel, and not all are children of Abraham because they are his offspring" (9:6–7a). God has always exercised his sovereign mercy, electing Isaac rather than Ishmael and Jacob rather than Esau, "though they were not yet born and had done nothing either good or bad—in order that God's purpose of election might continue, not because of works but because of him who calls" (v. 11). Therefore, our perseverance in faith is guaranteed by God's electing, redeeming, and calling grace. "So then it depends not on human will or exertion, but on God, who has mercy" (v. 16).

Although Peter denied Christ three times, Christ did not put out the smoldering wick or break off the bruised reed but brought him back to faith by his Spirit after the resurrection. Yet those who deny Christ to the very end, even though they may perhaps have outwardly been members of the visible church, are lost because they were never living members through faith. "They went out from us," says John concerning those who deny Christ, "but they were not of us; for if they had been of us, they would have continued with us. But they went out, that it might become plain that they all are not of us. But you have been anointed by the Holy One, and you all have knowledge" (1 John 2:19–20).

This is why the writer to the Hebrews warns Jewish Christians during tremendous persecution not to return to Judaism by appealing to the example of the wilderness generation under Moses:

> For good news came to us just as to them, but the message they heard did not benefit them, because they were not united by faith with those who listened. For we who have believed enter that rest.... So then, there remains a Sabbath rest for the people of God, for whoever has entered God's rest has also rested from his works as God did from his. (Heb. 4:2–3, 9–10)

Entering that rest means not only hearing but believing the gospel (Heb. 4:1–11).

In this light we are better able to understand the dire warnings against falling away in Hebrews 6. The writer describes those who belong only outwardly to the covenant community as "those who have once been enlightened, who have tasted the heavenly gift, and have shared in the Holy Spirit, and have tasted the goodness of the word of God and the powers of the age to come, and then have fallen away" (Heb. 6:4–6a). Those who apostatize have been beneficiaries of the Spirit's ministry through the means of grace even as merely formal or external members of the covenant community. Having been baptized ("enlightened"), they have also "*tasted* the heavenly gift" in the Supper and "*tasted* the goodness of the word of God and the powers of the age to come" (Heb. 6:4–5), but they have not actually received or *fed upon* Christ for eternal life, which Jesus linked to faith (John 6:27–58, 62–65).

According to Hebrews 6, then, those who apostatize by returning to the shadows of the law after Christ has come are basically "crucifying once again the Son of God to their own harm and holding him up to contempt" (Heb. 6:6). Belonging to the visible church places one in the very heart of the Spirit's activity of uniting sinners to Christ through the means of grace. It is a tremendous benefit; yet it is also a greater threat for those who do not actually trust in Christ. "For land that has drunk the rain that often falls on it, and produces a crop useful to those for whose sake it is cultivated, receives a blessing from God. But if it bears thorns and thistles, it is worthless and near to being cursed, and its end is to be burned" (vv. 7–8). The blessings of the covenant lead *ordinarily* to salvation, but when instead one hardens his or her heart to these blessings and does not receive the Christ who gives them, they become curses.

Happily, this severe warning is followed by the encouragement of verse 9: "Though we speak in this way, yet in your case, beloved, we feel sure of better things—*things that belong to salvation*" (Heb. 6:9, emphasis added). This salvation is exhibited in the case of these who are actually saved by the fruit that it yields (vv. 10–12). The writer then goes on to assure them of the unchangeable character of God's promise in Jesus Christ, so that "we who have fled for refuge might have strong encouragement to hold fast to the hope set before us" (v. 18). So these warning passages themselves target those who are visible members of the covenant community (professing believers and their children), in some sense benefiting from the Spirit's ministry, who have nevertheless failed to embrace the gift of salvation.

Engaging Other Views

Defended by Augustine in his treatise *On the Perseverance of the Saints,* this doctrine is taught not only in the Reformed and Presbyterian confessions but in the Thirty-Nine Articles (Anglican), the Savoy Declaration (Congregationalist), and the London/Philadelphia Confession (Calvinistic Baptists).[21]

Challenges to this doctrine usually appear in two broad forms. The first form is *synergism*, meaning "working together"; this view maintains that salvation is attained through a cooperative process between God and human beings. Representatives of this perspective are, therefore, neither fully Pelagian nor Augustinian but range somewhere between these positions. Though with their own distinct emphases, Eastern Orthodoxy, Roman Catholicism, and Arminianism are synergistic, teaching that the believer's security depends at least to some extent on his or her own cooperation with God's grace, and this grace may be finally lost.[22]

For them, the warning passages refer to those who were regenerated, justified, and even in the process of being sanctified, but at some point have lost their salvation through unbelief and serious (mortal) sin. According to the Catechism of the Catholic Church, "The children of our holy mother the Church rightly hope for the grace of final perseverance and the recompense of God their Father for the good works accomplished with his grace in communion with Jesus."[23]

The fifth point of the Remonstrant (Arminian) articles teaches:

> They who are united to Christ by faith are thereby furnished with abundant strength and succor sufficient to enable them to triumph over the seductions of Satan, and the allurements of sin; nevertheless they may, by the neglect of these succors, fall from grace, and, dying in such a state, may finally perish. This point was started at first doubtfully, but afterward positively as a settled doctrine.[24]

Neither the Roman Catholic and Orthodox nor the Arminian view is Pelagian. Both insist on the necessity of grace, but this grace is regarded as making final salvation merely possible; it becomes effectual only to the extent that the believer cooperates with its infused powers.

If these rival views of perseverance represent a consistent synergism, another important view can be identified as *inconsistent synergism*. Generally known as *eternal security*, this view seems in some respects indistinguishable from the perseverance of the saints. However, at least as it is articulated by many of its leading proponents, this view locates security in the believer's decision to accept Christ.[25] Although genuine Christians may fail to grow in their sanctification and persevere in their faith—in fact, they may never even begin to bear the fruit of righteousness—they are assured of eternal life. Such "carnal Christians" may leave the church, even deny Christ, and thereby lose the blessings of living as "victorious Christians" as well as the rewards in the next life for faithful service, but they will be saved, though "only as through fire" (1 Cor. 3:15).[26]

Although advocates often represent this position as *moderate Calvinism*, it is more appropriately identified as *moderate Arminianism*. This is why I have identified it as "inconsistent synergism." After all, it denies that human beings are incapable of responding to God in faith apart from a prior regeneration, bases election on foreseen faith, rejects the particular scope of the atonement, and maintains that the Spirit's sovereign call may be resisted. Even its teaching of eternal security is based on the believer's decision to accept Christ, which renders this view actually closer to Arminianism than to a Calvinist interpretation of perseverance of the saints.

Over every form of synergism, confessional Lutheranism strongly affirms a monergistic soteriology: God alone saves; it is not a process of human cooperation with God's grace. Nevertheless, from a Reformed perspective the Lutheran system represents an *inconsistent monergism*. Confessional Lutheranism affirms total depravity and unconditional election while nevertheless holding with equal rigor to a universal atonement and the possibility of resisting the Spirit's inward calling through the outward gospel. Lutheranism affirms with Reformed theology that the elect will persevere and "those who still take pleasure in their sins and continue in a sinful life do not believe" (Augsburg Confession, Art. 20); yet also holds that it is possible that (1) the elect may lose their salvation for a time (e.g., David, Peter), but not finally; and (2) others might once have truly believed, been regenerated and justified, but then lose all of these gifts through apostasy.[27]

According to some Lutherans, salvation can only be lost through unbelief, while according to others it may also be lost due to mortal sin.[28] How can one say that God alone saves, from beginning to end, while also affirming the possibility of losing one's salvation? It seems undeniable that this gift depends in some sense on the sinner's nonresisting, although this conclusion is rejected by confessional Lutherans.

The doctrine of the perseverance of the saints reflects a *consistently monergistic* view of salvation as entirely due to God's grace alone from beginning to end. With the writer to the Hebrews, we can acknowledge the tragic reality of apostasy or falling away from the covenantal sphere of the Spirit's activity through Word and sacrament without concluding that these visible members of Christ's body were actually regenerated branches of the vine. Although some professing members may be devoid of saving faith, those who *receive* the reality that is promised to them in Word and sacrament are assured that they will continue to trust in Christ. In spite of the weakness of our faith and repentance, we are "more than conquerors through him who loved us," so that nothing "will be able to separate us from the love of God in Christ Jesus our Lord" (Rom. 8:37, 39). Now that is a message that takes command of our hearts and minds, leading us to worship and out to our neighbors with the best news that they will ever hear!

SIX

CALVINISM AND THE CHRISTIAN LIFE

Calvinism may be the only stream of Christianity that has been repeatedly characterized as antinomian *and* legalistic. On one hand, it is asserted that so much emphasis on God's grace leaves people lax and passive. On the other hand, most of us have heard high school summaries of Calvinism as the engine of progress and activism in the cause of God's moral will because of a concern to prove their election. Calvinists, we are told, want to transform the nations of the earth into a theocratic empire under the divine law. Of course, these portraits are diametrically opposed; both cannot be true.

There have indeed been antinomians and legalists who identified themselves as Calvinists. However, for Reformed Christians, it is the creeds, confessions, and catechisms that summarize the faith we profess together as church bodies and hold each other to them. All of our doctrinal standards reject both errors in the clearest and strongest terms.

Calvinism rejects antinomianism as a serious error. Even though sin still clings to our best works even as Christians, when God accepts sinners for the sake of Christ and his righteousness, he also accepts their works—not as justifying, but as the fruit of his Spirit.[1] Although the civil and ceremonial laws are now obsolete, new covenant saints are still obligated to obey the moral law, not as the way *to* life but as the way *of* life.[2] The gospel alone remains the source of new obedience, but the moral law (summarized in the Ten Commandments, but also elaborated throughout the New Testament as the fruit of the Spirit or the law of love) remains the standard of what God requires.

There is no justification without sanctification; although we are justified through faith alone, that faith that clings to Christ immediately begins to bear the fruit of the Spirit. Nevertheless, there is no Christian whose faith and obedience are perfect. "In this life even the holiest have only a small beginning of this obedience. Nevertheless, with all seriousness of purpose, they do begin to live according to all, not only some, of God's commandments."[3] "Therefore it is so far from being true that this justifying faith makes men remiss in a pious and holy life, that on the contrary without it they would never do anything out of love to God, but only out of self-love or fear of damnation."[4]

Calvinism also rejects legalism as a serious error. Whether at the beginning, the middle, or the end of the Christian life, we never bring our works to God as that which could satisfy his holiness. Rather, we cling to Christ alone through faith.[5]

There are at least two kinds of legalism. One form treats God's commands in Scripture (whether the Ten Commandments or other calls to holy living) as the way to peace with God (i.e., justification). This is nothing less than "a different gospel" (Gal. 1:6). A second form may be identified as "a different law." Setting aside God's law, this legalism is actually antinomian at its heart, since it substitutes human wisdom for God's (Matt. 15:6; 23:1–28). This kind of "antinomian" legalism takes different shapes. Sometimes its focus is on personal piety (as in fundamentalism); in other cases on specific political policies (as in liberalism), with prohibitions and demands that are not clearly revealed in Scripture and are therefore left to Christian freedom.

It is often said that we are obligated not to "a bunch of laws," but to love and to seek justice, peace, and harmony in the world—as that is defined by a partisan political agenda that is nowhere prescribed in Scripture. Yet Moses and Jesus said that love of God and neighbor was precisely what the moral law stipulated (Lev. 19:18; Matt. 22:40). There is no basis in Scripture for setting love against law, and God's moral law remains his everlasting standard; although no one is justified by it, Christians are obligated to follow it.

Antinomians downplay the reality of the struggle with indwelling sin, but so do legalists by assuming that spiritual Christians can attain a moral perfection that no one can claim until glorification. Calvinists maintain, "This sanctification is throughout, in the whole man; yet imperfect in this life, there abiding still some remnants of corruption in every part; whence ariseth a continual and irreconcilable war, the flesh lusting against the Spirit, and the Spirit against the flesh."[6] Antinomianism and legalism miss the paradox of being simultaneously justified and sinful, genuinely renewed in every part yet still corrupt in every part.

So, does Calvinism generate passivity or activism in sanctification? Actually, both. Before God, we are always receivers. We cannot bring about our own regeneration, justification, or sanctification. These are inseparable gifts we receive through faith in Christ. That is why we emphasize God's work in preaching and the sacraments. Nevertheless, the gospel that we receive activates us for righteousness. Faith bears the fruit of righteousness. However, we do not present our works to God but to our neighbors. Receivers before God, we are active in the world.

Some modern thinkers have tried to explain the enormous energy of Calvinist activism in the world. The pioneer of sociology, Max Weber, famously argued that the Calvinist work ethic must have been based on the belief that believers proved their election by success in their worldly endeavors. Yet the "Weber Thesis" has fallen on hard times, especially since it lacks any documenting support. As Wilhelm Niesel reminds us, "The much discussed activism of Calvin is rooted in the fact that we belong to Christ and thus can go our way free from care and confess our membership in Christ; but it does not arise from any zealous desire to prove one's Christian faith by good works."[7]

Far from lodging good works in the fear of punishment and hope of rewards, Calvinism embraces the irony that can only be a scandal to the natural way of thinking. It is that true godliness can only begin when we cast off all confidence in our own obedience to the law. Not only at the moment of our justification but throughout the Christian life, says Calvin, "all our works are under the curse of the law if they are measured by the standard of the law!"

> But if, freed from this severe requirement of the law, or rather from the entire rigor of the law, they hear themselves called with fatherly gentleness by God, they will cheerfully and with great eagerness answer, and follow his leading. To sum up: Those bound by the yoke of the law are like servants assigned certain tasks for each day by their masters.... But sons, who are more generously and candidly treated by their fathers, do not hesitate to offer them incomplete and half-done and even defective works, trusting that their obedience and readiness will be approved by our most merciful Father, however small, rude, and imperfect these may be.... But how can this be done

amidst all this dread, where one doubts whether God is offended or honored by our works?[8]

A just judge cannot overlook violations of the law, but a good father is pleased with his children even though their obedience falls short of his standards. No longer under God's judgment, we are freed to love and serve our neighbors in his name and to live in his family as grateful heirs.

In the Reformed and Presbyterian heritage, we talk a lot about growing in Christ through the public means of grace: proclamation of the Word and administration of the sacraments. Our forebears have written some of the most stirring devotional works, encouraging regular prayer and meditation on Scripture in private, and especially in family worship. We speak of the importance of "returning to our baptism" in daily mortification of sins and revivification in righteousness. Baptism not only reminds you but "assure[s] you that Christ's one sacrifice on the cross is for you personally."[9] The Lord's Supper, too, lies at the center of Reformed piety. Catechisms (question-and-answer guides with Scripture references) were written to create structure to these habits and to pass the faith down from generation to generation. The Lord's Day has been set apart as the weekly Sabbath, resting in and with the triune God in communion with his people.

In short, Reformation piety always begins with God and his work and the Christian life is a "team sport." God is not only saving individuals but is creating a church. Furthermore, Reformed believers insist on Christian liberty—that is, freedom from commands that are not required by Scripture.[10]

However, when most evangelicals talk about piety, it is usually defined over against any formal ministry. Typically, such piety is understood in individualistic terms, without formal connection to church membership, the means of grace, and the disciplines that Scripture actually commands. Therefore, many Calvinists suspect that their non-Calvinist brothers and sisters are following humanly devised schemes for piety that are not directly based on Scripture while marginalizing or even ignoring the means of grace and spiritual disciplines that Christ has ordained. Missing a "quiet time" can provoke greater censure in some evangelical circles than missing church services on Sunday.

These differences account for some of the suspicions that Calvinists do not really care about piety, when it is really a question of what produces and what constitutes genuine devotion. When Reformed Christians talk about being baptized, catechized (not only in church but at home), learning to participate in public worship, making public profession, receiving the Supper, and loving our neighbors primarily through our vocations in the world, many evangelicals do not recognize their spiritual priorities on that list. We also talk about the gospel as the heart of sanctification, whereas it is often assumed by evangelicals that "presenting the gospel" is what we needed to get saved but is not our daily bread. This means that we may often be talking about the Christian life (piety or sanctification) when our brothers and sisters think we're talking about something else—and vice versa.

Not everything is contrast, of course. Reformed piety overlaps with the concerns of evangelicals more generally for personal witness to non-Christians, encouragement of fellow saints, regular Scripture reading, and prayer—in private as well as in family and corporate worship. If growth in Christ is not something we can do alone, it's also not something that happens without personal engagement—including private times of refreshment and meditation with the Lord.

SOME HISTORICAL BACKGROUND

The leading theologians of the Reformation were often pastors who also wrote devotional guides, hymns, prayers, and catechisms. Stories are told of coppersmiths debating fine points of theology at work and then singing psalms together on their way home at the end of the day. In fact, the spectacle of Christian neighbors being escorted to the flames singing psalms made such an impression on the bystanders that the officers of the Roman Inquisition demanded that their tongues be cut out beforehand.

Eventually, orthodoxy and pietism became warring factions in the Lutheran tradition. Lutheran pietists were often overreacting against a tendency to identify orthodoxy merely with doctrine and forms of worship. This is not to say that Lutheran orthodox clergy, families, and churches were uninterested in piety, or that pious families were not interested in doctrine. At least early on, it was difficult to draw a sharp line between the orthodox and the pietists. However, eventually extremes prevailed. Orthodoxy became somewhat suspicious of zeal while pietism became somewhat suspicious of doctrine and the formal ministry.

Yet in the Reformed tradition, there was less tension. For example, English Puritanism and the "Further Reformation" advocates in the

Dutch Reformed Church represented simultaneously a movement of Reformed orthodoxy and a call to further reformation in both corporate and personal devotion. Besides being among the formative shapers of the Calvinistic system of doctrine, they were concerned that the Reformation itself had not completed its work until all areas of life were penetrated by God's Word and Spirit. Dipping into the writings of William Perkins, Samuel Rutherford, Gisbertus Voetius, Wilhelmus à Brackel, Richard Sibbes, and John Owen, for example, leaves a deep impression that one is indeed, as J. I. Packer expresses it, among God's giants. The depth and richness are evident as much in the heart as in the mind.

In the past century or so, Calvinistic theologians, pastors, and writers have not only provided doctrinal tomes from which believers of various churches have drawn; they have also had a remarkable impact through their devotional writings, commentaries, hymns, and counseling guides.

THEOLOGY AND LIFE: KEY ASSUMPTIONS OF REFORMED PIETY

Calvinists have always underscored the importance of a personal relationship with Christ, including spiritual disciplines of private prayer and meditation on Scripture. However, these private practices are fed by broader streams from the public gathering of God's people. Where evangelical spiritualities tend to move from the individual to the family to the church, Reformed piety moves in the other direction: from the public means of grace to the family to the individual. Even more important, the direction of piety in many evangelical circles today is from the believer to God. How can I improve my relationship with the Lord? How can I serve the Lord? How is my walk? These become the primary questions and they can keep us narrowly focused on ourselves, when we should be focusing on Christ in faith and our neighbors in love.

However, in Reformed piety, the direction of the arrow is downward, from God to us, and then through us, out to the neighbors who need the gifts he has given us for their benefit. I cannot improve my relationship with the Lord. I cannot give him any gift that could obligate him to bless me; gifts come down, they don't go up (Acts 17:24–25; Rom. 11:35–36; Jas. 1:17). The triune God has chosen, redeemed, and called me into fellowship with the Son by the Spirit. Therefore, my concern is to hear his gospel promises, to receive his good gifts in Christ, and to be filled with the joy that the Spirit produces through this good news.

Of course, there are commands in Scripture as well. However, good works are not for my benefit or God's, but for others: my brothers and sisters in Christ, my family, and my neighbors in need of loving service and witness. This is why we focus so much on the means of grace—because only God's work for us can prepare us for our works for others. That means that when Reformed people talk about piety, it's often not the first things that other brothers and sisters think of as avenues of spiritual intimacy. "Yes, but you're talking about the church and formalities, but we're talking about growing in a personal relationship with the Lord." That is how it is often said, or at least implied, in many conversations I have had with others.

Reformed Christianity is not just a set of doctrines. It is a communal interpretation of the biblical story whose implications are summarized in doctrine and then become the world that we inhabit through faith, confession, lament, praise, and hope. This shapes our corporate worship and our activity in the world. Elsewhere, I have called this the web of drama, doctrine, doxology, and discipleship. None can be severed from the other threads without pulling the whole web apart.

It is not merely by looking at Reformed doctrines—especially when reducing them to "five points"—that one discovers this tradition's identity. To be sure, the doctrines of grace that we have focused on in this book are deeply formative of Christian practice. These truths shape our understanding of God, ourselves, and the world. However, particular practices have been just as formative as particular doctrines in shaping Reformed Christians for generations.

"The Earth is the LORD's and the Fullness Thereof"

Reformed piety is steeped in the biblical confession of the God of Israel as the only Creator, Preserver, Redeemer, and Consummator. While the nations look to various gods for their security—deities of sky and earth—Israel confesses, "The earth is the LORD's and the fullness thereof" (Ps. 24:1). Jesus Christ is not only the Savior, but the one in whom the world was created and through whom it holds together. Our Lord Jesus Christ announced, "I am the Alpha and the Omega ... who is and who was and who is to come, the Almighty" (Rev. 1:8).

We do not make Jesus our personal Lord and Savior. He *is* the Lord of all the earth and the Savior of the world. It is our calling to announce this to the world, calling all people everywhere to repent and to call on the name of Christ for salvation. The Roman empire would have left well enough alone if it were not for the fact that our Lord and his apostles appropriated Caesar's titles for Jesus of Nazareth. Jesus is not only enthroned in individual hearts, but is given "the name that is above every name, so that at the name of Jesus every knee should bow, in heaven and on earth and under the earth, and every tongue confess that Jesus Christ is Lord, to the glory of God the Father" (Phil. 2:9–11). Not only is heaven his throne; the earth is his footstool.[11]

Of course, as Hebrews 2:8 reminds us, "we do not yet see everything in subjection to him." We are still awaiting Christ's return, when he will consummate his kingdom in glory. "But we see him who for a little while was made lower than the angels, namely Jesus, crowned with glory and honor because of the suffering of death" (2:9), and he is now exalted as our priest in heaven (2:10–18). For now, it is a kingdom of grace and forgiveness, with the proclamation of the gospel going to the ends of the earth. Yet Christ already possesses the keys of death and hell (Rev. 1:18). He is Lord of all.

So the horizon of Reformed piety is not merely the individual heart or a personal relationship. Of course, it is that—but much more. Christ's saving work includes the whole created order—not only souls but bodies, and not only human beings but the natural world (Rom. 8:18–25). We are not looking for "the late, great planet earth," but for "the resurrection of the body and the life everlasting." Redemption is cosmic in its scale, even though for now its evidence is seen in the remission of sins and the gathering of a people from every nation in Christ's name.

This unfolding plan directs us away from an individual and introspective piety, concerned only with what is happening inside of us. We are directed outside of ourselves: looking up in faith toward God and out toward a world into which we are called in witness and service.

The sovereignty of God over all areas of life resists our tendency to compartmentalize our life into private and public, individual and corporate, sacred and secular. These distinctions are still valuable, of course. For example, we oppose any effort to support Christian faith and practice by public coercion or civil laws. In bringing the gospel to every person, we call each one to personal faith in Christ. We also affirm that there remains a distinction between the holy and the common.

However, at various points Reformed faith and practice resist the tendency to set these in opposition. Even in public, we are the Christians who must yield ultimate obedience to God alone. Even in the corporate body of Christ, we have a personal relationship with Christ. Even in our secular callings, we remain those who are "called ... out of darkness into [God's] marvelous light" (1 Peter 2:9). Our participation in the common life of working, raising a family, membership in secular organizations, political parties, and neighborhood watch programs is distinct from our holy calling in Christ, but it is nevertheless a gift and calling that have been given to us by God.

Election Is a Fountain for Godliness

It is a caricature to conclude that election leads to a lack of concern for the pursuit of godliness. On the contrary, it is a crucial impetus for it. As we have seen, many of the passages where election is more clearly explained lead the biblical writer to worship, like a hiker arriving at the summit from which the vista becomes overwhelming in beauty. "Oh, the depth of the riches and wisdom and knowledge of God!... For from him and through him and to him are all things. To him be glory forever. Amen" (Rom. 11:33, 36). Paul treats election in Ephesians 1 after praising God, as a way of specifying the blessings with which he has lavished us in heavenly places. Jesus teaches it as a way of shifting his disciples from a human-centered to a Christ-centered orientation (John 15:16). Election helps to raise our eyes from ourselves to God. Since there is no gift that we could offer to God for his favor, all that is left is wonder, praise, and the eagerness to share the gifts that he has given to us with others.

Assured that our salvation rests entirely on God's mercy, we are filled with thanksgiving. John Wesley said that he could not accept this doctrine because it would undermine the key motivation for holiness, which he took to be a fear of punishment and hope of reward.[12] "What is the direct antidote to Methodism, the doctrine of heart-holiness?" he asks. "Calvinism: All the devices of Satan, for these fifty years, have done far less toward stopping this work of God, than that single doctrine. It strikes at the root of salvation from sin, previous to glory, putting the matter on quite another issue.... Be diligent to prevent them, and to guard these tender minds against the predestinarian poison."[13] It is difficult to reconcile Wesley's caricature with the obvious concern for godliness among the Puritans, or their heirs among Wesley's contemporaries—such as Augustus Toplady, John Newton, the Countess of Huntington, and many others.

More important than historical evaluations is the fact that election is treated as a vital support to holiness in Scripture. Paul reminds us, "For you did not receive the spirit of slavery to fall back into fear, but you have received the Spirit of adoption as sons, by whom we cry, 'Abba! Father'" (Rom. 8:15). How could the knowledge that God "predestined us for adoption" as sons (Eph. 1:5) lead to anything other than a longing to embrace all of the treasures of God's house? When we realize that we are part of God's "chosen race, a royal priesthood, a holy nation, a people for his own possession" (1 Peter 2:9), it changes the way we think, feel, and act in the world.

Why should we walk in works of love toward our neighbor? Because "God prepared beforehand, that we should walk in them" (Eph. 2:10). We were not chosen by good works but unto good works. We have been "predestined to be conformed to the image of [God's] Son" (Rom. 8:29). God "chose [us] as the firstfruits to be saved, through sanctification by the Spirit and belief in the truth" (2 Thess. 2:13). "Put on then, as God's chosen ones, holy and beloved, compassionate hearts, kindness, humility, meekness, and patience" (Col. 3:12).

There is therefore nothing in the doctrine itself that would lead to complacency, pride, or indolence in the Christian life. Yet it has to be acknowledged that those of us who defend this doctrine have not always exhibited these characteristics of compassion, kindness, humility, meekness, and patience. Although election teaches that "God chose what is low and despised in the world" (1 Cor. 1:28), we can exude an ungodly pride as if God has chosen the high and privileged. We may not praise our good works, but we do often give the impression that we are "in the know" and everyone else is sub-Christian. While pointing out the splinter in our brother or sister's eye, we can be as pharisaical in missing the log in our own.

Justification and Sanctification Found in Christ Alone

Like election, justification and sanctification are found in Christ alone. As we have seen, Calvin no less than Luther regarded the justification of the ungodly as the heart of the gospel. His coworkers and heirs not only proclaimed this truth but also defended it in the face of perpetual challenges. More than that, however, Reformed theology sees justification not only as relevant to how we are saved, but to the whole Christian pilgrimage from sanctification to glory. We do not embrace

Christ for justification and then move on to someone or something else for our sanctification. In Christ alone are hidden all of the treasures of salvation and life: at the beginning, in the middle, and at the end. We do not find some spiritual gifts in Christ, through faith, and then other gifts somewhere else. If we cling to Christ, we are beneficiaries of everything Christ himself possesses. We hold these treasures in common with him as coheirs.

So while Reformed theology distinguishes justification (a legal verdict) from sanctification (a process of gradual conformity to Christ), it recognizes them as inextricably linked. The same faith that clings to Christ for justification also clings to him for sanctification. Justification always remains the basis for sanctification. Only because we are in every moment already declared righteous before God apart from works is it possible for us now to bear the fruit of faith, namely, works that glorify God and serve our neighbor in love.

Calvin believed that "justification ... is the principal hinge by which religion is supported" and "the sum of all piety."[14] "Whenever the knowledge of it is taken away, the glory of Christ is extinguished, religion abolished, the Church destroyed, and the hope of salvation utterly overthrown."[15] With the Scriptures, Calvin held that works and faith are totally opposed when it comes to the question of how we are justified before God. There is no "balance" to be sought here, or as Calvin put it, "There is nothing intermediate between being justified by faith and justified by works."[16] Not even free will can be admitted as a means of justification: "Whatever mixture men study to add from the power of free will to the grace of God is only a corruption of it; just as if one should dilute good wine with dirty water."[17]

Rome taught (and teaches) that justification is a process of actually becoming holy. In baptism, we receive the first justification, washing away the guilt and corruption of the soul. Then, as we cooperate with grace we merit further justification and then, if we have cooperated well, final justification on judgment day. Justification is viewed as an *infused* righteousness that enables us to cooperate with God's grace. In other words, justification is collapsed into sanctification. The same tendency is evident in Arminian treatments, as I point out below.

The Reformers did not deny sanctification; they simply distinguished it from justification. Justification is a verdict, a declaration, that one who is actually unrighteous in oneself is righteous before God solely on the basis of Christ's righteousness being credited through faith alone. Therefore, justifying righteousness is not infused into us but imputed to us. It is not enabling but saving. It is not partial but complete. It is not the goal of the Christian life but the source. Calvin wrote, "Therefore, we explain justification simply as the acceptance with which God receives us into his favor as righteous. And we say that it consists in the remission of sins and the imputation of Christ's righteousness."[18]

Calvin believed that the whole letter to the Romans can be summarized as saying "that man's only righteousness is through the mercy of God in Christ, which being offered by the Gospel is apprehended by faith."[19]

> All things around us are in opposition to the promises of God: He promises immortality; we are surrounded with mortality and corruption: He declares that he counts us as just; we are covered with our sins: He testifies that he is propitious and kind to us; outward judgments threaten his wrath. What then is to be done? We must with closed eyes pass by ourselves and all things connected with us, that nothing may hinder or prevent us from believing that God is true.[20]

When Paul speaks of Christ's being crucified for our sins and raised for our justification in Romans 4:25, Calvin observes, "For if justification means renovation, then that he died for our sins must be taken in the same sense, as signifying that he acquired for us grace to mortify the flesh, which no one admits.... He therefore still speaks of imputative justification."[21]

The faith that receives Christ is a mere act of receiving a gift. Rome holds that in order to attain the status of justifying, faith has to become an act of love. In other words, faith not only bears the fruit of love; it is not justifying until it is this obedient act.

However, Calvin defines faith as "a sure and steadfast knowledge of the fatherly goodwill of God toward us, as he declares in the gospel that for the sake of Christ he will be our Father and Savior."[22] Further, faith "is a steady and certain knowledge of the Divine benevolence towards us, which, being founded on the truth of the gratuitous promise in Christ, is both revealed to our minds and confirmed to our hearts by the Holy Spirit."[23] "With respect to justification, faith is a thing merely passive, bringing nothing of our own to conciliate the favor of God, but receiving what we need from Christ."[24] Apart from any virtues or actions that might improve our inherent moral condition, "faith adorns us with the righteousness of another, which it seeks as a gift from God."[25]

This faith is not justifying because it is virtuous, but because of its object: namely, Christ. Even a weak faith clings to a strong Savior. In fact, Calvin adds, "some portion of unbelief is always mixed with faith in every Christian."[26] Especially against the Anabaptists, Calvin taught, "our faith is never perfect ... we are partly unbelievers."[27]

Nevertheless, the same act of faith that looks to Christ for justification also receives sanctification. Christ's righteousness is imputed and imparted. Although our growth in righteousness is incomplete in this life, we live on the basis of the perfect righteousness that we already have in Christ. Calvin says:

> Christ was given to us by God's generosity to be grasped and possessed by us in faith. By partaking of him, we principally receive a double grace: namely, that being reconciled to God through Christ's blamelessness, we may have in heaven instead of a Judge a gracious Father; and secondly, that sanctified by Christ's spirit we may cultivate blamelessness and purity of life.[28]

> This alone is of importance: having admitted that faith and good works must cleave together, we still lodge justification in faith, not in works. We have a ready explanation for doing this, provided we turn to Christ to whom our faith is directed and from whom it receives its full strength.[29]

The believer does not keep one eye on Christ for justification and the other eye on his or her own works, but looks to Christ for both. "You cannot grasp this [justification] without at the same time grasping sanctification also."[30]

Calvin was especially concerned about the tendency among the Anabaptists to turn faith into a work and to imagine that faith, much less loving obedience, could be perfect in this life. He warned, "Beware of the intrigues of Satan ... for we see that some leave the Church because they require in it the highest perfection ... and seek to form for themselves a new world, in which there is to be a perfect Church.... They depart from God himself, and violate the unity of the Church."[31] Yet since we are justified already by Christ's perfect righteousness, we are free to pursue holiness—however imperfect. "Being at a great distance from perfection, it behooves us to make continual advances; and being entangled in vices, we have need to strive against them every day."[32] Justification is declared once and for all in a moment, but conversion is a process. "Christ by his Spirit does not perfectly renew us at once, or in an instant, but he continues our renovation throughout life."[33]

Sanctification and the Means of Grace

One of the most striking differences I have encountered as an evangelical coming into the Reformed communion was the emphasis on the church and the means of grace. If I had been asked to draw up a list of aids to sanctification as a younger Christian, I would have ranked my daily quiet time above preaching, baptism, the Lord's Supper, and church membership. In fact, often the public preaching of the Word was made subordinate to my own quiet time, baptism was not only distinguished from but was contrasted with the new birth, and the Lord's Supper was not a regular means of grace but at most another opportunity for me to dive into my own heart in introspection and deeper determination to stir up my pious commitment.

For a while at least, my family attended regularly a house church where there were no sermons, no sacraments, and no formal officers. In fact, there was no membership. All of this was considered "churchianity": an inauthentic formalism that threatened the spontaneous, free, inward, and deeply personal relationship with Christ. Even fellowship with other believers was valuable only insofar as it helped to facilitate my personal spiritual growth. The concept of growing up into Christ as one body, through the means of grace that Christ commanded and administered by duly called officers to whom we were accountable—all of this was nothing more than the trappings of man-made religion.

When you start with the triune God and his gospel, sanctification cannot be seen as a process of our ascending a ladder of mystical experience or moral achievement. Rather, it is the outworking of God's descent to us in our own flesh, into our misery. Becoming incarnate, Jesus Christ fulfilled the law in our place, bore our debt, rose triumphantly, and now sits on the throne of all authority, where he pours out his gifts by the Spirit. Even now, he still takes all of the steps toward us: he sends a preacher and delivers Christ to us in baptism and the Lord's Supper. The arrow of activity points downward, from God to us, not upward. This means that there is nowhere for our good works to go except outward, to our neighbors who need us. God does not need our good works, but he wants our good works to serve our neighbors.

Sanctification is not just individual but covenantal; no one is an island. And sanctification is not our striving for divine approval but the outworking of that approval that we already possess. This is why the means of grace are not only there at the beginning of the Christian life but throughout. Every week, the gospel puts wind in the Christian's sails. Although baptism is administered only once, its effects continue; Reformed Christians speak of returning to our baptism for the daily mortification of the flesh and vivifying life of the Spirit. In the Supper, God perpetually ratifies to our conscience the pledge that he is our gracious Father in Christ.

Like the other Reformers, Calvin said that the marks of the true church are "the pure preaching of God's Word and the lawful administration of the sacraments."[34] "Wherever we find the word of God purely preached and heard, and the sacraments administered according to the institution of Christ, there ... is a Church of God."[35] To be sure, the Reformers emphasized the importance of personal salvation through faith in Christ. However, they would have been as baffled as the apostles with the dichotomy between "a personal relationship with Christ" and "belonging to a church." "God's glory and the salvation of the Church are things almost inseparably united."[36]

Reformed faith and practice recognize the implications of the doctrines of grace for sanctification by emphasizing that preaching and sacraments are not our means of commitment, but God's means of grace. Of course, God's work always calls forth an appropriate Spirit-wrought human response. There is a place for our response of faith and repentance, praise and commitment to his commands. However, the means of grace come first. Apart from God's saving work, there can be no grateful response.

The Regulative Principle

It is by Scripture alone that we come to know the truth of who we are by nature in Adam and by grace in Jesus Christ. The gospel is not something we can discover or figure out by speculation, observation, or experience. It is an announcement about God's saving work in Christ, and as such it has to be proclaimed to us by a herald. On this point, Reformed and Lutheran churches have been agreed.

However, from the beginning Reformed Christians have insisted on a broader application of the sufficiency of Scripture (*sola scriptura*). Scripture is the only norm for faith and practice—not only for understanding the gospel but for everything that it teaches. Not only with respect to how we are saved from death and judgment, but with respect to worship, outreach, and personal discipleship, the church is to speak where God has spoken and to remain silent where God has not given us his Word. When it comes to public worship, it is not merely that we cannot do what is forbidden in Scripture, but that we cannot add to or take away from that which it prescribes. In his Great Commission, Jesus commanded the disciples to proclaim the Word, administer the sacraments, and teach people "to observe all that I have commanded you" (Matt. 28:20). Nothing may be added or omitted from what he has revealed in his Word.

Throughout the Old Testament, God's holiness was to be taken with the utmost seriousness. When the Israelites found God's Word too difficult to bear, they convinced Aaron to commission a golden calf around which they could dance in revelry. Only when Moses interceded did God withhold his consuming judgment. God's law prescribed every detail of his worship: from the furniture and drapes to the sacrifices to the liturgies pertaining to each sacrifice and the rituals that distinguished the common from the holy. Like their father Aaron, Nadab and Abihu provoked God's anger when they added a ceremony to God's worship. However, these high priests died on the spot. False worship in Israel always began with compromising the form of worship (violating the second commandment) and culminated in idolatry (violating the first commandment).

Reformed Christians have drawn on such biblical instances to warn against adding to or subtracting from God's commands in his public service. After all, it is God's work and it is for our own good that we leave him to his own methods! Calvin exhorted, "God's service is corrupted if any strange invention be mingled with it. Let us ... learn not to intrude our own inventions in God's service."[37] Calvin also detected the craving for idolatry in the early church. Paul reminded Timothy constantly to ignore his critics and give himself entirely to the preaching of the Word. "They had such an itch for novelty that hardly any space was left for edification."[38]

Jesus scolded the religious leaders of his day for subverting the Word of God by adding their own rules and worship. "We see the extraordinary insolence that is displayed by men as to the form and manner of worshiping God; for they are perpetually contriving new modes of worship."[39] In his polemics Calvin accused the medieval church not of traditionalism but of a craving for innovation and novelty. In contrast with the ancient fathers, the medieval church was adding "strange fire" to God's prescribed worship, multiplying ceremonies, regulations, and superstitions.

It may be easier for us to detect such novelties in other traditions, but Protestants have developed this "itch for novelty" in their own way. Did God prescribe altar calls, sinner's prayers, parachurch campaigns, patriotic celebrations, pageants, and countless other elements that often replace the public reading and preaching of Scripture, public prayers, the sacraments, and congregational singing of the Word?

God's character has not changed in the new covenant. He is still holy. We dare not, therefore, make the fatal mistake of separating the God of the Old Testament from that of the New. It is the same God who will not give his glory to another who addresses us from Mount Zion, calling us to embrace no other prophet, priest, and king than Jesus Christ. We no longer offer sacrifices for guilt; rather, we offer the living sacrifice of thanksgiving and praise. We no longer go through a gauntlet of ritual washings to be ceremonially clean before the Lord, but we are baptized into Christ and receive him through faith, signified and sealed to us in the sacraments. Christ has determined by his authority how we are to worship, how we are to plant and organize churches, and how we are to live in fellowship with the saints and in our daily lives in the world.

So nothing can be done in public worship that is not commanded in Scripture, either directly or by good and necessary inference drawn from Scripture. It is a solemn assembly of the Lord, gathered in joy but also "in reverence and in awe." It is not our gathering. It is not a meeting of friends, relatives, coworkers, or any other natural association. It is convened by the Father, in the Son, by the Spirit, as the site where he promises to bless his people and to add to the church.

To be sure, there is a valid distinction between elements and circumstances. *Elements* are those aspects of the public service that are directly laid down in the New Testament. Not only in the evangelistic mission but in regular Lord's Day worship, Christ has commanded certain elements: preaching of his Word, baptism, the Lord's Supper, prayers, singing, and offerings for the saints. We dare not clutter God's service to his people with our own inventions. The triune God knows what he is up to, and it is best simply to get out of his way as he dispenses his gracious gifts on his own terms, through his own means of grace.

Of course, there are also circumstances. *Circumstances* are left up to the church's wisdom. There are no passages in Scripture that tell us what time to meet, the specific order of the liturgical elements, the architecture of the church building, and other discretionary matters.

One of the implications of the regulative principle is that believers are freed from the burden of doctrines and rules that their leaders tend to multiply. Christ alone is King. The same one who has given his life for his people is their ruler. He does not forgive their sins and release them from bondage to sin and death only to hand them over to religious despots, clever marketers, or entrepreneurial empire-builders. The good Shepherd refuses to surrender his ongoing priesthood. He is our prophet, priest, and king.

This also means that we are obligated to obey God's Word in every matter he addresses us, but we are free from the doctrines and rules of human beings. When Christ's ministers proclaim his Word, administer his sacraments, and guide us on the basis of his Word, we are bound, but the church has no authority to create its own teachings or laws. To be bound to Christ is to be liberated from all other masters and to be, in him, servants of all.

Communal Disciplines

The church is a covenant community, not just a collection of pious individuals and activists. We talk a lot as evangelicals about spiritual disciplines, but what about church discipline? All of us are under church discipline to some degree, submitting to the yoke of Christ through his pastors, elders, and deacons. Disciples are made in the church, not in conferences, movements, or parachurch ministries. We are not self-feeders but sheep to whom the good Shepherd has provided undershepherds for our lifelong growth.

As I have pointed out, Reformed piety affirms private disciplines of prayer, meditation on God's Word, and memorizing Scripture even in song. But whereas a lot of evangelical piety starts with the individual, rising up to God, Reformed piety starts with the descent of the triune God in his judgment and salvation. Consequently, it moves from the corporate and public worship of the covenant community on the Lord's Day to the daily instruction and worship in the family to the personal times of prayer and meditation. At the least the tendency of evangelical devotion is to move in the opposite direction.

From this public fountain the stream of grace flows into our homes. There, often at the family table, we feed on God's Word, learn its truths, and respond in prayer and praise. One of my favorite portraits of Luther has him playing the guitar as his family is sitting around the dinner table with the Scriptures open. From Calvinist homes one could hear the psalms being sung by young and old alike—and many of these believers went to their executions with these songs on their lips and in their hearts.

Luther complained that in making his rounds, he discovered that most families did not even know the Apostles' Creed, the Lord's Prayer, and the Ten Commandments. So, following the example of the ancient church, he wrote his Small Catechism, which is still used widely. Calvin, too, wrote a catechism, and Reformed and Presbyterian churches eventually adopted the Heidelberg Catechism and the Westminster Shorter and Longer Catechisms. Written in question-and-answer formats, these instruction guides remain unsurpassed as summaries of Christian faith and practice. As busy as they were, Luther, Calvin, and other Reformers took it as a responsibility of their office to personally teach the catechism throughout the week to the youth. However, the main venue was the home, where parents led their children through the questions and answers along with the attached scriptural references.

This stream flows not only into the home, but into the hearts of each believer in private prayer and meditation. Here once more, though, it is always grounded in the gospel, with Christ as the mediator. How else can we dare to approach God's throne? Only when Christ comes forward as the mediator do we have any hope. "Till we have a persuasion of being saved through the grace of God there can be no sincere prayer."[40] "Our prayers are acceptable to God only insofar as Christ sprinkles and sanctifies them with the perfume of his own sacrifice."[41]

In public worship we are trained to pray properly: with the whole church, according to forms that are either taken from Scripture or are based on Scripture itself. Then in private study, we pore over the same Word and pray—even in private—with the whole church, with Christ as head. Instead of being a dull routine, such practices are merely opportunities to be more fully and deeply immersed in God's Word and to speak back God's Word in prayer.

It is significant that God gave us a whole book of the Bible—the Psalms—in order to form our prayers properly. They are filled not only with praise, but also with lament, supplication, questions, frustrations, hopes, and fears. "Prayer digs out those treasures that the gospel of the Lord discovers to our faith," Calvin reminds us.[42] Unlike the narrow range of emotion that we often bring repetitively into worship these days (usually in the "victory" mode), the psalms give us a wider horizon, a richer vocabulary, and a deeper experience. Calvin notes, "We are permitted to pour into [God's] bosom the difficulties that torment us, in order that he may loosen the knots that we cannot untie."[43]

In fact, in many places Calvin emphasizes God's fatherly condescension to us in our weakness. He speaks of the Scriptures as "baby talk," where God stammers like a mother to a child. So why should we allow our own embarrassment to keep us from talking to God? "When God descends to us he, in a certain sense, abases himself and stammers with us, so he allows us to stammer with him."[44]

So the stream comes down from God to us in the public service, into our homes, and into every nook and cranny of our personal lives. Then where does it go? *Out into the world, where God has posted us in our callings to our neighbors.*

Piety does not begin with the lonely individual in his or her apartment, nor does it end there. Our works do not go up to God but out to our neighbors. God is already completely satisfied with us in Jesus Christ. Christ is our "righteousness and sanctification and redemption" (1 Cor. 1:30). Not only in the beginning but throughout our lives as Christians, it is not our works, but Christ's, that we bring to God for acceptance—and even this faith that embraces Christ is never the basis but the God-given means of embracing Christ with all of his treasures. So when it comes to our relationship to God, good works have no place; but when it comes to God's relationship to the world, he loves and serves our neighbors through our good works. This means that our good works do not really serve God or us but our neighbors.

The first neighbors, of course, include our immediate family. Yet it also includes the communion of saints—not only locally but in all times and places. We are united by "one Lord, one faith, one baptism" in "one Spirit" with Christ as our head (Eph. 4:4–5). Pastors feed us, elders guide us, and deacons care for our physical needs. From these ministries, each member of the body is equipped for the general office of prophets, priests, and kings: testifying to Christ, interceding for each other in prayer, and reigning with Christ over sin and death.

Through generosity, hospitality, discernment, and other spiritual gifts, each believer is made a crucial part of Christ's body. Created out of nothing by God's Word and Spirit, we become a holy temple made up of living stones in Christ (1 Peter 2:4–5). The first place where our good works go is to our brothers and sisters, in fellowship, mutual admonition and instruction, and loving service. But then the stream flows further out, into the world, through our common vocations as we live and work side by side with others. God serves even the most hardened atheist with gifts of common grace through the callings that he has given us.

KEY DIFFERENCES BETWEEN REFORMED AND ARMINIAN DOCTRINES OF SANCTIFICATION

On each of the key assumptions of Reformed piety I have mentioned, there are comparisons amid greater contrasts. We do not disagree about everything concerning the Christian life, of course. However, it is just at this point that we discern some of the most important practical implications of Calvinist and Arminian schemes.

From my own reading, it is not entirely clear where John Wesley stood on justification. In some sermons, he defends this evangelical truth as robustly as Luther and Calvin. In others, however, he redefines justification to the point that it is more identifiably Roman Catholic than Reformed. In still others, he seems confusing.

By his own admission, Wesley did not even understand the gospel of free grace in his early ministry until he heard Luther's preface to *Commentary on Romans* being read in a chapel. Yet even after this experience, he continued to send mixed signals about his understanding of justification. Often justification appears to be eclipsed by sanctification or even to include sanctification. In any case, Wesley seemed to be more worried that Calvinists were preaching antinomian heresy than that Arminians were preaching works-righteousness.

Differences already begin to emerge even on the nature, much less the importance, of justification in relation to sanctification. In contemporary discussions, the differences between Arminian (especially Wesleyan) views of the Christian life become apparent.[45] According to Laurence W. Wood, justification is not only forgiveness (he does not mention imputation); "justification is freedom from the acts of sin."[46]

> Incidentally, I suspect Protestants in general misinterpret the Council of Trent in its statement that we are justified by faith and good works. For Roman Catholic theology, justification has to do both with our initial acceptance of God in Christ and the entire life of the Christian until death. Consequently, in the end we will be justified if through faith and obedience we have so conducted our life. Perhaps, after all, Wesley was not that far away from his Anglo-Catholic roots when he stressed that justification by faith and a life lived in obedience to God were both necessary for salvation. In this respect, we are renewed in the image of Christ (sanctified) so that we are enabled to do good works.[47]

At this point, the Wesleyan view parallels the Roman Catholic confusion of justification and sanctification. Calvinism affirms as vigorously as Arminians that there is no justification without consequent sanctification, but wonders why justification has to become sanctification in order to make this point. Salvation encompasses both justification and sanctification (as well as glorification), but justification and sanctification remain distinct divine acts. Yet, according to Wood, "to be justified by faith is to experience forgiveness of sins *and to be enabled through the power of the Spirit to live a life of victory over sinning*" (emphasis added).[48]

Another parallel with Roman Catholic teaching on justification is evident in the way in which Wesleyan theology teaches a perfect holiness only by lowering the standard of the law. Here we encounter the famous doctrine of Christian perfection, which holds that believers can be so completely filled with God's love that they live above all known sin. "If sin means any deviation from the perfect will of God, then obviously all believers commit sin daily.... This is why Wesley made a distinction between voluntary sins and involuntary sins. For Wesley, justified believers do not voluntarily sin against God."[49] As in the Roman Catholic view, Wesley seems to reflect a Platonist conception of sin as due to the weakness of the body and its appetites.[50]

In any case, according to Wood, the Reformation had too low an estimate of the perfection of which believers were capable through the Spirit's inner working. "Luther's assumption was that one cannot be freed from a sinful heart of pride.... The Wesleyan tradition, along with the Anglo-Catholic tradition, perceives the New Testament to maintain a different stance; namely, that one can be justified and truly sanctified."

In any event, justification is not central. "Contemporary New Testament exegetes such as Krister Stendahl and Rudolf Bultmann maintain that Paul's overriding interest was not in justification by faith, but rather with sanctification by the Spirit."[51]

Pentecostal theologian Russel P. Spittler displays admiration for Luther's verve in advancing the idea that believers are "justified and sinful simultaneously" (*simul iustus et peccator*), but worries that this is too good to be true. "But can it really be true—saint and sinner simultaneously? I wish it were so … I simply fear it's not."[52] Offering a response from the contemplative tradition, Baptist scholar E. Glenn Hinson judges that Luther's view takes "a narrow view of grace, seeing it as something given rather than as the living God invading our lives and transforming us."[53] The Reformation interpretation represents "Pauline imperialism.… Brilliant as Paul was and great as his contribution was … the Gospels give a rather different slant to things than did the apostle to the Gentiles."[54]

In the Reformed view of sanctification, every believer is a saint and a sinner simultaneously. Defined by our union with Christ, we are already justified and are also regenerated, so that we are not what we were before. Nevertheless, we still struggle with sin—and will do so for the rest of our lives. We take our ultimate confidence not from our own victories over sin but Christ's victories. Arminian theologies of sanctification, however, tend to divide Christians into "victorious" and "carnal." Instead of one act of faith receiving a complete justification and a sanctification that is partial in this life, there are two acts of faith. In this way, evangelicals easily return to the medieval division between "the perfect" (i.e., monks) and the average layperson, who lives a secular life.

In fact, Hinson complains that the Puritans encouraged every believer to embrace their status as a saint and live accordingly. However, "only those who really want to and are willing to surrender themselves fully can become saints."[55] By contrast, even when writing to a seriously compromised Corinthian church, Paul begins, "To the church of God that is in Corinth, to those sanctified in Christ Jesus, called to be saints together with all those who in every place call upon the name of our Lord Jesus Christ, both their Lord and ours" (1 Cor. 1:2). Only because they already *are* saints can he rebuke them for living inconsistently with that profession. Since all believers are holy in Christ alone (1:30), sainthood is not the goal attainable for a select few but is the privilege of every member.

Differences arise also over the means of grace. Wesley seems to have held the sacraments in higher esteem than many of his spiritual heirs. Whereas Sinclair Ferguson speaks of the sacraments as "means of grace" in sanctification, Spittler says that for Pentecostal Christians, "there is no high doctrine of the sacraments. The highest motive for their practice, for the most part, is 'because Jesus told us to do it.'"[56] Classic Arminianism itself abandoned a Reformed understanding of the sacraments, aligning itself more with Erasmian and Anabaptist views. All of this is understandable when the emphasis shifts from God's sovereign grace, dispensing gifts to us, to the human response of faith and obedience. It is no wonder, then, that "means of grace" commanded explicitly by Christ become subordinate to "means of commitment" that are not instituted by our Lord.

Luther's well-known contrast between "theologies of glory" and "theologies of the cross" challenged the ascent of the soul upward to God. Rather, a theology of the cross recognizes that God has descended to us in a manger, at the cross, and now in the Word, water, bread, and wine. However, Hinson's chapter, "Climbing the Ladder of Love," exhibits the similarities between evangelical spirituality and the medieval piety that Luther had in mind.[57] Lutheran theologian Gerhard Forde responds to Hinson's essay much as Luther might have done:

> When you come back from the mountain and tell your admirers that the trip was totally by grace, but then answer questions on how to make the trip by talking about surrender, humility, self-abandonment and all sort of spiritual exercises, the emphasis has slipped from grace to human effort. The protestations about grace appear simply an anti-Pelagian codicil, a mostly verbal protest whose substance is not apparent.[58]

In his response, Sinclair Ferguson shows that in spite of different nuances, the churches of the Reformation are at one over against "theologies of glory":

> We neither ascend into heaven or descend into the deep in order to know God (Rom. 10:6–7).... In Reformed theology and its view of Scripture, the gospel is not, "God loves you. Love God back," as Dr. Hinson suggests of the contemplative tradition. Rather, it is, "God was reconciling the world to himself in Christ, not counting men's sins against them.... God made him who knew no sin to be sin for us

> ... that in him we might become the righteousness of God" (2 Cor. 5:18, 21).[59]

Ferguson adds, "Direct knowledge of God's essence is sought only by fools, Calvin wrote boldly." We know God only in Christ, through the gospel.[60]

In the late nineteenth century, especially in the wake of the visits of D. L. Moody and Ira Sankey, the Keswick movement was born in England. Through this movement the Wesleyan emphasis on entire sanctification became more mainstream in evangelical circles. Through a second crisis experience (a "second blessing"), a believer enters a higher stage of Christian life that many of the movement's leaders called "the victorious Christian life" or "the higher life." Keswick teaching therefore distinguished between "carnal Christians" and "victorious Christians."[61] Princeton's B. B. Warfield devoted most of a hefty volume, *Perfectionism*, to a close analysis and critique of the Keswick view of sanctification.

One of the most articulate recent spokespersons of this movement, Robert McQuilkin, maintains that "classical Wesleyan teaching and the Keswick approach are quite compatible." Both affirm that Christian perfection (victory over all known sin) is possible in this life, but again this claim requires a redefinition of sin:

> If sin is any falling short of God's glorious character, no one is perfect. Yet, every Spirit-empowered believer may consistently refrain from deliberately violating God's known will.... Should they fail to maintain this loving, obedient relationship, they no longer experience sanctification in the sense of spiritual growth, and they need a fresh encounter with God, a renewal that could be described as a second crisis experience.[62]

McQuilkin quotes the 1890 Convention speaker H. W. Webb-Peploe: "Before, I expected failure, and was astonished at deliverance; now I expect deliverance, and am astonished at failure."[63] "Consecration is the theme, and people are challenged, in the light of their own failure and inability and in the light of God's full provision, to surrender unconditionally to God." The normal Christian life is "consistent success in resisting the temptation to violate deliberately the known will of God."[64] McQuilkin realizes, "The problem seems to lie in the definition of sin"; he adds, "Keswick clearly teaches that Christians, by the power of the indwelling Spirit, have the ability to choose consistently not to violate deliberately the known will of God."[65] Questions at the heart of justification and its relation to sanctification are held at bay.

> Are church members living in sin saved, or are they lost? Have they been saved? Will they prove to have been saved? Have they lost their salvation? I have opinions—even convictions—about the theological answers to some of those questions, but since the Holy Spirit did not feel it necessary to answer them directly in Scripture, I feel under no compulsion to do so in the context of addressing professing Christians who are living in sin.[66]

Yet McQuilkin does assume a particular view of justification. First, he says that in the Keswick interpretation of Scripture, "*faith* might be more accurately rendered *faithful* in most instances ... obedience and trust [are] aspects of saving faith."[67] Where the Reformers spoke of faith as personal trust in Christ, McQuilkin repeats the mechanical images replete in the writings of the Keswick leaders: "Faith throws the switch, releasing the current of divine power."[68] Over against Rome, the Reformers taught that although faith bears the fruit of love, in justification it is merely trusting in Christ. However, McQuilkin broadens the definition of saving faith: "That is, true faith involves understanding, love, and decision."[69] "Thus, the essential element of faith for one who is disobedient is obedience. The unyielded person must surrender."[70] It is the act of decision itself that saves.[71]

Once again, we also encounter the more mystical spirituality of the inner self over against the outer Word and world in which God acts:

> The inner mind is the primary arena of growth.... God does influence our minds directly, but His primary method of bringing about growth is through what are commonly called "means of grace," or conduits of divine energy. In these means we are not passive but must participate actively.[72]

These means are "prayer, Scripture, church, and suffering."[73] There is no mention of the sacraments or even preaching.

Wesleyan theologian Melvin E. Dieter acknowledges the similarity with the Wesleyan view. It is the will that is perfected by the Spirit in the "second blessing."[74] This seems to go to the heart of it. In the Reformed perspective, any transgression of God's revealed will is at its heart an act of the will. It is not merely an external mistake but arises from the corruption that still clings to us.

Representing what he calls an "Augustinian-Dispensationalist" perspective, John F. Walvoord argues for "regeneration as a result of believing." This is ironic, given the fact that the "Calvinist" position he challenges is in fact the Augustinian view. "The Synod of Dort seems to teach that regeneration precedes faith, and in this case the sovereignty of God prevails and a person, for all practical purposes, is a robot who does not actively participate in his or her own salvation."[75] For his own part, McQuilkin, also a dispensationalist, concludes that "the doctrine of sanctification as enunciated by John Walvoord is in harmony with the Keswick approach."[76]

Through this series of interchanges we begin to see how a diverse spectrum of evangelicalism is indebted to Arminian (largely Wesleyan) views of sanctification. Included in this range of perspectives are the following conclusions (drawn by many, if not all, of the representatives cited): Salvation is by grace, but we must believe before we are regenerated. Faith is obedience and sanctification is included in justification. Although some Christians may remain "carnal"—that is, beset by spiritual and moral defeat—those who draw on the energy of the Spirit within them can enter into a higher level of sanctification and live above all known sin. From beginning to end, the Christian life is supported by grace but dependent ultimately at every stage on our activity. Human activity is not a response to God's work as much as it is a cooperation with God's work that actually determines the outcome of one's salvation—at least the level of heaven that one occupies.

The difference between these varied versions of the Arminian paradigm and the Reformation (both Lutheran and Calvinist) could not be clearer. It is often said in evangelical circles that one should go to the Calvinists for a robust doctrine of sin and grace, to "high churches" for a robust doctrine of the sacraments, and to the Arminians for a robust view of the Christian life. However, it has been my goal in this chapter to show the inconsistency of this maxim.

The doctrines of grace—along with other emphases just as dear to the Reformed system—engender their own type of piety. At the end of the day, the choice remains between theologies of glory and the theology of the cross and resurrection, between our ascent through spiritual practices and God's descent through his means of grace and our being raised with Christ, seated with him in heavenly places.

SEVEN

CALVINISM AND CHRISTIAN MISSIONS

Not everyone has the same feelings about Calvinism when it comes to evangelism and missions. How can you really throw yourself into proclaiming the gospel to everyone if you are convinced that only some people are chosen and redeemed and will be effectually drawn to saving faith? It may be good news for the elect, but is it good news for the whole world? Furthermore, wouldn't such doctrines dampen our motivation to pray for and labor over the plight of the lost? After all, God will save whomever he will, and there isn't much you or I can do about it!

These are understandable first impressions, but they are misunderstandings of the Calvinist position. Before trying to correct them directly, I want to take a step back and suggest a more helpful starting place, namely, the historical fact that Calvinism has encouraged a host of evangelistic and missionary enterprises.

CALVINISTIC EVANGELISM: AN OXYMORON?

The above-mentioned charge has been leveled not only by those first encountering Calvinism but also some who have not sufficiently investigated the history of missions. For example, Southern Baptist church historian William R. Estep, a noted authority on Anabaptism, asserts that "logically, Calvinism is anti-missionary." If election is true, he argues, "evangelism and missionary effort are exercises in futility."[1] The premises in Estep's article do indeed follow logically to his conclusion. If election eliminates personal responsibility for responding to the gospel and the gospel itself is not to be proclaimed indiscriminately to every person, of course the missionary enterprise would be a fool's errand. However, none of the premises is actually held by Calvinists. But they are widely assumed by non-Calvinists. It is a caricature of Calvinism that leads to the conclusion that, on logical grounds, it is inimical to missions.

The first way to challenge this caricature is by looking at the history. If in fact Calvinists have played a prominent role in modern missions and evangelism, they are either doing so in spite of their theological convictions or because of them. Before defending the latter, I want to focus on the actual history of Calvinism and missions.

HAS CALVINISM BEEN DEATH TO MISSIONS? A HISTORICAL SURVEY

The charge that Calvinism is inimical to missions would surprise those in Presbyterian and Reformed churches—both leaders who know their history and are personally engaged in missions as well as laypeople regularly involved in close relationships with missionaries sent and supported by their churches.

The Reformation Era and Missions

It is often said that the Reformation showed little interest in missions. However, this verdict depends on what one thinks the Reformation was in the first place. If this movement was no more than an internecine debate over the finer points of theology, then it was a distraction from missions. But if it was in fact a recovery of the gospel of God's free grace in Jesus Christ, then it was the greatest missionary movement since the apostle Paul. That is exactly how millions of Christians saw the matter, which is why they were willing to give their lives in its defense.

Admittedly, the first wave of missionaries sent to far-flung regions in the early modern period were Roman Catholic monks. Historian of missions professor Ruth Tucker observes concerning the Reformers, "Just holding their own in the face of Roman Catholic opposition and breaking new ground in Europe were significant achievements in themselves, and there was little time or personnel for overseas ventures." Tucker also points out that Roman Catholic missionaries traveled under the protection of explorers, merchants, and conquistadors, while the Lutheran and Reformed churches were landlocked and did not yet have "a ready-made missionary force like the Roman Catholic monastic orders."[2] Fred Klooster adds:

> We know how difficult it was for [the Reformers] to propagate the gospel even within Europe under governments usually controlled by Roman Catholic princes, kings, and emperors. Practically every door to

> the heathen world was closed to Calvin as well as to the other Reformers because the world of Islam to the south and east was guarded by Turkish armies while the navies of Spain and Portugal prevented access to the recently discovered new world. Pope Alexander VI in 1493 gave the Spanish and Portuguese crowns exclusive rights to these areas and later popes and treaties reaffirmed those donations.[3]

In addition, notes Tucker, "Martin Luther was so certain of the imminent return of Christ that he overlooked the necessity of foreign missions." Lutherans did become involved in early Protestant missions, especially those within the rise of Lutheran pietism. "Calvin himself, however, was at least outwardly the most missionary-minded of all the Reformers. He not only sent dozens of evangelists back into his homeland of France, but also commissioned four missionaries, along with a number of French Huguenots, to establish a colony and evangelize the Indians in Brazil." In fact, these were the first Protestant missionaries to have set foot in the New World. The renegade leader of the company defected to the Portuguese "and left the few remaining defenseless survivors to be slain at the hands of the Jesuits."[4]

One of these missionary martyrs was Jean de Lery, one of Calvin's favorite theology students. Calvin and the other pastors in Geneva—as well as in other Reformed churches—believed that missionaries should be thoroughly prepared, trained to read the Bible in the original languages, and steeped in sound theology. The mission field deserved no less than the quality of ministers expected at home.

Meanwhile, at home Reformed churches became centers for refugees fleeing persecution throughout Europe. Philip E. Hughes explains:

> Calvin's Geneva, however, was something more than a haven of refuge for the afflicted: it was also a school, in which, with the aid of regular lectures and daily sermons, the people were instructed and built up to be strong in the Christian faith. Even more significantly, it was a school of missions: it was open not only to receive fugitives but also to send out witnesses who would spread the teaching of the Reformation far and wide.... It was a dynamic centre of missionary concern and activity.[5]

Hughes observes that the records of the Genevan church during this period demonstrate the impressiveness of this missionary activity.

In addition to the successive waves of graduates from Calvin's Academy who were sent to almost certain martyrdom in France, many others came from Italy, Poland, England, Scotland, and elsewhere in order to return as evangelists in their native land. Historians often observe the remarkable growth of Reformed churches, often under hostile conditions, during this period. In 1561, for example, 142 graduates were commissioned by the church in Geneva as missionaries. Graduates often joked uneasily that their diplomas from the Geneva Academy were a death warrant.

In his native France, the tiny bands of evangelical Christians who had escaped martyrdom swelled to over three million by 1562, and Calvin was in close and regular correspondence with the pastors and missionary-evangelists leading the efforts. Frank James III remarks, "Far from being disinterested in missions, history shows that Calvin was enraptured by it."[6]

This passion is evident in Calvin's sermons. In commenting on the command not to forsake "to meet together" with Christ's body (Heb. 10:25), Calvin exhorted that this has as much to do with bestowing "so much labor on those who are yet aliens to the flock of Christ" as on nurturing those within.[7] In a sermon on 1 Timothy 2:3–5, Calvin declared:

> Thus we may see what St. Paul's meaning is when he saith, God will have His grace made known to all the world, and His gospel preached to all creatures. Therefore, we must endeavor, as much as possible, to persuade those who are strangers to the faith, and seem to be utterly deprived of the goodness of God, to accept salvation. Jesus Christ is not only a Savior of few, but he offereth Himself to all.

"As often as the gospel is preached to us," Calvin reminded his congregation, "we must labor as much as possible to draw those to salvation who seem to be afar off."[8]

In a sermon on Matthew 28:19, Calvin said, "This is the point of the word *go* (*exeundi*): the boundaries of Judea were prescribed to the prophets under the law, but now the wall is pulled down and the Lord orders the ministers of the gospel to go far out to scatter the teaching of salvation throughout all the regions of the earth."[9]

Calvin was hardly unusual in his missionary zeal. The Heidelberg Catechism (1564), itself an evangelistic tool, was translated into Dutch, Saxon, Hungarian, English, Greek, French, Polish, Lithuanian, and Italian—within only twenty-five years of its initial publication. Tremellius (d. 1580), a great Reformed theologian converted to Christ from Judaism, was professor at the University of Heidelberg and translated the Catechism into Hebrew with the express purpose of bringing the gospel to the Jewish people. Similarly, the Greek translation, sent to the Patriarch of the Greek Orthodox Church, was for the purpose of evangelization. In fact, the Patriarch officially adopted the Catechism (and the Canons of Dort!), although this act was repudiated by later leaders.

In the post-Reformation era, the Heidelberg Catechism was translated into Malay, Javanese, Portuguese, Spanish, Singhalese, Tamil, Chinese, and Japanese (later, into Navaho, Zuni, Tiv, and Hausa). This demonstrates the vast breadth of Reformed missionary activity during this early modern era, even prior to the rise of the modern missionary movement. In fact, the Jesuit Order (often called "God's Marines") was founded to further the aims of the Counter-Reformation. Its impressive missionary, educational, and spiritual enterprises were a direct attempt to stem the expansion of Protestant—especially Calvinist—faith and practice.

The Modern Missionary Movement

The London Missionary Society, organized in 1795, became a major seedbed of the modern missionary movement. Self-consciously Calvinistic, the group's first meeting included a speech by George Burder, recalling how

> "the apostolic spirit revived in the glorious Reformers" following the "long and awful night" of medieval superstition and decline. Luther, Calvin, other great lights of the Reformation recovered the gospel in their day. "But oh! Where is the primitive zeal? Where are the heroes of the church—men who would willingly spend and be spent for Christ; who have the ambition not to tread in a line made ready for them, but to preach Christ, where, before, He was not named?"[10]

As he spoke, William Carey was preaching on the banks of the Ganges River in India.

But before we turn to Carey, the modern missionary movement has earlier precedents. As Reformed and Presbyterian churches gained political toleration and, in some cases, even national privilege, missions abroad picked up at a remarkable pace.

The story of the modern missionary movement can hardly be told without the impressive contributions of the Dutch Reformed. In some ways, this expansion paralleled Spanish and Portuguese practice of sending missionaries with merchant ships, and the Dutch East India Company was especially dominant during this period. This was an uneasy relationship, as the Synod of Dort had ruled that no baptized person could be held in slavery. (However inadequate theologically, this policy was at least a significant advance beyond Roman Catholic practices at the time.) The missionaries were also to be given room and board at the expense of the Company. A school was established in Leyden simply for the training of missionaries.

The missionary success throughout Southeast Asia, Ceylon (Sri Lanka), Sumatra, and other regions was remarkable. Kenneth Stewart observes that many in attendance at the Synod of Dort itself, like Gisbertus Voetius, were zealous advocates of missions. In fact, the Canons of Dort explicitly underscore the missionary mandate. The Dutch Reformed also reestablished a worshiping community in Brazil, but again this work suffered setbacks from Roman Catholic missionaries and the Portuguese government.

The New England Calvinists set out early on to evangelize natives in the New World. In fact, this was included in many of the early charters, such as that of the Massachusetts Bay Colony—namely, "to wynn and incite the natives of the Country to the Knowledge and obedience of the only true God and Savior of Mankinde, and the Christian fayth."[11]

We may bristle justly at the confusion of Christ and empire, but the General Court of Massachusetts encouraged evangelization in the mid-1600s. One who responded to the call was the Calvinist pastor John Eliot (1604–1690). Eventually he left his Roxbury pastorate and settled permanently among the Indians, preaching and teaching catechism to the children. Partly in response to his work, the English Parliament authorized the founding of the Society for the Propagation of the Gospel in New England. Soon, Eliot was joined by assistants who, like him, learned the Algonquian or Mohican language, and together they translated an Indian catechism, a Psalter for singing, and finally the whole Bible. Some 3,600 natives were converted, and before long native pastors were ordained. Tucker asks:

> What was the secret behind Eliot's exceptional life of service? What carried him through the years of opposition, hardship, and disap-

> pointment? Three characteristics are worth noting: his unbending optimism, his ability to enlist the help of others, and his absolute certainty that God, not he, was saving souls and was in control of the bad times as well as the good.[12]

The Mayhew family also came from England in the 1630s, and Thomas Mayhew Sr. purchased Martha's Vineyard and became its governor. After studying for the ministry, his son, Thomas Jr., learned the native language and settled among the Indians on the island. With his new convert and associate, Hiacoomes, three hundred converts were worshiping Christ and a school was established. Thomas Mayhew Jr. was lost at sea on a trip to England, but his father—now seventy years old—took over his work, followed by his grandson, John Mayhew, and then his great-grandson, Experience.[13]

Early on, Calvinistic missionaries were glad to work with other evangelicals in the missionary cause. In fact, there was correspondence between New England ministers and the leader of the Lutheran pietists, August Francke, particularly with regard to news that the King of Denmark was encouraging missions to India (although in this case there does not seem to have been a political motivation, the king simply being an ardent pietistic Lutheran). Calvinistic missionaries established vast networks of Bible translation and distribution throughout Central and South America.

David Brainerd (1718–1747) was another Calvinist minister noted for his remarkable mission to the Indians in western Massachusetts, under the Scottish Society for the Propagation of Christian Knowledge. In 1749, Jonathan Edwards (also for a time a missionary to the Indians) provided a close report of Brainerd's work in *An Account of the Life of the Late Reverend David Brainerd*. Brainerd himself noted in his diary, "It was surprising to see how their hearts seemed to be pierced with the tender and melting invitations of the gospel, when there was not a word of terror spoken to them."[14] In the mid-1700s, Eleazer Wheelock sought to bring Indians and white settlers together for mission training in Hanover, New Hampshire. The school was eventually named Dartmouth College, after its English benefactor (Earl of Dartmouth), and was chartered to educate natives and white settlers together. In its heyday, Yale was a major missionary training-and-sending center, along with Andover and the Log College (later named Princeton).

Soon, Calvinists were looking to Africa and Asia as the new frontier of missions. Although there were already Dutch Reformed missionaries in the south, Presbyterian Robert Moffat (1795–1862), reared by Scottish parents on the Catechism and missionary stories, was the first to penetrate the African interior, together with his wife Mary.

Moffat's more famous son-in-law, David Livingstone (1813–73), became the more famous pioneer of African missions. When the *New York Herald* sent a reporter, Henry Stanley, to find Livingstone "dead or alive," the half-dead missionary was greeted with the famous words, "Dr. Livingston, I presume." Although Stanley's medicine and food restored Livingstone's health for a while, he died a year later. Yet through that encounter, Stanley became deeply impressed with the message and the messenger: "I was converted by him, although he had not tried to do it."[15] Tucker points out that these missionaries, "more than any other outside influence, fought against the evils of colonialism and imperialism" that sought to corrupt the missionary enterprise.[16]

One of the catalysts in the modern missionary movement was the Evangelical Awakening in England and Wales. Out of a Calvinistic awakening in Wales in 1772, a decision was made to send missionaries to natives and settlers in pre-Revolution America. The broadly Calvinistic London Missionary Society, mentioned at the beginning of this section, led the way toward an expanded missionary thrust.[17] Another Scottish Presbyterian, Mary Slessor (a self-proclaimed "wild lassie"), became a pioneer missionary to West Africa in 1876 at only twenty-seven years of age. Although she was honored as the first female vice-consul of the British Empire, she considered her commissioning as a missionary more distinguished. In 1915, at age sixty-six, she died in her mud hut.[18]

Reformed and Presbyterian (as well as Calvinistic Baptist and Anglican) churches pioneered missions also to the Far East. Robert Morrison was the first Protestant missionary in China, the son of staunch Scots-Presbyterian parents, and among his remarkable achievements was the first translation of the Bible in Chinese.[19]

German Reformed missionary Karl F. A. Gutzlaff was commissioned by the Netherlands Missionary Society, sent to Indonesia, Thailand, and beyond (Manchuria, Korea, Formosa); he translated the whole Bible into Cambodian and Laotian languages. Eventually, he established a base in Hong Kong, where in six years he trained more than three hundred Chinese workers as missionaries. "People everywhere were flocking to hear the gospel messages, and the greatest news of all was that no fewer than 2,871 converts had been baptized 'upon examination and satisfactory confession of their faith.'"[20]

Jonathan Goforth, "China's most outstanding evangelist," was, together with his missionary wife Rosalind, a staunch Canadian Presbyterian.[21] While the Roman Catholic missionaries were offering political and economic enticements to those who would convert, Goforth countered, "We could offer no such inducements, and we have a horror of making 'rice Christians.' We cannot fight Rome by competing with them in buying up the people."[22] Nevertheless, God blessed this work remarkably; even tens of thousands who had joined Rome converted to the evangelical faith. As theological liberalism made its way into China in the 1920s, Goforth said he "felt powerless to stem the tide" and could only "preach, as never before, salvation through the cross of Calvary and demonstrate its power.'"[23]

In the mid-nineteenth century, a young student at Princeton Seminary became convinced to go to the mission field after a lecture by Charles Hodge, in which the great theologian challenged the idea that God would convert the nations by his "extraordinary agency" rather than through the ordinary ministry of the Word. This student, Ashbel Green Simonton, led not only many natives to Christ but also many Roman Catholic settlers, including priests. Although he died at age thirty-four, within eight years Simonton established the Presbytery of Rio de Janeiro and the Brazilian Presbyterian Seminary in 1867. Today, there are well over a million communicant Presbyterians in Brazil.

Space does not allow mention of the many other Calvinists who pioneered missions in the South Pacific, Asia, Africa, and Central and South America. In fact, in 1950 a noted British Methodist missionary to India, N. Carr Sargant, could say, "To praise Arminianism and to reproach Calvinism is the conventional judgment. In respect of missions, however, rigid Calvinism and the warm Arminianism of the Wesleys were in substance the same."[24] In fact, Sargant complained that while Methodist missions focused on inculcating Wesleyan distinctives to nominal Christians, Calvinist missionaries were being sent "to the heathen."[25]

The renewed interest in missions among British and American evangelicals was spurred on by the Evangelical Revival in the mid-eighteenth century. Although John Wesley's distinguished name is significant in this movement, it was largely led by Calvinistic Anglicans, Presbyterians, and Baptists. (In fact, the Welsh Revival gave rise to the otherwise apparently paradoxical name, "Calvinistic Methodists.")[26]

However, it is William Carey (1761–1834) who is celebrated as the founder of the modern missionary movement. It is true, indeed, that he was at first opposed by a hyper-Calvinistic Baptist, John Ryland Sr., who reportedly answered Carey's call with the retort, "Young man, sit down. When God pleases to convert the heathen, He will do it without your aid or mine."[27] However, Carey was a Calvinistic Baptist, not a hyper-Calvinist. God works through means. Christians are converted and grow in their faith through the ministry of the gospel; why would we imagine that it would be any different in another part of the world?

Happily, John Ryland did not have much support, and Carey won the day among his Calvinist cohorts, founding the Baptist Missionary Society in London. In spite of enormous hardships, Carey's mission in India was enormously successful. He translated the Bible into "some 40 languages and dialects never before used for this holy purpose," notes Timothy George.[28] On every page of his own testimonies to that work, he exhibits all of the convictions of someone enthralled with the doctrines of God's sovereign grace. He believed that the modern missionary movement was carrying on the impulse and message of the Protestant Reformation.[29] His associate, Andrew Fuller, was in his own right another important leader in Calvinistic Baptist missions.

It is significant that among Baptists it was the Calvinists who led the way in missions. According to Timothy George, although the General (Arminian) Baptists were vigorous in planting churches in England early on, they had mostly died out or had lost their evangelical theological convictions by the mid-eighteenth century, denying Christ's deity and the Trinity. In any case, they refused to subscribe to any confessions, including the Apostles' and Nicene Creeds.[30] "Particular [Calvinistic] Baptists, on the other hand, resisted such liberalizing tendencies and affirmed strongly the orthodox Calvinist theology set forth in their First (1644) and Second London Confessions (1677, 1689)." Like John Bunyan before them, Carey and all of the Baptist pioneers of missions in this circle were ardent advocates of this second stripe.[31]

Presbyterians were also involved early on in the pioneering mission to India. Alexander Duff arrived in Calcutta with his wife in 1830. In addition to planting churches he established a network of schools (including colleges) whose only drawback was that they attracted many who were interested only in the secular education and not in the Christian faith.[32]

When Calvinists criticized some of these efforts, it was rarely the charge leveled by John Rylands Sr. Rather, it was a concern that these missionary endeavors were becoming too loosely connected to churches and instead to more free-floating voluntary societies. This remains a Reformed concern, but it has never dampened the zeal of Reformed and Presbyterian churches to sponsor their own missions programs. Reformed missions have been especially distinguished by an insistence on planting churches, not just producing conversions. It is this robustly New Testament view of the church that has contributed to such longevity and stability of Reformed missionary endeavors in many parts of the world.

One of the most remarkable stories of Reformed and Presbyterian missions is the Korean peninsula. Prior to 1945, the Presbyterian Church was the principal denomination. In fact, despite the fact that the Presbyterian Church remains the largest denomination in South Korea, the bulk of its members were (at least in mid-century) in what is now North Korea.[33] According to reports in the 1930s, entire villages embraced the gospel.[34]

During its heyday of orthodoxy, the Presbyterian Church in the USA (PCUSA) was a major engine of world missions, including the pioneering work in Islamic nations like Egypt.[35] We think of the Dutch-American Reformed missionary Samuel Zwemer, "the Apostle to Islam," whose work in the Arab world continues to bear fruit. He himself summarized his theology of mission in these words: "With God's sovereignty as basis, God's glory as goal, and God's will as motive, the missionary enterprise today can face the most difficult of all missionary tasks — the evangelization of the Moslem world."[36]

In fact, Presbyterians have been more involved than any other tradition in missions to the Middle East. In Bahrain, the majority of Arab Christians (and some Indians) are members of the National Evangelical Church, which is Reformed in tradition.[37] The pioneer mission agency in Iran was jointly Presbyterian and Congregationalist, forming the Evangelical Church in 1855. Until recently, it was the largest Protestant church in the country and has a disproportionate influence, especially through a network of schools, services, and a medical school.[38] The Reformed Church in America pioneered missions to Iraq in 1889 and, joined by the Evangelical and Reformed Church and the Presbyterian Church, became the United Mission.[39] The oldest missionary work in modern Palestine was sponsored by the Church of Scotland in 1839, and the first mission in Kuwait and Oman was established by the Reformed Church in America in 1903.[40] The largest Protestant membership in Syria and Lebanon is Presbyterian and the largest in Morocco is Reformed.[41]

So profoundly engaged were the Reformed and Presbyterian churches in early missions that it never seems to have occurred to anyone to calculate its full extent. Scottish church historian T. M. Lindsay, in a meeting of the Reformed and Presbyterian Alliance (1896), claimed that at least 25 percent of the missionaries on the field at that time were from such churches.[42] This did not take into account the vast number of Calvinistic Anglicans, Congregationalists, and Baptists.

Missions Today

With growing interest in Calvinism in Southern Baptist circles, some leaders have expressed alarm that it will dampen the denomination's enthusiasm for evangelism and missions. However, according to a *PCA News* report, there is no cause for worry.[43] According to its official website, the Southern Baptist Convention sponsors "about 5,000 home missionaries" and "more than 5,000 foreign missionaries."[44] For a denomination of sixteen million, this comes to approximately "0.000625 missionaries per capita."

> By contrast, the 310,000 member Presbyterian Church in America (which believes the Bible teaches predestination) has "about 600 foreign missionaries." That is 0.001935 foreign missionaries per capita commissioned and supported by the PCA. Although the PCA also has many home based missionaries, those statistics were not readily available. Thus, the PCA supports three times more foreign missionaries per capita than the SBC supports foreign and domestic missionaries combined.[45]

In fact, according to a report in *Christianity Today*, the PCA gives twice as much per dollar to international missions compared with the SBC.[46] The same was true of the Orthodox Presbyterian Church (OPC).[47] According to this same report, the Associate Reformed Presbyterian Church (ARP) comes in second among all U. S. denominations in missions support. So a high commitment to Calvinistic distinctives is an incentive rather than obstacle to missions. Moreover, the formation of the OPC was precipitated by a missionary concern. When it was known that liberal missionaries were being commissioned, Princeton New Testament professor J. Gresham Machen founded the Independent Board of Foreign Mission and was put on trial for insubordination by the PCUSA. This action led to the founding of the OPC.

Even over the last several decades, centuries of labor has borne fruit in many parts of the world. Today, there are more confessional Reformed Christians in Nigeria than in all of North America; the same can be said of Mexico, not to mention South Korea. As we have been reminded repeatedly of late, explosive growth of Christianity has shifted from the north to the south of the globe, and this is as true of the Reformed and Presbyterian churches. We in North America used to speak of the day when we would need missionaries to come to us, and already missionaries are being sent to the United States from these churches abroad.

As a minister in the even smaller and more recent United Reformed Churches in North America, I am impressed with the steady planting of new churches at home and abroad. Although the denomination has its roots in Dutch immigration, the growing membership of these young churches comes almost entirely from non-Reformed and even non-Christian backgrounds. In many cases, apologetics and evangelism classes are held during the week and are well-attended.

Around the world today there are many evangelists and missionaries who embrace without hesitation or embarrassment the doctrines of grace, otherwise nicknamed "Calvinism." Yet, as Timothy George reports, "there are still 1.3 billion persons on earth who have never heard the name of Jesus for the first time."[48] He adds:

> Today, more than a new program of missionary training or another strategy for world evangelization, the Church of Jesus Christ needs a fresh vision of a full-sized God—eternal, transcendent, holy, filled with compassion, sovereignly working by His Holy Spirit to call unto Himself a people out of every nation, kindred, tribe, and language group on earth. Only such a vision, born of repentance, prayer, and self-denial, can inspire a Carey-like faith in a new generation of Christian heralds.[49]

SHOULD CALVINISM BE DEATH TO MISSIONS? THE LOGIC OF CALVINISM

It is indisputable that convinced Calvinists have contributed significantly to missions and evangelism. However, many critics still wonder *how* this could be, given the emphasis on God's sovereign grace. Yet if history testifies to Calvinist enthusiasm for missions, could it be that critics have misunderstood what Calvinism teaches and where such teachings lead logically in action?

The apostle to the Gentiles related that he was motivated in his missionary zeal by the confidence that wherever he went, the Lord had his elect who would believe the gospel. "I endure everything for the sake of the elect, that they also may obtain the salvation that is in Christ Jesus" (2 Tim. 2:10). It was Paul's responsibility to preach the gospel to Lydia, but the Spirit "opened her heart to pay attention to what was said by Paul" (Acts 16:14). Election is the source, but God works through means. The Spirit raises those "dead in ... trespasses and sins" (Eph. 2:1) through the preaching of the gospel (Rom. 10:17; 1 Peter 1:23, 25). "How are they to hear without someone preaching? And how are they to preach unless they are sent?" (Rom. 10:14–15a).

So there is no contradiction between God's sovereign grace in salvation and the imperative of the Great Commission. In fact, the former is the basis for the latter. Given the bondage of the will to sin, no one would respond affirmatively to the gospel apart from God's regenerating grace. If God had not chosen, redeemed, and called a people for his Son, no one would have made the slightest move toward God. So the doctrine of grace motivates mission by giving us confidence that our witness will have an impact that it otherwise could never have.

Because Christ's saving work is not hypothetical but actual, we can proclaim to everyone with confidence, "God so loved the world, that he gave his only Son, that whoever believes in him should not perish but have eternal life" (John 3:16). There is not a single New Testament invitation to Christ that Calvinists cannot employ with all joy and seriousness. In fact, we are able to proclaim to sinners not that Christ has made them savable or possible, but that he has actually accomplished the salvation of all who trust in him.

Again, as we have seen, particular redemption does not limit the *sufficiency* of Christ's death. With the New Testament, advocates of particular redemption can cheerfully proclaim, "Christ died for sinners," "Christ died for the world," and "Christ's death is sufficient for you," acknowledging also with the Scriptures that the assurance, "Christ died for you," is to be given only to professing believers. When we assure people that "Christ died for you," we are telling them that they are redeemed, that their sins have been blotted out, and that they are no longer subject to God's condemnation.

The doctrines of grace also motivate a missional outlook in terms of their message. There is no greater good news that we can bring to our loved ones, friends, and neighbors than that the triune God has accomplished everything for our salvation from sin and death. We are not inviting people to cooperate with God in their redemption or new birth. We are not telling them that if they clean up their lives sufficiently, display enough zeal, and exhibit a perfect faith, they will be saved. Rather, we are given the privilege of announcing to them, like a herald returning from the battle, that God has achieved victory over Satan, death, and hell. And because God has chosen and redeemed and is effectually calling a people for himself, we are assured that our witness will not be in vain.

Election reminds us that God is the original missionary and that we have the privilege of serving alongside him in his execution of that plan. The church is God's creation, not ours. A lot of churches today are designed for different groups. There are churches for different age demographics, for people who like a certain type of music or belong to a similar marketing niche. Churches grow more quickly, we are told, when they target specific groups. So today, even in the same neighborhood, there may be a number of different churches that are similar in their beliefs yet are divided by racial, generational, political, socioeconomic, and cultural preferences. Often, a particular church today reflects the personal preferences, tastes, and cultural location of the minister. They are more a circle of friends than a communion of saints. This reflects a human-centered approach, where the church is not a miracle but a predictable result of business principles.

Election reminds us that salvation—and therefore the church—is in fact a miracle. "Salvation belongs to the LORD" (Jon. 2:9). It comes from above, not from below (John 3:5). Christ is praised in heaven because he has "by [his] blood ... ransomed people for God from every tribe and language and people and nation" (Rev. 5:9). While the epithet "chosen race" was restricted to the nation of Israel in the old covenant, it is expanded in the new covenant to include all of the elect from every nation who form Christ's body (1 Peter 2:9). It is a church made up not of people whom we have chosen but of those whom God has chosen for himself and for us as our brothers and sisters. The only nation that has any elect status today is the international remnant from Israel and the nations, united to Christ.

To invoke "chosen people" for any particular ethnic group or nation today is therefore contradictory to the eternal purpose of God.

Election affords assurance not only of our salvation but of God's ability to overcome the unbelief of friends and loved ones, no matter how hard their hearts. In the evangelical Arminian view, the new birth is entirely in our hands. Sufficient prevenient grace is given to everyone so that they can choose (or not choose) to be born again. However, in the Calvinist understanding, the new birth is the Spirit's gift in Jesus Christ. We do not believe so that we can be born again; we are born again so that we can believe. According to the Arminian perspective, the new birth is essential for salvation and yet it is something that we must bring about by our decision. Why, in that case, would we pray for the conversion of others? Why wouldn't God say, "I did my part and now it's up to your friend." Every time we pray for God to save someone, we are assuming that the new birth is a gift of God prior to the act of faith.

Arminians offer a false dilemma: (premise 1) If God alone saves, apart from our willing and running, then (premise 2) this divine work must exclude any creaturely means. Therefore, (conclusion) Calvinism is anti-missions. However, the second premise is rejected vigorously by Calvinists. The Canons of Dort declare, "Moreover, the promise of the gospel is that whosoever believes in Christ crucified shall not perish, but have eternal life. This promise, together with the command to repent and believe, ought to be declared and published to all nations, and to all persons promiscuously and without distinction."[50]

It is not God's secret predestination but the revealed gospel that is the province of the church's proclamation. The gospel is not, "Come, if you are elect," but "Come to me, all who labor and are heavy laden, and I will give you rest" (Matt. 11:28). And yet, in the previous sentence, Jesus said that "no one knows the Father except the Son and anyone to whom the Son chooses to reveal him" (v. 27). The elect are effectually called *through the proclamation of the gospel.* God uses means, as Paul reminds us in Romans 10:14–17, for "faith comes from hearing ... the word of Christ" through the mouth of preachers who have been sent.

Yet even if God works through means, including our witness, how can we proclaim the gospel freely and indiscriminately to every person if we do not know for whom Christ died? This is a good question, but the answer is clear enough from Scripture: nowhere are believers called to find the elect. Nor is there any New Testament precedent for assuring people that they are forgiven apart from faith in Christ. Rather, our mandate is to proclaim the gospel to every creature and call them to place their faith in Christ for the assurance of salvation.

Everyone who believes in Christ is assured that his death has secured their redemption—and even the faith that the Spirit bestows on them to receive Christ and all of his benefits. Christ purchased all of the gifts of salvation, leaving nothing to be attained by free will, pious experience, or works. We know that we are God's elect, redeemed to all eternity, because we rest in Christ alone for our salvation. Because Christ's death is sufficient to save a thousand worlds, no one can say "there was no redemption for me." Christ died for all who believe. The success of his death does not lie in the hands of the believer. Jesus announces from heaven, "I am ... the living one ... and I have the keys of Death and Hades" (Rev. 1:18). In this confidence, we can announce Christ's finished work to the world with joy.

It is not surprising, then, that Calvinists have been among the most zealous missionaries and evangelists in church history. Paul himself sought, through many trials, to bring salvation to the elect (2 Tim. 2:10) and was motivated in his evangelistic zeal by Christ's promise spoken directly to him, "I have many in this city who are my people" (Acts 18:10).

Charles Spurgeon recognized the significance of the objection, "How can you, sir, upon that theory, go to preach the Gospel unto every creature?" He replied:

> I could not go upon any other theory, for I dare not go on that fool's errand of preaching a redemption that might not redeem ... a salvation that might not save. I could not go to a man and say, "Believe and thou shalt be saved." He would ask me, "Do you think you are going to be in heaven?"
>
> "Yes."
>
> "Why?"
>
> "Because Christ died for me."
>
> "But he died for everybody, so my chances are therefore as good as yours."
>
> And after he had accepted my declaration, he might reply, "Is there any real reason why I should rejoice? Some for whom Christ died are in hell. What makes me so sure I will not go there? It is rather a faulty piece of good news, because it is nothing positive; it is a grand uncertainty you have proclaimed to me."

Therefore, Spurgeon concluded, the evangelistic message is clear: "If you believe on the Lord Jesus Christ, you shall be saved; if you do not, you shall be lost, and lost forever. You are not redeemed—you are not saved—there is no salvation or redemption for you."[51]

Because God finds us even when we are fleeing his presence and redeemed us even while we were enemies, we can be confident that he will achieve the full realization of his purposes in Christ through our witness. No heart is so hard, no mind so closed, no rejection so stubborn that God's sovereign love cannot melt, open, and embrace.

In the Gospels and the book of Acts, the call is to repent and believe in Christ. As we saw above, the Canons of Dort reject anything like a hyper-Calvinistic position and affirm that the gospel is to be preached "promiscuously" and "indiscriminately" to all. There is a full, free, and sufficient pardon in Christ's cross for every person who has ever lived or will ever live. Again, the phrase that has been used for centuries, long before the Synod of Dort, is apt: Christ's death is "sufficient for all, efficient for the elect only."

Note that no one in Scripture is told, "Christ died for you," much less, "Christ died to make your salvation possible." Christ's sheep hear his voice and they come to him, and not one of them will perish (John 10:11, 15). No one is called to discern whether they are among Christ's sheep, but they are called to repent and believe in Christ. Christ proclaims himself the Savior of all humanity, and he invites each and every person to embrace him through our proclamation of the gospel. No one can say on the last day that he or she wanted to be saved by Christ but was not among the elect.

This gives us confidence, since we know that nothing is impossible for God. The hardest heart can be melted; the closed mind can be opened; the most obstinate will can be healed. Only because God is the sovereignly gracious missionary are we able to take up our responsibility and privilege of witness to his gospel. And only because he alone is the Savior can we bear that responsibility with humility and freedom rather than slavish guilt or self-righteous pride.

Finally, election reminds us that there are many who have yet to hear that saving gospel. Christ not only died for us, but "to gather into one the children of God who are scattered abroad" (John 11:52). Called out of our ingrown churches, we are drawn by the hope of that new song of praise to the Lamb in heaven:

Worthy are you to take the scroll
  and to open its seals,
for you were slain, and by your blood you ransomed people for God
  from every tribe and language and people and nation,
and you have made them a kingdom and priests to our God,
  and they shall reign on the earth. (Rev. 5:9–10)

EIGHT

CALVINISM TODAY: A SWOT ANALYSIS

We know from daily experience that our greatest strengths can also become our greatest weaknesses. Persistence can become stubbornness; sympathy can devolve into sentimentality; and genuine concern for others sometimes turns into an obsequious craving for approval. Remarkable gifts of leadership and creativity can be used for good or for ill, depending on the motivation and the goals. The same is true of movements, since they are largely the collective activity of people like us.

It has become popular for businesses and organizations to conduct a periodical "SWOT" analysis, exploring **S**trengths, **W**eaknesses, **O**pportunities, and **T**hreats. Since acrostics appeal to "TULIP"-loving Calvinists, this kind of analysis may be a useful in-house evaluation, although I do not presume to speak for anyone other than myself.

STRENGTHS AND WEAKNESSES

I've selected a few areas of strengths that can also become—and have been—potential dangers.

Intellectual Boldness/Cold Intellectualism

Even critics point out the intellectual rigor and curiosity of Reformed Christians. Far from elitist, Reformed churches have insisted from the beginning on the importance of educating the whole body of Christ—and indeed, society more generally. Historians observe that Lutheran and Reformed churches played a crucial role in the rise of modern literacy and universal public education. They expected their ministers to be fluent in the original languages, yet the Reformers translated the Bible in the common languages of the people.

Stories have been told of blacksmiths getting worked up over fine points of theology. In fact, the rise of the ancient practice of catechism instruction was restored by the Reformers, who worked this into their busy daily schedule as pastors. In Reformed church orders, the pastor is typically designated the principal catechist. It is no wonder that the youth felt a connection with the wider body, in contrast to the situation today where many younger believers know their youth leader but not the pastor.

Reformed education also encompassed higher learning, and its centers were the busiest beehives of publishing. Ancient universities like Oxford and Cambridge were "restored to their ancient splendor," as one historian puts it, under the supervision of Martin Bucer and Peter Martyr Vermigli: two Reformed leaders whom Edward VI lured to England. The University of Heidelberg was similarly transformed and became a center for law, medicine, arts, and sciences along with theology. From nascent theology academies, Reformed institutions grew into major European liberal arts institutions, such as the universities of Zurich, Geneva, Leiden, Utrecht, and Edinburgh. In fact, the Jesuit Order was founded in large measure as a Counter-Reformation educational program to stem the rapid growth of Reformed colleges.

The New England Puritans first built a church, then houses, and then a college—named after the minister, John Harvard, who donated his library. When Harvard College began to tolerate Arminianism and eventually Unitarianism, the faithful founded Andover and Yale. In New Jersey, the Presbyterians founded the Log College for the training of ministers, which became Princeton College. The Reformed tradition has always insisted on a ministry steeped in learning, not only in the languages and theology, but in the arts and sciences more generally. Its centers for the training of ministers therefore became the nucleus for broader liberal arts education. The Dutch Reformed founded Rutgers, a Puritan pastor and missionary founded Dartmouth, and Calvinistic Baptists founded Brown. Especially in its defense of orthodox Christianity against the steady assault of liberalism, evangelicals from many different denominations and traditions have relied on the resources of Reformed scholarship.

Even critics (both of Reformed theology in particular and of conservative evangelicalism in general) recognize this healthy inquisitiveness and intellectual rigor. For example, Brian McLaren writes:

> When I was growing up, there was anti-intellectualism rampant in Evangelical Christianity. At that time it was mostly in the Reformed churches (Presbyterian, Christian Reformed, etc.) that one found much intellectual vigor and life of the mind. Reformed writers and speakers like Francis Schaeffer, R. C. Sproul, Ravi Zacharias, Os Guinness, J. I. Packer, and others gave me a challenge and permission to think, and, forever grateful, I made use of that permission.[1]

McLaren's recollections are similar to my own. One of the things that attracted me from the beginning to this tradition is the interest it has in the whole breadth of life and the questions that are faced in the world, not just in the church. Coming from a rather narrow church background, where even theology was thought to produce intellectual pride and division, the new vista was breathtaking—and still is to me.

Because of these strengths, however, Reformed Christians must always be on guard against intellectual pride and the reduction of the faith to sound doctrine. First, it can lead to a smugness, for we can assume we do not really have to reach out to others and understand their points of view because we are the ones who write the textbooks and sooner or later everybody borrows from our tradition. Aside from its arrogance, this assumption is no longer true—if it ever was. The memory of Old Princeton as the ivy-covered bastion of scholarly orthodoxy has faded, and Arminian evangelicals have been doing just fine writing their own theological works, biblical commentaries, and practical guides to ministry and the Christian life.

Second, while we are eager to remind our fellow Christians of the call to love God with our mind as well as our heart, sometimes we forget the heart. In some of our circles, the public ministry of Word and sacrament seems more like a lecture, and fellowship sometimes strikes newcomers as an exam. In such settings, each sentence is carefully edited so as not to say the wrong thing—or the right thing in the wrong way. The (hopefully unintended) consequence is the impression that we are privy to the answer key and are grading everyone else's work. I am glad to say this is less common than it may have been a few decades ago, but we should do everything we can to avoid giving life to the caricature. Our churches need to be hospitals for sinners and welcoming settings for honest questions.

A critical, questioning attitude is one of the hallmarks of Calvinism. Non-Calvinists often feel the brunt of this criticism, but anyone who has spent time within these circles knows how self-critical we can be. It is an asset. There is always a kind of uneasiness with the way things are that encourages further reformation. However, it can also become a liability when our concern for getting the gospel *right* is disconnected from the zeal to get the gospel *out.*

Precision is important, especially when we are talking about central doctrines. It is often noted that in the ancient debates over whether Christ is of the same essence (*homoousios*) or of a similar essence (*homoiousios*), the line between Christianity and heresy was as thin as a single vowel. However, once you catch the precision bug, it can become difficult to know when it is wiser to surrender to mystery or at least to say, "I don't know." We can lose a sense of proportion, as if precision about the order of the decrees is as important as precision about justification or the Trinity. "Getting it right" can become the end rather than a means to the greater end of trusting, praising, and obeying the God to whom these doctrines refer.

Third, there is sometimes in our circles a concern for doctrine that nevertheless leaves people as cold as ice. This is not the way the apostles proclaimed the great truths of Scripture. For them, the gospel was not just a true proposition to which we are to yield assent, but the good news—an announcement of what God had done for us in Jesus Christ.

Similarly, the first question of the Heidelberg Catechism asks, "What is your only comfort in life and in death?" What a great question! It assumes from the start that doctrine is not abstract contemplation of eternal principles but concerns the ultimate issues of personal interest. Periodically, after a series of questions and answers, the Catechism interjects, "What does this mean for you?" It doesn't ask, "What does this mean *to* you?" as if our subjective experience could determine truth, but it does press us to recognize the relevance of truth for our lives, individually and corporately. At its best, Reformed theology does not force a choice between concern for God's glory and our own comfort and happiness. After all, as the first answer of the Westminster Shorter Catechism has it, "The chief end of man is to glorify God *and to enjoy him* forever."

Intellectualism can also be driven back by drawing on biblical emphases that we also see clearly in our own confession. For example, we believe (in the words of the Heidelberg Catechism) that the Holy Spirit "creates [faith] in our hearts by the preaching of the holy gospel and confirms it by the use of the holy sacraments." There is a strong emphasis historically on preaching as a means of grace, not just a means of instruction. "The preached Word is the Word of God," says the Second Helvetic Confession. In this event, the minister is not merely educating the congregation in doctrine and applying it in exhortation, but is speaking resurrection-life into the dead, as Ezekiel did in his famous vision (Ezek. 37).

Similarly, baptism and the Lord's Supper are public ceremonies in which God shows up to ratify his covenant promises, strengthening our faith and filling our hearts with the gratitude that fuels loving obedience and service to our neighbors. As we are knit more closely in covenantal bonds with Christ, a deeper communion of saints emerges, so that their fellowship transcends anything that could be duplicated in a natural society, family, or community. Each Lord's Day is a local "community theater" in which God renews his covenant promises to us and we respond in joyful thanksgiving and fellowship with God and each other. It is a covenantal dialogue: God speaks his promises and commands, and we respond.

The Reformed tradition has a rich heritage of liturgical forms and prayers in which both the minister and the rest of the congregation speak and answer back the very words of Scripture. Especially in the singing of the psalms, Reformed worship has widened the scope of the ministry of the Word to include every aspect of the service. It has sought to follow Paul's counsel of making "the word of Christ dwell in you richly ... singing psalms and hymns and spiritual songs, with thankfulness in your hearts to God" (Col. 3:16).

However, in more recent generations, especially in the English-speaking world, a more "Zwinglian" drift has tended to turn preaching into mere teaching, the service of the Word merely to the sermon, and the Lord's Supper into an infrequent opportunity merely to remember Christ's death as a prod to greater faithfulness. What is lost is a sense that the regular gathering of the Lord's people is chiefly *his* covenant service to us: a radical in-breaking of the powers of the age to come that shower us, individually and corporately, with the treasures of heaven in Jesus Christ and by his Spirit.

I have suggested in various places that there are four coordinates that must always be kept in view: the drama, the doctrine, doxology, and discipleship. It is the dynamic *drama* of creation, fall, redemption, and the consummation that sweeps us into the unfolding plot. From this drama arise stable *doctrines* that identify the characters and interpret the meaning of the events in a coherent whole. In the process, we find ourselves not merely as spectators assenting to facts but as believers trusting in Christ. No longer "strangers and aliens" we are written into the script as children and heirs. Thus, the goal of sound doctrine is faith and hearts filled with *doxology* (praise and thanksgiving), which yields the fruit of active love and service (i.e., *discipleship*) in the world. There is a tendency for Christians to camp out on one of these instead of moving back and forth between these coordinates simultaneously.

Reducing the richness of Reformed faith and practice to the "five points" can easily abstract these doctrines from the biblical drama. As a result, they become more like dry propositions than implications drawn from the dynamic history of God's activity. Instead of pulsing, the blood dries in one's veins and the body becomes stiff. In addition, this tendency cuts off the circulation from doctrine to doxology. Although some of the key biblical passages explaining the doctrines of grace end in praise, we sometimes seem content if such explanations lead merely to assent. Good theology is meant to be sung.

Furthermore, reducing the faith to doctrinal statements shrinks our horizon, excluding the life that we are called to lead in our discipleship. On one hand, we lose a sense of the relevance that doctrines have for our lives; on the other hand, it deprives our discipleship of direction and motivation. We may believe great doctrines, but do we worship a great God, embrace a great gospel, and live in the world as those who are shaped by the gracious work that these truths proclaim? It is easy to become schizophrenic (another word for it is hypocritical), assenting to doctrines that are nevertheless contradicted by our hearts and our actions. Zeal without knowledge is blind; knowledge without zeal is dead.

If it is true that God has accomplished everything for our salvation, then how should we *feel* about that and how should we *live* as a result? There is a long tradition of connecting these coordinates in the Reformed tradition. The Puritans were especially concerned to integrate these aspects of knowing, experiencing, and doing. We can learn from their wisdom.

Love for Truth/Factionalism

We dare not miss our Lord's point when he says that the second commandment (love of one's neighbor) "is like [the first]" (love of God) (Matt. 22:39). In the Scriptures, love of truth is ultimately love of God *and* neighbor. It is possible to be selfish and human-centered even in the way we defend what we believe to be a God-centered interpretation of Scripture. We do not cherish propositions and principles, but we place our trust in Christ and embrace each other in that love that he has won for us.

I have to check my motives. Why am I so eager to convince this brother or sister of a Reformed position? Am I trying to win the argument or the person? Am I concerned that this brother or sister for whom Christ died experience a fuller astonishment at God's amazing grace, or do I want to convince them that my position is right and theirs is wrong?

Sometimes we are properly admonished to curb our enthusiasm, to exercise patience and self-control toward brothers and sisters. Yet I have also found that such admonitions themselves can be driven by a reverse kind of pride. If it is arrogant for us to pontificate where God has not spoken, it is just as proud to refuse to accept what God had revealed.

There is nothing in Calvinism itself that makes it inherently contentious. Whenever someone has invested considerable time and energy, especially on a subject that has altered their lives, passion can boil over into fanaticism. Recent converts from any belief, position, or party can be among the most polemical in their rhetoric and extreme in articulating their new views. Often, they are hardest on those who remain in the group that they left. Recent converts from Roman Catholicism are not usually the best missionaries to their Roman Catholic friends and family members. Ex-atheists are often obsessed with refuting atheists. Peter reminds us to always be ready to have an answer. However, he adds, "yet do it with gentleness and respect" (1 Peter 3:15). This is a challenge for anyone who is still nursing old wounds.

It works in the other direction as well. Former evangelicals often make the most zealous converts to Rome, and many of the most strident secularists were reared in staunchly conservative—even fundamentalist—homes. At a time when shrill voices command the radio and TV airwaves, Christians should be especially concerned to listen and respond to people with respect.

However, the stakes are raised in any debate when one is convinced that a particular interpretation of Scripture is God-centered rather than human-centered; when one has exchanged a religion of "salvation by works" for "salvation by grace." Regardless of the fairness of contrasting Calvinism and Arminianism in this way, many new converts to Calvinism express their transition in precisely those terms. It is not only a doctrine here or there but their whole orientation that is affected. The upside of this is obvious, but it often encourages one to draw a line in the sand between those who "get it" and those who don't. It is easy to caricature other views—and to forget how recently I learned these teachings myself.

Again, this is true in the case of anyone who experiences a radical change. However, the wise course is neither to ignore the issues, stifling discussion and debate, nor to encourage a divisive and immature spirit; rather, we should together open God's Word and pray for the Spirit's illumination. Convinced Arminians are just as passionate as convinced Calvinists—always ready for a good discussion and even debate of the issues. However, it is the massive group in between—the professing "undecided" vote—that usually regards any mention of these questions as igniting a powder keg. It is not uncommon for them to react with hostility—sometimes strong hostility—to those who raise them even in a spirit of charity.

Self-righteousness and pride can hide behind zeal for the truth, but frustration can also be the shell-shock that comes from believing that much of what you had learned was wrong and now you see everything in an entirely new light. Especially among pastors, we call this the "cage phase." During this period, the usual counsel from veteran Calvinists is to listen, learn, question, praise, and serve. It is an opportunity to learn the whole counsel of God, allowing all of the Scriptures to shape our faith and practice rather than to see election under every verse. There will be plenty of time to present the case for the doctrines of grace, but at this stage we always think we have arrived at the summit when there are still ranges behind with their staggering peaks.

In my own experience, I recall articulating these doctrines with certain hyper-Calvinistic elements. I was overreacting. And even when I was less extreme in my views, I sometimes expressed them with a sense of frustration with those who did not hold them. As Calvinists, we can be liberated from the fear of thinking that it's ultimately up to us to convert non-Christians, while, ironically, beating brothers and sisters over the head until they cry "Uncle!"

We have to distinguish between a God-centered perspective and thinking that you have God on your side (which implies that he's against fellow brothers and sisters). Unfortunately, we can turn God into a mascot for our team while extolling his sovereignty, glory, and grace. One of my seminary professors, Ed Clowney, used to say that we Calvinists are the only people who often seem proud of knowing they're totally depraved!

The same impetus that makes us inquisitive and questioning can also make us smug and self-confident in what we know—or think we know. For all sorts of good reasons, we can be misguided in our approach, and we can do all sorts of nasty things "for the glory of God."

When you are overwhelmed by a sense of being claimed by God and his Word—in ways that were obscure even through years of church life—it is easy to develop something like a "messiah-complex." Sometimes we mistake confidence in the truth with self-confidence. Some Christians confuse humility with imbecility: a lazy shrug in the face of important questions for which God has given us answers. However, others—including Calvinists—can confuse confidence in God's Word with confidence in our own interpretations. Genuine humility allows people to doubt themselves even while they are confident in the truth. And we can always do with more of both.

Respect for Tradition/Traditionalism

Like other Christians, Calvinists love the communion of saints. I'll never forget the new vistas that opened when Calvinist writers introduced me to ancient teachers, reformers, mystics, missionaries, and other godly men and women through the ages. At first, I was a little put off by it all. I had been under the impression that church history was pretty dark until D. L. Moody. I'm exaggerating, but there was little sense of belonging to a communion of saints between the apostles and Billy Graham.

Like a love of learning, a love for the tradition we have inherited is a strength. However, this virtue too can be turned into a vice. Sometimes in Reformed circles it may sound as if a quote from Luther, Calvin, the Puritans, Jonathan Edwards, or some other notable figure in history should settle a matter. We can treat confessions that way as well, although there is more reason to appeal to these professions of what we hold together. (It is interesting that the Reformed and Presbyterian confessions and catechisms that we subscribe to do not include any of Calvin's writings, while Wesley's sermons and his revision of the Thirty-Nine Articles hold confessional status.) Nevertheless, in actual practice, we love to quote great leaders from the past and sometimes treat their conclusions as normative.

Respect for tradition enriches us, but we can also become hero-worshipers. We can ignore the blemishes of our heroes and thereby fail to learn from their mistakes as well as their wisdom. Placing these heroes on pedestals is an odd thing to do to people who emphasized that we are all sinful—even as believers—and that God is the only real hero of the story.

One of the great benefits of the recent celebration of the tercentenary celebration of Calvin's birth has been a spate of high-quality historical studies. It is important to put the Reformation in general and Calvin and Calvinism in particular in historical context. On one hand, it challenges caricatures; on the other, it challenges rosy portraits that brush away the warts of history. The Reformers themselves often fell short of the marvelous teachings to which they gave eloquent witness. I relish sitting at Calvin's feet, reading his sermons and commentaries, but I am glad that I do not live in sixteenth-century Geneva. In many ways, Geneva and other great centers of the Reformation were exceptional exhibitions of God's gracious work; in others, they reveal the flaws of sinful people. However, this should come as no surprise to Calvinists, who believe that all of us—including our heroes—have feet of clay.

This is yet another reason why it is better to subscribe to confessions of faith than to venerate traditions and individuals. Nothing in our Reformed confessions and catechisms brings embarrassment to Calvinists to confess in our own day. They remain for us rich and enduring summaries of "the faith that was once for all delivered to the saints" (Jude 3). Yet each generation needs to rediscover the fountain from which they flow as well as our own context that makes us especially prone to wander, sometimes in ways that are different from our predecessors.

OPPORTUNITIES AND THREATS

Like strengths and weaknesses, opportunities and threats are usually two sides of the same coin.

Revived Interest in the Doctrines of Grace/ Replacing the Church with a Movement

I have already mentioned the "New Calvinism" movement, which appreciates its strengths. While defending the doctrines of grace in this book, I have also warned against reducing Reformed theology to "five points." There is more to being Reformed than appreciating Jonathan Edwards and reveling in the sovereignty and glory of God's grace.

My concern with this is not about who owns the trademark. If a label is used chiefly to lionize "us" and demonize "them," we'd be better off without it. Rather, my concern is that the richness and breadth of Reformed faith and practice are being reduced to a few doctrines. In the process, even those doctrines lose much of their supporting rationale. In fact, their meaning changes at crucial points. For example, I believe that the doctrine of election is inextricably bound up with covenant theology and with the covenantal life that is shaped in the New Testament by the means of grace. As I have argued, even "eternal security" is different from the doctrine of perseverance.

There is a widespread assumption among Christians today—even among many "New Calvinists" I encounter—that Reformed theology offers a lot of sound doctrine, but we have to look to other traditions for piety or for our eschatology or for our worship principles. Yet this assumption often rests on an ignorance of the Reformed confession, which is more easily accommodated by having reduced Calvinism to the five points. One may still disagree with the basic convictions of Reformed approaches to the Christian life. However, one cannot say that the Reformed tradition has not fleshed out its doctrinal convictions in particular approaches to piety, mission, eschatology, church government, or the application of Christian doctrine to all areas of life.

Like summer storms, movements come and go. However, Jesus has created his church and promised that the gates of hell will not prevail against it. His church is the kingdom that outlasts all of the kingdoms, cultures, movements, and trends of this passing age. Even a Calvinist movement is a tumbleweed compared to the ecclesial tree that Christ has planted near living streams. People may be swept into a movement for the moment, but they are baptized, catechized, nurtured, and fed with Christ's everlasting life in the visible communion of saints.

There is a danger even of turning churches into movements. Before long, movements—led by charismatic personalities—become corporations. Gifted ministers become CEOs. We even speak of churches in the "entrepreneurial" phase, followed by the "managerial" phase. However, this is not only language but categories from the business world transferred to the church. We should praise God for impressive preachers and ministries that have attracted people to the faith on a wide scale. Nevertheless, the greatest number of people through the ages have actually been evangelized, formed, encouraged, comforted, and challenged in their Christian faith by participating in faithful, though often small and unimpressive, churches over a lifetime. I don't have a lot of confidence in the longevity or depth of a "New Calvinism" movement that does not become a feeder for actual churches.

A New Interest in Sound Doctrine/A New Fundamentalism

Christians are neither conservatives nor progressives. We do not have a God's-eye view of reality. We do not know anything the way God knows it. There is absolute knowledge, but it belongs to God, not to us. With that much, we can agree with postmodern critiques. However, there is a God who transcends the world, created the world, sustains it, has redeemed it, and will return to consummate his reign in and over it. This God has revealed himself to us and has given us his interpretation of reality. Of course, even this revelation is accommodated to our creaturely capacity, and its scope is limited to that which he considers necessary for our salvation and life.

All of this means that we are not those who hold stubbornly to the status quo or worship at the altar of progress and innovation. God has given us a transcendent revelation by which we can evaluate all of our times and places under the sun. Therefore, we conserve some things, reform or even dispense with others, and grow in our personal and corporate faith through our own lives and through the generations as Christ's body.

Both of these tendencies—conservatism and progressivism—belong to "this passing age," while the Word of God constantly breaks up the powers of this age from above. This age—whether modern or postmodern—is either unaware of or does not believe that the great turning point in history has occurred in the resurrection of Jesus from the dead. There is only an old creation, struggling to preserve its past or improve its present. However, Christians believe in a new creation and even now participate in it by union with the risen Christ.

Ironically, Counter-Reformation theologians thought they were defending a conservative position, but the Reformers were right: the Counter-Reformation was simply codifying the unscriptural innovations in doctrine and worship that had accumulated in the medieval period. A false progressivism draws the church away from biblical teaching, while a false conservatism ensures that such innovations will become a formal and unquestioned feature of faith and practice. The real question is not whether we are conservative or progressive, but whether we are Reformed and always being reformed by God's Word.

The apostle Paul gives us the proper coordinates in 2 Timothy 1:8–14:

> Therefore do not be ashamed of the testimony about our Lord, nor of me his prisoner, but share in suffering for the gospel by the power of God, who saved us and called us to a holy calling, not because of our works but because of his own purpose and grace, which he gave us in Christ Jesus before the ages began, and which now has been manifested through the appearing of our Savior Christ Jesus, who abolished death and brought life and immortality to light through the gospel, for which I was appointed a preacher and apostle and teacher, which is why I suffer as I do. But I am not ashamed, for I know whom I have believed, and I am convinced that he is able to guard until that Day what has been entrusted to me. Follow the pattern of the sound words that you have heard from me, in the faith and love that are in Christ Jesus. By the Holy Spirit who dwells within us, guard the good deposit entrusted to you.

Paul begins by reminding Timothy of the importance of properly understanding the *message*. In this passage, as elsewhere (Rom. 1:16; 1 Cor. 1:22–24; 2:2; Phil. 3:7–9), Paul says that he is not ashamed of the gospel. Although he suffers for it, he is saved by it. He knows its power. It is not the power that one can find through any system of religion, philosophy, or ethics. It is the power of God for salvation.

Just where the gospel is an offense, it gets interesting—even for unbelievers. They are bored—understandably bored—by everything else that passes for religion and that we think is relevant in reaching them. Here, as elsewhere, Paul defines this gospel in sharp contrast to human striving. Notice how Paul cannot even refer to his suffering on behalf of Christ without preaching the gospel. Our whole ministry centers on the extrapolation, defense, and application of the gospel. This is why the gospel is *good news*. In contrast to our works, this gospel announces a salvation that has been secured by God's eternal election and in these last days is now revealed in Christ's death and resurrection.

The gospel is not a self-improvement program but the announcement of everlasting life—"immortality," including the resurrection of the body. This is why the minister is a herald or reporter—even more than that, an ambassador, that is, someone who is designated and officially empowered to announce good news on behalf of the king. *Proclamation* fits *news*. It comes to you from the outside, like the headline announcing the defeat of the Axis powers: "Victory in Europe!" This is why Christianity turns not on good advice or good instructions or good intentions, but on good *news*. News by definition is objective. It announces something that has happened in the external world and not just in the experience of a given individual. It is the announcement of something that has happened (i.e., the indicative) and not the exhortation to obedience (i.e., the imperative) that brings life and immortality to light.

Only through the faith that the gospel creates in the human heart can anyone respond faithfully to the imperatives of God's law. Not the imperatives of God's law, but the indicatives of the gospel alone, bring life and immortality to light.

Yet for Paul there is no false choice between getting the message *right* and getting the message *out*. In other words, there is no dichotomy between the message and the mission, doctrine and life, creeds and deeds. Before his conversion, he was distinguished by his conservatism, as he relates in Philippians 3. At the same time, he was not a radical. After all, the gospel is the fulfillment of the promises that God made to Abraham. For Paul, the radical character of his ministry was determined not from within himself, by his own constitution or by a concern to "re-vision" the faith for first-century experience, but by the new, definitive, and unrepeatable event of Christ's resurrection. He had been accosted by the ascended Christ on his way to another purge of Jesus' followers. *This* was definitive for everything that he now thought with respect to the past, present, and future.

Precisely because the gospel announces God's salvation from heaven, there is an urgent imperative to take this message to every human being. A false progressivism often advertises itself as missional, while a false conservatism comforts itself in the thought that it is preserving true doctrine while failing to distribute the riches. Paul was neither a conservative nor a progressivist, but he was captivated by the strange work that the triune God was doing within history, of which he was an ambassador. Ambassadors do not create policy; they announce it.

The gospel has a particular office for its faithful delivery on God's behalf. We are not on our own mission and are therefore not free to determine what the great need of our day happens to be. God has already determined what that great need is in every day. It is *God's* ministry to which we are called: "for which I *was appointed* a preacher and apostle and teacher." Paul was willing to suffer not because it was a good cause or because once he started something he finished, but because God had appointed him to this charge.

But even more, Paul was confident because of the gospel: "I am not ashamed, for I know whom I have believed, and I am convinced that *he is able to guard* until that Day what has been entrusted to me" (2 Tim. 1:12, emphasis added). Of course, he must remain faithful to his calling. Nevertheless, this sacred trust (God's grace to save and keep sinners) was the basis for this sacred mission (God's grace to save and keep the ministry of this gospel). It was not his confidence in his own powers of holding on to Christ and the gospel, but of the efficacy of God and his testimony to see the covenant through to the end.

This parallels the latter part of Paul's argument in Romans 10:14: "How then will they call on him in whom they have not believed? And how are they to believe in him of whom they have never heard? And how are they to hear without someone preaching?" In other words, if the message is all good news of something that has already been fully accomplished by someone else for sinners, where are the heralds? God even takes the responsibility upon himself of getting the word to us! "And how are they to preach unless they are sent? As it is written, 'How beautiful are the feet of those who preach the good news!'... So faith comes from hearing, and hearing through the word of Christ" (10:15, 17).

The Word of God gives us a transcendent place to stand, beyond conservatism and progressivism. It allows us to see that these are simply two stances or temperamental tendencies of this passing age and do not really take their coordinates from God's heavenly voice of judgment and salvation. When God speaks, bare conservatism is exposed as just another form of self-justification, refusing to have its barrenness broken up and impregnated by the seed of heavenly life.

It is easy to be distracted from the gospel by conservatism as well as by progressivism. In *The Screwtape Letters*, C. S. Lewis refers to the tendency of churches to adopt a "Christianity And ..." approach. The devil tells his apprentice:

> What we want, if men become Christians at all, is to keep them in the state of what I call "Christianity And." You know—Christianity and the Crisis, Christianity and the New Psychology, Christianity

> and the New Order, Christianity and Faith Healing, Christianity and Psychical Research, Christianity and Vegetarianism, Christianity and Spelling Reform ... Substitute for the faith itself some Fashion with a Christian colouring. Work on their horror of the Same Old Thing. The horror of the Same Old Thing is one of the most valuable passions we have produced in the human heart—an endless source of heresies in religion, folly in counsel, infidelity in marriage, and inconstancy in friendship.... Cruel ages are put on their guard against Sentimentality, feckless and idle ones against Respectability, lecherous ones against Puritanism; and whenever all men are really hastening to be slaves or tyrants we make Liberalism the prime bogey.[2]

Today, there are all sorts of claims being promoted in the name of Christ and on the authority of his Word that are not found in Scripture or "by good and necessary consequence deduced therefrom." The assumption (evident on both the left and the right) is that the gospel is not sufficiently relevant. Christianity must establish its credentials elsewhere, by its contribution to Western civilization or by its progressive spirit.

Abraham Kuyper spoke of the danger of a moribund conservatism in his own movement: the separation from the national Reformed Church in the Netherlands. In a sermon preached in Utrecht in 1870, Kuyper complained that a generic conservatism had replaced a genuine Reformed impulse in the church. He relates:

> Gradually recovering from a befuddled spirituality that vaporizes everything, people have ever more insistently called for the appearance of a Christianity with firm forms, and through a threefold struggle involving church elections, church property, and churchly baptism, the demand has been put with mounting urgency to our ecclesiastical apparatus either to give us back a church of Christ or to dissolve and so to disappear from the scene.[3]

Kuyper referred to the Reformation, where Christians returned to the source of Scripture—in the face of struggle and suffering. We are called to hold on to what we have. "Hold on to it, but not in the spirit of a killing conservatism which, under the motto of 'safe and sound,' causes life to wither. This fallacious preservation has nothing in common with the true sort. Conservatism and orthodoxy, terms which are often confused, need to be most sharply distinguished today."[4]

Like Paul, Kuyper saw the source of the church's life in the gospel itself. "Christianity came to save. Salvation is the hope-giving word that it unfurls on its banner. Precisely as a power of salvation it militates against destruction."[5] It renews rather than obliterates nature.

> Precisely because it seeks to save, Christianity detests a false conservatism that adorns itself with the name of Christianity but is devoid of its power. Who would save the sick by keeping the patient in the status quo? He will die before your eyes, with your false conservatism responsible for his death. To be conservative in that sense, to preserve in that sense, is to block Christianity from pursuing its goal. In a world of sin, that which is cannot remain as it is.[6]

It is true, a false progressivism closes its eyes to the past, but a false conservatism falls into the opposite error: "Quenching life, we find our peace solely in the past."[7] This type of conservatism tries merely to hold on to the "ever-diminishing influence still left to us" from our forebears.[8] This is an exercise in "repristination": the mere repetition of past utterances as if this could magically preserve the truth for the next generation. Advocates of this approach alternate between triumphalism and despair:

> They force themselves outside of their own time at the cost of having any influence on the life that surrounds them. In the end they turn against their own brothers, fragmenting even more the little power that remains. Worst of all, their own spiritual life has to suffer, and as a result of continual disappointment, the grave of their dearest wishes must become the grave of their faith itself. No, you men who honor the fathers: first seek to have for yourself the life your fathers had and then hold fast what you have. Then articulate that life in your own language as they did in theirs. Struggle as they did to pump that life into the arteries of the life of our church and society. Then not being a dead form but a living fellowship will unite you with them, faith will be a power in your own life, and your building project will reach complete success.[9]

Kuyper recalls the decline of many within his own circle toward false conservatism. First, they singled out a few slogans. "To save that, not to ask for more; to take a firm stand for that, not to reach for more, became the slogan of these folks. They venture not to create anything new; the old they cannot call back; what else can they do, then, but devote all their love to what has been preserved, firmly resolved to strike back every hand reaching out to rob them of that jewel?"[10]

New demands came, but these churches were not ready to meet them, for they did not even understand—and did not try to understand—them.

> Then everyone began to swear by his own slogans and wander down his own paths, and all too cruelly the carefree circle of brothers had to pay the penalty for opting to be a circle of friends rather than a church. People now discovered that for public life spiritual affinity is not enough; one needs the bond of a confession.... "Hold fast to what you have" was still the rallying cry, but *what* people had in Christ remained uncertain for the heart and undecided for the mind.... From that moment on a nervous scrupulosity hindered every step; mutual distrust blocked every demonstration of power. People were doomed to inaction. They kept gliding over the surface, fearing that if they immersed themselves more deeply they would drown. And so, internally divided, now swinging one way, now another, they could not stand firm, much less show a character that compelled respect from the enemy.... Neither was there any power in it.... Not, beloved, it is not the frozen waters but the foaming streams which carry life and bring salvation![11]

A false conservatism, therefore, does not really take a stand. It threatens, "This far and no further"; but when that boundary is crossed, they take a step back and repeat the threat.

> First it was the attempt to uphold the *Confession*. When that was lost, people were prepared to hold the line on *Scripture*. When that was lost, some *six fundamental truths* would serve as our shibboleths. When that too proved untenable, people were prepared at least to stand by the *miracles*. In the end they also surrendered those forward trenches and made the *Resurrection of Christ* the breastwork of Christianity, but that too was lost. Today the adversary has already laid hands on our *Baptism*—but people get used to everything and they still have not found "the formula for resistance." Thus the line of defense was shrunk again and again.[12]

In the conservative movement Kuyper discerned "no swimming against the current" in the totality of Christian faith and practice.[13]

"True: there is still a semblance of unity but it will last only as long as it pleases the enemy to unite us by his opposition."[14]

However, the gospel is not a series of "beautiful ideas." Rather, it "strikes its roots into existing reality by a series of mighty acts. It is after all a historical phenomenon." The church lives in the power of these historical acts of God in Jesus Christ. This means, says Kuyper, that the church cannot exist in the present, much less extend into the future, without going through the past that creates it. For that reason, we must indeed preserve the past, but we cannot return to it or re-create it. Instead, "the past lives on in the present." "The centuries are not juxtaposed to each other as airtight compartments; what was then works on now. The miraculous historical facts by which Christianity was begun have impregnated succeeding centuries with their power."[15]

It is not by nostalgia for a supposedly golden age (even the Reformation), but by returning to the founding events of Christ's saving work that each generation can experience the liberating power of the gospel for its own time and place. A false conservatism holds on to reality "as it is." "True conservatism seeks to preserve what is in terms of what it will become in Christ, that is, resurrected from the dead." Against all forms of salvation by human effort,

> the battle for the Bible must necessarily end in suicide if it does not unconditionally yield to the Word of God and open its eyes to the totally unprecedented, totally other new life of which that Word shows us the beginning, the substance, and the final goal, the life whose typical patterns and movements it portrays for us, and for whose recognition it offers the only genuine touchstone.[16]

Modernism is radical, pioneering, and utterly destitute of the Word of God that brings genuine life. However, false conservatism is lazy and shallow and is content merely to hold on to remnants of its shattered heritage. Genuine Christianity "must be concerned to keep not just a few blossoms that have budded on the plant but the plant itself." Kuyper adds:

> The plant must be preserved not on the assumption that our hands must create the ripe fruit and then tie it to the branches but in the firm belief that the plant already contains that fullness of fruit within. It must hold on to the Christ not merely to maintain a distinct life, not only as the absolute principle of that life, but equally as

> the Eternal One in whom the fullness of that life is already present, also for yourselves. Orthodoxy is unfaithful to that eternal principle if it shrinks from saying, as our fathers did, that in Christ we already have everything and need not first acquire it.[17]

To be sure, genuine orthodoxy is continuous with the faith of our fathers and mothers in Christ. "Still it is our calling to hold fast what we have in Christ in our own time, not in theirs.... That labor is enormous, Congregation, especially where so much of it has been neglected."[18] It is an orthodoxy that refuses a dead repetition of dull routine, but asks what it believes and why it believes it. It returns to the source of its life—not only for the church's sake, but for the benefit of the world.

Kuyper concluded this final sermon to his Utrecht congregation: "Do not bury our splendid orthodoxy in the treacherous pit of false conservatism.... And now, Congregation, before I pronounce the Amen, receive my final 'Farewell.' May the Lord never take away the candlestick He so marvelously gave you, but may His light shine from it ever more brightly."[19]

TOWARD A NEW REFORMATION

The creeds, confessions, catechisms, and dogmatics of our churches serve the ministry of word and sacrament, not vice versa. It is because God has spoken good news and has appointed ambassadors to the errand of announcing it that the specific content of that proclamation must be protected, defended, and clarified so that it can be widely disseminated through proclamation. In other words, evangelism is the penultimate goal of theology, whose ultimate end is the glory of God. If much of evangelicalism today surrenders important aspects of the message in the name of relevant mission, the opposite danger is to glory in the fullness of the message as a satisfactory compensation for neglecting the imperative of the Great Commission.

The gospel has a particular form for its faithful repetition in the life of God's people. In Paul's advice to Timothy quoted above, the church today hears its own imperative: "Follow [hold fast] the *pattern of the sound words* that you have heard from me, in the faith and love that are in Christ Jesus" (2 Tim. 1:13, emphasis added). Already the church was formulating the truth of God's Word in simple but not simplistic statements that could provide the perimeters of faithful preaching, teaching, and life. Sound words were essential but not sufficient; there needed to be a pattern, a way of saying things in the manner in which they *should* be said, in order to avoid error and to build up the body in unity. "Hold fast" is a command to preserve, not to innovate. "By the Holy Spirit who dwells within us, *guard* the good deposit entrusted to you," he concludes (1:14). The truth must be guarded, so that it may be dispensed to others in ever-widening circles as the life-giving Word that it always is in its very essence.

Are we conservative or Reformed? Although many of his criticisms are based on caricatures, Brian McLaren correctly presses us to answer the question:

> So what happens when Protestants get tired of protesting? What happens when they want to protest their own protesting? If they simply form another elite sect that protests Protestant protesting, they're still stuck in the cycle, doomed to become the next Protestant sideshow, super-Protestants, nothing more. Is there an alternative?[20]

In an interview, church historian Jarolav Pelikan famously said:

> Tradition is the living faith of the dead; traditionalism is the dead faith of the living. Tradition lives in conversation with the past, while remembering where we are and when we are and that it is we who have to decide. Traditionalism supposes that nothing should ever be done for the first time, so all that is needed to solve any problem is to arrive at the supposedly unanimous testimony of this homogenized tradition.[21]

Our calling is not to simply repeat slogans, but to clarify and, on the basis of Scripture, at times even modify our understanding and practice in order to achieve greater precision in teaching and obeying God's Word faithfully.

The past is not necessarily weighty because it is past. Arianism, Pelagianism, and other heresies also have an ancient pedigree. Rather, it is to the living stream of God's Word that we step in the present, as did our forebears, to be washed from the accumulated superstitions and lies of our own time and place. False conservatism cannot even sustain its own irrelevant existence. Without a *confessional* consciousness and a *confessing* heart, the disintegration of a clear common enemy gives way to sectarian rivalry.

Churches today stand in need of a new reformation. There is no need to rehearse the statistics here. Evangelicalism in the United States is plagued by ignorance of Scripture and confusion concerning the nature of the human plight and its solution in the gospel. Worship, church life, and outreach are determined by the whim of the market, just as the Word was buried under medieval innovations.

At the same time, many Reformed and Presbyterian churches seem content to live off of the capital of the past, without having to return for themselves to the streams that fed the great renewals of apostolic faith and practice in the past. It is not enough to invoke the slogans of the Reformation and to settle for the pristine confession of "the five points of Calvinism." We need to recover the fullness of biblical faith and practice in our own time and place. Like children, we need to ask even the most basic questions anew, in the light of the specific challenges and opportunities in our own age.

We are not caretakers of a cemetery or guardians of a heritage; rather, we are ambassadors of the ever-living and ever-active King in heaven, sent into our families, neighborhoods, and nations with the life-giving message of Christ. We cannot take this inheritance for granted. It is not a treasure merely to be guarded but to be put on display each week, shared among the saints, and distributed to a world that lies under the domain of sin and death.

Like Paul's advice to Timothy, Kuyper's heartfelt call reminds us that the challenge for Reformed believers—indeed, for all Christians—is to draw our strength for our own day from the deep wells of the apostolic gospel. Luther will not save us. Calvin's words help us to understand God's Word, but we must return to the well from which he drew in his own time and speak to our generation as directly as he did to his. We are *confessional*, but we also must *confess* the faith in our own time and place and not be content to boast in the purity of a book whose expressions are not the treasure of our own hearts. Far from exhibiting sectarianism, the "form of sounds words" to Paul calls Timothy to provide both the magnet for unity and the boundaries within which faithful preservation of God's truth can serve the ever-wider, ever-more-joyful, ever-zealous proclamation of that truth to every person—until the glory of God covers the earth as the waters cover the sea.

AFTERWORD

"If you have any unconfessed sin when you die—or Jesus returns—you'll probably go to hell."

Those were the comforting words I was given to ponder as I walked home from school that day. And as if that wasn't enough to frighten me into confession on the spot, my seventh-grade Christian school teacher added a warning against entertaining sinful thoughts: "So if you're walking home from the bus stop today entertaining a vile thought, remember . . . He knows . . . He knows."

It was enough to give any middle school student the creeps.

I was reared in a Baptist family, and my mother had a fairly good grasp of the core teachings of the Bible, so I knew that something was wrong with what he had said, but I was still confused. I didn't really know what to believe. The church we were attending at the time was mostly of the "doctrine divides, so let's not talk about those issues" school, so we rarely heard anything controversial on Sunday mornings. For those rare times when we'd encounter unusual teachings like this, my mom would always say to me, "Let's go back to the Bible and see what it says." It was the best advice she ever gave me.

At the time, my oldest brother (by twenty years) had just embraced what he called "the doctrines of grace." He had advised me to spend some time reading Paul's letter to the Romans. Everything would become clear for me if I would just read Romans, he said. *Read Romans?* I wondered. *Is it that simple?* If the Bible is so clear, why am I getting so many different interpretations from the different authority figures in my life?

Still, I took his advice and I read Romans. And then I read it again. And again. I think it's safe to say that at some point reading Romans became an obsession for me. That section of my Bible soon began to fall out of the binding. Something began stirring in my own heart, but I wasn't sure what was happening.

I remember one night, after throwing my Bible across the room, I saw it had fallen open to Romans 9. *Great,* I thought, *now my salvation has been taken completely out of my hands. Not even my decision to accept Christ is something I can claim.* I found myself more and more identifying with the experience of Jonathan Edwards, who said that at first God's sovereign grace seemed terrible to him, but afterward it became the sweetest song of his heart.

I understand that people come to embrace the doctrines of grace—the teachings of Calvinism—for different reasons. Some people are raised to believe these doctrines and never question their beliefs. Others may believe the teachings of Calvinism, but they never wrestle with them at a heart level—they remain nothing but an academic exercise for them. My own experience—like many other believers I have met over the years—felt more like a matter of life and death. Either it was *all* of grace, or I had no hope. I knew I had reached a decision point: it was going to be "Christ alone," or I would just walk out on everything and leave my faith behind.

Thank God, my brother was right: Romans is clear. And so is John, and Genesis, and the rest of the Scriptures. In fact, the more I began to read the whole Bible in the light of the central message of the gospel, the more I became convinced of Jesus' own testimony, that this was a book *about him.* For the first time, I began to understand that the Bible was not just a book of commands, principles, and moral teachings. It was a drama of unfolding redemption centered around the person and work of Jesus Christ.

I was now ... gasp ... becoming a "Calvinist."

Sadly, as my interest in Reformed theology and the doctrines of grace began to grow, I became pretty hard to live with. My father would make an ostentatious exit whenever I began debating doctrine with my mom. In an ironic twist, at that very moment in my life when I became convinced that I couldn't convert anybody and had to trust the Spirit to work as he chose through my witness, I grew impatient with my own fellow Christians. Where I had been liberated by a fresh view of God and his gospel of grace in Christ, I was now imprisoned by my own pride. Perversely, I was proud of knowing that I was totally depraved, helpless, and saved by grace alone. How blind were other Christians who didn't "get it"!

Although I reveled in the election passages I read in the Scriptures, it hadn't quite sunk in that God chose the *foolish* to shame the wise and the *weak* to shame the powerful. I had still not allowed these wonderful doctrines of grace to humble me before God and other people, to fill me with praise instead of pride. I had not learned to trust patiently in the Spirit's persuasion through his Word instead of my own dogmatism.

Sin runs so deep in our hearts that sadly, we can twist even the best of the Spirit's gifts into weapons of the flesh. Spiritual pride is so deeply entrenched in us, even as Christians, that we can rebound from moral legalism to intellectual legalism in the blink of an eye. I wish I could say after all these years of writing and teaching about the doctrines of Calvinism that I have outgrown my spiritual immaturity. What I *can* say is that these truths captivate me in new ways, each day. They continue to surprise, challenge, and uproot me from my inborn tendency to defend *myself* under the guise of defending the *truth*.

The doctrines and teachings of Arminianism shouldn't be defined by their aberrations any more than Calvinism should. Yet I will say this: even the most evangelical forms of Arminian theology fail to adequately deal with the whole teaching of Scripture or the serious depth of the heart's depravity. They fail to account for the ongoing struggle with sin that is a daily part of our Christian experience. I personally know many Arminians who look resolutely to Christ alone, who praise God's glorious grace, and who do *not* in fact lean on their own willing and running. However, I remain as convinced as ever that Arminianism as a theological system is inconsistent with that genuine profession.

Wherever we encounter expositions of the doctrines of grace in Scripture itself, they lead to surprise (sometimes even frustration), joy, thanksgiving, witness, comfort, and godly living. And yes, they can also lead to debate. Many of Jesus' own followers left him when he began preaching difficult doctrines and saying things like, "No one can come to me unless the Father who sent me draws him" (John 6:44). Anything that is important will inevitably lead to debate. Only inconsequential matters can be ignored, pushed aside, and left on the shelf.

Yet real truth should always lead us to the Truth—the person who is Love Incarnate. All of us are called to "grow in the grace and knowledge of our Lord and Savior Jesus Christ" (2 Peter 3:18). Because these are questions that Scripture clearly and frequently addresses, the positions that we historically label as "Calvinism" and "Arminianism" cannot simply be ignored.

Yet it is tragic when, out of zeal for truth, we misrepresent the truth about the positions that others hold. One of the main fruits of adopting the position we call "Calvinism" should be a realization that all of our blessings in Christ are a gift. Perhaps we need to hear Paul's rebuke once again: "What do you have that you did not receive? If then you received it, why do you boast as if you did not receive it?" (1 Cor. 4:7). In our zeal for truth, Calvinists need to remember that we didn't invent the doctrines of grace. In fact, it is easy to forget our own ignorance of these truths when we react against criticism. God is gracious with us, in our sinful failings, just as he is with our Arminian brothers and sisters. Together, we are pilgrims on the way, not masters who have arrived.

In defending these doctrines, we would do well regularly to ask ourselves whether we're trying to win an argument ... or if our heart's desire is to truly share the gift we have received from God. In my experience, there is a world of difference between the two, between seeking further assurance in God's grace and scoring points on the debate scorecard. Sound doctrine is never an end in itself. It should lead us on to a deeper experience of the Father, in the Son, through the Spirit, together with the communion of saints.

As you continue your study of Calvinism, I pray that you will receive the blessing of God's grace in a way that will transform your heart and mind. May the triune God lead us by these truths to a clearer sight of the Truth to whom all believers are led by the Spirit to cry, "Lord, be merciful to me, a sinner!"

NOTES

Introduction: Calvinism and Arminianism: Why Bother?

1. Clark Pinnock, "From Augustine to Arminius: A Pilgrimage in Theology," in *The Grace of God, The Will of Man: A Case for Arminianism*, ed. Clark H. Pinnock (Grand Rapids: Zondervan, 1989), 23, 26, 27: "It is my strong impression that Augustinian thinking is losing its hold on present-day Christians. It is hard to find a Calvinist theologian willing to defend Reformed theology, including the views of Calvin and Luther, in all its rigorous particulars now that Gordon Clark is no longer with us and John Gerstner is retired." Pinnock concedes that his changes are part of a growing accommodation to the secular mind: "We are finally making peace with the culture of modernity."

2. John Calvin, *Institutes* 3.2.28. All references are from *The Institutes of the Christian Religion* (1559), Library of Christian Classics 20–21; ed. John T. McNiell; trans. Ford Lewis Battles (Philadelphia: Westminster, 1959).

3. Ibid., 3.2.29.

4. Charles Spurgeon, *The Autobiography of Charles H. Spurgeon* (Cincinnati: Curts & Jennings, 1898), 1:172.

Chapter One: The Essence of Calvinism

1. Kenneth J. Stewart, *Ten Myths about Calvinism* (Downers Grove, IL: InterVarsity Press, 2011), 75–96.

2. Calvin, *Institutes*, 3.2.1; 3.11.1; and "Sermon on Luke 1:5–10," in *Corpus Reformatorum* (CR), ed. C. G. Bretschneider, H. E. Bindseil, et al. (New York: Johnson, repr. 1964), 46:23.

3. See, for instance, Heinrich Bullinger, *De testamento seu foedere Dei unico et aeterno* (1534); cf. Philip Melanchthon, *Loci communes* (1543), where the covenant concept repeatedly appears as a unifying factor.

4. B. B. Warfield, *The Westminster Assembly and Its Work* (New York: Oxford Univ. Press, 1931), 56.

5. John H. Leith, *Creeds of the Churches*, 3rd ed. (Louisville: Westminster John Knox, 1983), 38–39.

6. Martin Luther, *The Bondage of the Will* (Grand Rapids: Revell, repr. 1990).

7. Despite his friendship with Calvin, Philip Melanchthon eventually came to question reprobation and taught a form of synergism (conditional election) that (in addition to his more Calvinist understanding of the Lord's Supper) led to a strong reaction against him on the part of Luther's orthodox followers. Their conclusions, summarized in the Formula of Concord, reject reprobation and affirm the resistibility of (and possibility of falling from) grace. At the same time, the Formula sharply rejects the synergism associated with Melanchthon's view. See Charles Porterfield Krauth, *The Conservative Reformation and Its Theology* (Minneapolis: Augsburg, 1963), 322–24. Nevertheless, some Lutherans rejected this confessional position in favor of Melanchthon's view (conditional election, based on foreseen faith). See Heinrich Smid, *Doctrinal Theology of the Evangelical Lutheran Church*, trans. Charles A. Hay and Henry E. Jacobs (Minneapolis: Augsburg, 1889), 272–73.

8. Arminian (Remonstrant) theology, as it evolved into a system, rejected unconditional election and, consequently, its monoergistic emphases. The Counter-Reformation of the Roman Catholic Church offered yet another perspective on the divine decree. In between the classic Thomistic-Augustinian position defended by the Dominicans and the more Semi-Pelagian position adopted by the later Franciscans are the so-called "Molinists," named after Molina who, with Sũarez, defended a position identified as "middle knowledge" (*scientia media*). For a contemporary defense of this view see William Lane Craig, "The Middle Knowledge View," in *Divine Foreknowledge: Four Views* (Downers Grove, IL: InterVarsity Press, 2001).

9. Roger Olson, *Arminian Theology: Myths and Realities* (Downers Grove, IL: InterVarsity Press, 2006), 53.

10. Richard Watson, *Theological Institutes* (New York: Phillips and Hunt, 1887), 2:392–449; Thomas N. Ralston, *Elements of Divinity*, ed. T. O. Summers (New York: Abingdon-Cokesbury, 1924), 278–327; William B. Pope, *A Compendium of Christian Theology* (New York: Phillips and Hunt, n.d.), 1:317–19; John Lawson, *Introduction to Christian Doctrine* (Grand Rapids: Zondervan, 1967, 1980), 206–35. See also Roger Olson, *Arminian Theology*, 18: "Contrary to confused critics, classical Arminianism is neither Pelagian nor semi-Pelagian! But it is *synergistic*."

11. Olson, *Arminian Theology*, 57.

12. Followers of this movement were radical Protestants who rejected all dogmas that they thought were inconsistent with reason and practical morality. Forerunners of modern Unitarians, Socinians denied the Trinity, the deity of Christ, and the substitutionary character of Christ's atonement. They held that in order to affirm free will, God's foreknowledge must include only necessary truths rather than the contingent decisions and acts of human beings. See the citations from the Racovian Catechism in William Cunningham, *Historical Theology* (Edinburgh: Banner of Truth, 1996), 2:173. Similar views at least on these points are advanced today in the movement known as "open theism," particularly in the work of Clark Pinnock, John Sanders, and Gregory Boyd.

Chapter Two: Of Regents and Rebels: The Human Condition

1. Calvin, *Institutes* 1.1.1.

2. *Catechism of the Catholic Church* (New York: Doubleday, 1997), 405, 418.

3. Calvin, *Institutes* 2.2.10.

4. Ibid., 2.2.11.

5. Ibid., 2.1.9. See also 2.2.11 and 1.16.8.

6. John Calvin, *Commentary on the First Book of Moses Called Genesis*, trans. John King (Grand Rapids: Baker, repr. 1996), 112–13.

7. Ibid., 95.

8. Ibid., 97–98.

9. Ibid., 100.

10. This characteristic emphasis of Reformed anthropology can be found among many of Calvin's students, as in J. I. Packer, *Christianity: The True Humanism* (Waco, TX: Word, 1986).

11. Calvin, *Institutes* 1.15.8.

12. Ibid.

13. The Canons of Dort, Third and Fourth Heads of Doctrine, Art. 1, in the *Psalter Hymnal: Doctrinal Standards and Liturgy of the Christian Reformed Church* (Grand Rapids: Board of Publications for the Christian Reformed Church, 1976), 102. See also Michael S. Horton, "Post-Reformation Reformed Anthropology," in Richard Lints, Michael Horton, and Mark Talbot, eds., *Personal Identity in Theological Perspective* (Grand Rapids: Eerdmans, 2006), 45ff. I treat this historical development at greater length in my *Lord and Servant* (Louisville: Westminster John Knox, 2005), chapters 4 and 5.

14. The Belgic Confession, Art XIV, in the *Psalter Hymnal*, 75.

15. Calvin, *Institutes* 2.1.5.
16. Ibid., 2.1.6.
17. Ibid., 2.1.7.
18. Ibid., 2.1.8.
19. See Edmund Schlink, *Theology of the Lutheran Confessions*, trans. Paul F. Koehneke and Herbert J. A. Bouman (Philadelphia: Fortress, 1961), 47 and 59, with ample citations from the Book of Concord and Lutheran orthodoxy.
20. Calvin, *Institutes* 2.2.15.
21. Ibid., 2.2.16.
22. Ibid., 2.3.5.
23. Ibid., 2.2.6–7.
24. Ibid., 2.2.6.
25. Ibid., 2.3.10.
26. Ibid., 2.3.14.
27. Ibid., 1.3.3.
28. Ibid.
29. John Calvin, *Commentary on the Epistle of Paul the Apostle to the Romans*, trans. and ed. by John Owen (Grand Rapids: Baker, repr. 1996), 71.
30. Ibid.
31. Calvin, *Institutes* 1.5.1.
32. Ibid., 1.6.14.
33. Calvin, *Romans*, 73–74.
34. Ibid., 80.
35. Ibid., 88.
36. Calvin, *Institutes* 2.3.4.
37. Ibid., 3.23.4–5.
38. Ibid., 2.2.11.
39. Ibid.
40. Calvin, *Romans*, 68.
41. Calvin, *Institutes* 2.3.13.
42. Ibid., 1.2.1.
43. Ibid., 2.6.1.
44. Ibid., 2.6.2–3.
45. Ibid., 2.6.4.
46. Ibid.
47. See the statistics offered in David F. Wells, *Above All Earthly Pow'rs: Christ in a Postmodern World* (Grand Rapids: Eerdmans, 2005), 299.
48. Christian Smith with Melinda Lundquist Denton, *Soul Searching: The Religious and Spiritual Lives of American Teenagers* (New York: Oxford Univ. Press, 2005).
49. Olson, *Arminian Theology*, 30.
50. C. Fitzsimons Allison, "Pastoral Care in the Light of Justification by Faith Alone," in *By Faith Alone: Essays on Justification in Honor of Gerhard O. Forde*, eds. Joseph A. Burgess and Marc Kolden (Grand Rapids: Eerdmans, 2004), 309–12.

Chapter Three: Loved before Time (Election)

1. John Stott, *God's New Society* (Downers Grove, IL: InterVarsity Press, 1982), 20.
2. Luther, *The Bondage of the Will*, 217.
3. John Calvin, on Acts 13:46 in *Commentary on Acts* in *Calvin's Commentaries*, trans. and ed. by John Owen (Grand Rapids: Baker, 2009), 1:551. All references to Calvin's commentaries that follow are from this series.
4. John Calvin, *Commentary on the Synoptic Gospels*, 3:378.
5. Louis Berkhof, *Systematic Theology* (Grand Rapids: Eerdmans, 1996), 119 (cf. p. 120 for an excellent summary of the two views).

6. Canons of the Synod of Dort, Chapter V, Conclusion, 115.

7. Olson, *Arminian Theology*, 128, from Richard Watson, *Theological Institutes* (New York: Lane & Scott, 1851), 2:435.

8. See, for example, Clark Pinnock, "Systematic Theology," in *The Openness of God: A Biblical Challenge to the Traditional Understanding of God*, ed. Clark Pinnock et al. (Downers Grove, IL: InterVarsity Press, 1994), 121–23; Clark Pinnock, *Most Moved Mover* (Grand Rapids: Baker, 2001), 100; William Hasker, "An Adequate God," in *Searching for an Adequate God: A Dialogue between Process and Free Will Theists*, ed. John B. Cobb Jr. and Clark H. Pinnock (Grand Rapids: Eerdmans, 2000), 218–19. These writers insist that this view still affirms God's omniscience, but they fail to demonstrate how "all-knowledge" can exist when God is said to be ignorant of the vast majority of future actions (namely, those brought about by human decision).

9. See, for example, Robert Shank, *Elect in the Son: A Study of the Doctrine of Election* (Minneapolis: Bethany, 1970); William Klein, *The New Chosen People: A Corporate View of Election* (Grand Rapids: Zondervan, 2005).

10. Ben Witherington, *The Problem with Evangelical Theology: Testing the Exegetical Foundations of Calvinism, Dispensationalism and Wesleyanism* (Waco, TX: Baylor Univ. Press, 2005), 62–3.

11. I owe this observation to Terrance Tiessen in personal correspondence.

12. Charles Hodge, *Systematic Theology* (Grand Rapids: Eerdmans, 1946), 1:547: "It is vain to argue that a holy and benevolent God cannot permit sin and misery, if sin and misery do in fact exist. It is vain to say that his impartiality forbids that there should be any diversity in the endowments, advantages, or happiness of his rational creatures.... So it is utterly irrational to contend that God cannot foreordain sin, if he foreordained (as no Christian doubts) the crucifixion of Christ. The occurrence of sin in the plan adopted by God is a palpable fact; the consistency, therefore, of foreordination with the holiness of God cannot rationally be denied."

13. Pinnock, *Most Moved Mover*, 4.

14. Ibid., 6.

15. Ibid., 142.

16. Pinnock, "From Augustine to Arminius," 27.

17. Clark Pinnock, "From Augustine to Arminius: A Pilgrimage in Theology," in Clark Pinnock, ed., *The Grace of God and the Will of Man* (Grand Rapids, Mich.: Zondervan, 1989), 24.

18. Calvin, *Institutes* 1.17.2, see esp. footnote 7: "Cf. Calvin, *De aeterna Dei praedestinatione*, where he assails the 'Sorbonnist dogma that ascribes to God absolute power' dissociated from justice.... Similarly, in Sermons on Job lxxxviii, on Job 23:1–7: 'What the Sorbonne doctors say, that God has an absolute power, is a diabolical blasphemy which has been invented in hell' (CR XXXIV. 339f.)." Although open theism appears at times to separate God's love from his justice, Calvin will not allow that either God's love or sovereignty is unhinged from his justice.

19. *Institutes*, 1.17.1.

20. Ibid., 1.17.2.

21. Ibid., 1.17.9.

22. Berkhof, *Systematic Theology*, 105.

23. Ibid., 103.

24. Francis Turretin, *Institutes of Elenctic Theology*, trans. G. M. Giger; ed. J. T. Dennison Jr. (Phillipsburg, NJ: Presbyterian and Reformed, 1992), 1:529.

25. Ibid., 1:530.

26. Ibid., 1:531.

27. Quoted in ibid., 104.

28. Luther, *The Bondage of the Will*, 217.

29. William Twisse, *Riches of Gods love unto the vessels of mercy, consistent with his absolute hatred or reprobation of the vessels of wrath* (Oxford, 1653), 2:170–81.

30. Ibid., 1:64.
31. *Mennonite Confession of Faith* (Crockett: Rod and Staff, 1966), 96.
32. Calvin, *Institutes* 3.24.1.
33. Ibid., 3.24.4.
34. Ibid., 3.24.5.
35. Ibid., 3.24.3–4.
36. Ibid., 3.24.5.
37. John Calvin, *Commentary on Isaiah*, 4:146.
38. Canons of Dort, First Head of Doctrine, Art. 17, 95.
39. Thirty-Nine Articles of the Church of England, Art. 17.
40. Luther, *The Bondage of the Will*, 217.
41. Westminster Confession 3.8, in *The Book of Confessions* (Louisville: PCUSA).
42. Formula of Concord, Solid Declaration, Article XI ("Election"), Para. 2. See http://bocl.org?SD=XI–2.
43. Ibid., Para. 8. See http://bocl.org?SD-XI–8.
44. Ibid., Para. 12. See http://bocl.org?SD-XI–12.
45. Ibid., Para. 43–46.
46. Ibid., Para. 48, 50–51.
47. Formula of Concord, Solid Declaration, Article XI ("Election"), Para. 52.
48. Turretin, *Institutes of Elenctic Theology*, 1:16. Calvin's attitude toward speculation is well-known, as is his emphasis on God's condescension and accommodation to us, revealing God not as he is in himself but as he is toward us—not in his being but in his works. "Better to limp along this path," Calvin cautioned, "than to dash with all speed outside it" (*Institutes* 1.6.3).
49. Turretin, *Institutes of Elenctic Theology*, 1:252.
50. See Calvin, *Institutes* 3.21.2.
51. Ibid., 3.21.1, 5.
52. Calvin, *Commentary on Zechariah-Malachi*, 482.

Chapter Four: Mission Accomplished (Atonement)

1. Martin Hengel, *The Atonement in New Testament Teaching* (Philadelphia: Fortress, 1981), 36–38, 49.
2. Gustav Aulen, *Christus Victor: An Historical Study of the Three Main Types of the Idea of Atonement*, SPCK Classics (London: SPCK, 2010).
3. See Walter Wink's works, especially *The Powers That Be: Theology for a New Millennium* (New York: Doubleday, 1999); N. T. Wright, *Evil and the Justice of God* (Downers Grove, IL: InterVarsity Press, 2006), and Brian McLaren, *Everything Must Change: Jesus, Global Crisis, and a Revolution of Hope* (Nashville: Nelson, 2007). *Christus Victor* is also the favored interpretation of liberation theologies and in recent Anabaptist defenses of a nonviolent atonement. See, e.g., J. Denny Weaver, *The Nonviolent Atonement* (Grand Rapids: Eerdmans, 2001).
4. I explore this cosmic eschatological aspect in *Covenant and Salvation* (Louisville and London: Westminster John Knox, 2007), 289–302.
5. St. Anselm, "Cur Deus Homo," in *Anselm: Basic Writings*, trans. S. N. Deane, 2nd ed. (London: Open Court, 1998), 192–252.
6. Berkhof, *Systematic Theology*, 385.
7. Ibid., 386.
8. Ibid.
9. Immanuel Kant, *Religion and Rational Theology*, in *The Cambridge Edition of the Works of Immanuel Kant*, ed. Allen W. Wood and George di Giovanni (Cambridge: Cambridge Univ. Press, 1996), 76–97, 104–45.
10. H. Orton Wiley, *Christian Theology* (Kansas City, MO: Beacon Hill, 1952), 2:241.

11. Referring to the penal substitution theory as "the Calvinistic theory" (2:241), Wiley (ibid.) asserts, "It is in this attempt to impute our sin to Christ as His own that the weakness of this type of substitution appears" (245). "Our final objection to the satisfaction theory is based upon the fact that it leads logically to antinomianism," for the following reasons: "(1) It holds that Christ's active obedience is imputed to believers in such a manner that it is esteemed by God as done by them. They are, therefore, righteous by proxy. (2) This imputation in reality makes Christ's suffering superfluous; for if He has done for us all that the law requires, why should we be under the necessity of being delivered from penalty by His death? (3) If Christ's active obedience is to be substituted for that of believers, it shuts out the necessity of personal obedience to the law of God.... Man is therefore left in the position of being tempted to license of every kind, instead of being held strictly accountable for a life of righteousness" (249). Wiley points out that John Miley "is the outstanding representative of the governmental theory in modern times" (255). Wiley denied that Christ's death involved "a substitution in penalty as the merited punishment of sin" (257).

12. Cf. Berkhof, *Systematic Theology*, 368.

13. Ibid., 369.

14. Charles G. Finney, *Systematic Theology* (Minneapolis: Bethany, repr. 1976), 31, 179–80, 236. Arminian theologian Roger Olson points out that Finney's theology is much closer to Pelagianism than to Arminianism (*Arminian Theology*, 28, including footnote 20).

15. Finney, *Systematic Theology*, 206.

16. Ibid., 209.

17. Ibid.

18. George Lindbeck, "Justification and Atonement: An Ecumenical Trajectory," in *By Faith Alone: Essays on Justification in Honor of Gerhard O. Forde*, ed. Joseph A. Burgess and Marc Kolden (Grand Rapids: Eerdmans, 2004), 205.

19. Ibid., 205–6. He adds, "Those who continued to use the *sola fide* language assumed that they agreed with the Reformers no matter how much, under the influence of conversionist pietism and revivalism, they turned the faith that saves into a meritorious good work of the free will, a voluntaristic decision to believe that Christ bore the punishment of sins on the cross *pro me*, for each person individually. Improbable as it might seem given the metaphor (and the Johannine passage from which it comes), everyone is thus capable of being 'born again' if only he or she tries hard enough. Thus with the loss of the Reformation understanding of the faith that justifies as itself God's gift, Anselmic atonement theory became culturally associated with a self-righteousness that was both moral and religious and therefore rather nastier, its critics thought, than the primarily moral self-righteousness of the liberal Abelardians. In time, to move on in our story, the liberals increasingly ceased to be even Abelardian" (207).

20. Ibid.

21. I interact at length with these views in my *Lord and Servant: A Covenant Christology* (Louisville: Westminster John Knox, 2005), 178–207.

22. See, e.g., Clark Pinnock, *A Wideness in God's Mercy: The Finality of Jesus Christ in a World of Religions* (Grand Rapids: Zondervan, 1992), esp. 49–80; Clark Pinnock and Robert Brow, *Unbounded Love: A Good News Theology for the 21st Century* (Downers Grove, IL: InterVarsity Press, 1994), esp. 100–105.

23. Note how John Wiley refers to "The Penal Satisfaction Theory, generally known as the Calvinistic theory," in his *Systematic Theology* (New York: Hunt and Eaton, 1892), 241. Pinnock observes that his adoption of Arminianism led him to reject the classical doctrine of the substitutionary atonement: "Obviously it caused me to reduce the precision in which I understood the substitution to take place.... It caused me to look first at the theory of Anselm and later of Hugo Grotius, both of whom encourage us to view the atonement as an act of judicial demonstration rather than a strict or quantitative substitution as such.... It is my strong impression that Augustinian thinking is losing its

hold on present-day Christians. It is hard to find a Calvinist theologian willing to defend Reformed theology, including the views of Calvin and Luther, in all its rigorous particulars now that Gordon Clark is no longer with us and John Gerstner is retired." Pinnock concedes that his changes are part of a growing accommodation to the secular mind: "We are finally making peace with the culture of modernity" ("From Augustine to Arminius: A Pilgrimage in Theology," in *The Grace of God, The Will of Man: A Case for Arminianism*, ed. Clark H. Pinnock [Grand Rapids: Zondervan, 1989], 23, 26, 27).

24. John Knox, *The Death of Christ: The Cross in the New Testament History and Faith* (New York: Abingdon, 1958), 145. Of course, Christ's death does disclose God's love, more than any other divine work. However, it does so precisely because its purpose is not only to disclose or reveal God's love but to save sinners by God's loving movement toward us in Jesus Christ.

25. Calvin, *Institutes* 2.16.5.

26. See *The Seven Ecumenical Councils*, vol. 14 in *Nicene and Post-Nicene Fathers*, ed. Henry R. Percival (Grand Rapids: Eerdmans, repr. 1971).

27. Karl Barth, *Church Dogmatics* II/2, 417–423; III/2, 136; IV/1, 91, 140, 410. For responsible evaluations, see especially G. C. Berkouwer, *The Triumph of Grace in the Theology* of *Karl Barth*, trans. H. R. Boer (London: Paternoster, 1956), 215–34; Garry J. Williams, "Karl Barth and the Doctrine of the Atonement," in *Engaging with Barth: Contemporary Evangelical Critiques*, ed. David Gibson and Daniel Strange (Nottingham: Apollos, 2008), 232–72.

28. Wiley, *Christian Theology*, 2:246.

29. Lewis Sperry Chafer, "For Whom Did Christ Die?" reprinted in *Bibliotheca Sacra* 137 (Oct.-Dec. 1980): 325.

30. Robert Lightner, "For Whom Did Christ Die?" in *Walvoord: A Tribute*, ed. John F. Walvoord and Donald K. Campbell (Chicago: Moody Press, 1982), 162.

31. John Owen, "The Death of Death in the Death of Christ," *Works of John Owen* (Edinburgh: Banner of Truth Trust, 1966), 10:233.

32. See Stephen M. Baugh, "Galatians 3:20 and the Covenant of Redemption," *Westminster Theological Journal* 66:1 (2004): 49–70.

33. Herman Bavinck, *Reformed Dogmatics*, ed. John Bolt; trans. John Vriend (Grand Rapids: Baker, 2006), 3:469.

34. See B. B. Warfield, *The Plan of Salvation* (Grand Rapids: Eerdmans, 1942 [repr. 1980]), esp. 95.

35. Canons of Dort, Second Head of Doctrine, Art. 3, 99.

Chapter Five: Called and Kept (Effectual Calling and Perseverance)

1. Calvin, *Institutes* 3.1.4.

2. Reflecting Arminian presuppositions, much of contemporary evangelicalism understands the new birth as something that is in our power (at least partially) to effect. Especially in its American expression, this form of synergism (cooperative regeneration) is combined with a pragmatic and almost technical apparatus of formulae for being born again. For example, this can be seen even in the title of a best-selling book by Billy Graham from the 1970s, *How to Be Born Again* (Nashville: Nelson, 1977, 1989); cf. Billy Graham, *The Holy Spirit: Activating God's Power in Your Life* (Nashville: Nelson, 1978, 1988, 2000). Shaped by the Keswick "Higher Life" movement, this broad stream of contemporary evangelical piety tends to treat the Spirit's person and work as a resource that we can access, activate, and manage through various steps and techniques. For a critique of this view see esp. B. B. Warfield, *Studies in Perfectionism* (Phillipsburg, NJ: Presbyterian & Reformed, 1958), and J. I. Packer, *Keep in Step with the Spirit* (Old Tappan, NJ: Revell, 1987), 146–63.

3. Roger Olson offers a helpful distinction between evangelical and rationalistic Arminianism ("Arminianism of the heart" and "Arminianism of the head," respectively) in his *Arminian Theology*. He quotes John Mark Hicks' comparison and contrast

of Arminius and Philip Limborch in this respect: "For Arminius man is deprived of the actual ability to will the good, but for Limborch man is only deprived of the knowledge which informs the intellect, but the will is fully capable within itself, if it is informed by the intellect, to will and perform anything good" (quoted on p. 57). Olson comments that at least indirectly, "Limborch's interpretation of the effects of original sin is very similar to Charles Finney's" (57).

4. Wiley, *Christian Theology*, 2:419.

5. The Reformed scholastic Heidegger, for example, writes, "The word is the same which man preaches and which the Spirit writes on the heart. There is strictly one calling, but its cause and medium is twofold: instrumental, man preaching the word outwardly; principal, the Holy Spirit writing it inwardly in the heart." Quoted by Heinrich Heppe, *Reformed Dogmatics* (trans. G. T. Thompson; London: Allen & Unwin, 1950), 518. Heidegger adds, "The first effect of calling is regeneration" (ibid.).

6. See, e.g., the Heidelberg Catechism, Q. 65: "It is by faith alone that we share in Christ and all his blessings; where then does that faith come from? A. The Holy Spirit produces it in our hearts by the preaching of the holy gospel and confirms it through our use of the holy sacraments" (*Ecumenical Creeds and Reformed Confessions* [Grand Rapids: CRC Publications, 1988], 41).

7. Second Helvetic Confession, Ch. 9 (Free Will), in *The Book of Confessions* (Louisville: PCUSA).

8. Westminster Confession of Faith, chap. 11.

9. Ibid., chap. 12 (Effectual Calling).

10. Canons of the Synod of Dort (1618–19), *Psalter Hymnal*, Third and Fourth Head of Doctrine, Art. 16, p. 106.

11. Owen, *The Works of John Owen*, 3:319.

12. Calvin, *Institutes* 1.13.18.

13. Canons of the Synod of Dort, Third and Fourth Heads, Art. 11, 104.

14. Ibid., 105.

15. For this reason, anthropomorphic theologies (such as Moltmann's) actually end up deepening the causal scheme, as if God (or each divine person) is a humanlike subject acting on or in relation to another. God's omniscience, omnipresence, wisdom, eternity, immutability, aseity, as well as Trinity, ensure that his omnipotence is *not* like the overpowering of one person by another.

16. Bavinck, *Reformed Dogmatics*, 3:230.

17. Calvin, *Institutes* 3.2.14.

18. Ibid., 3.2.36.

19. Berkhof, *Systematic Theology*, 498.

20. Augustine, "On The Gift of Perseverance," in Philip Schaff, ed., *A Select Library of the Nicene and Post-Nicene Fathers of the Christian Church*, vol. 5: *Anti-Pelagian Writings* (Edinburgh: T&T Clark, repr. 1991), chap. 16.

21. For a fine recent defense of this doctrine, see Thomas R. Schreiner and Ardel B. Caneday, *The Race Set Before Us: A Biblical Theology of Perseverance and Assurance* (Downers Grove, IL: InterVarsity Press, 2001).

22. William B. Pope, *A Compendium of Christian Theology*, 3:137–47. A contemporary defense of the dominant Arminian position may be found in Shank, *Elect in the Son*.

23. See *Catechism of the Catholic Church*, 489.

24. Cited by Wiley, *Christian Theology*, 351.

25. Lewis Sperry Chafer, *Major Bible Doctrines*, rev. John Walvoord (Grand Rapids: Zondervan, 1974), 214, 220, 222, 230–35. Though representing what he calls the "moderate Calvinist" position (in defense of eternal security), Norman L. Geisler presupposes a basically Arminian scheme: "God's grace works synergistically on free will.... Put in other terms, God's justifying grace works cooperatively, not operatively" (*Chosen but Free* [Minneapolis: Bethany, 1999], 233). Elsewhere he writes, "Indeed, God would save all men if He could.... God will achieve the greatest number in heaven that He possibly

can" ("God, Evil, and Dispensations," in *Walvoord: A Tribute*, ed. Donald K. Campbell [Chicago: Moody Press, 1982], 102, 108). I interact with Norman Geisler on this issue in J. Matthew Pinson, ed., *Four Views on Eternal Security* (Grand Rapids: Zondervan, 2002).

26. Chafer, *Major Bible Doctrines*, 283–86. Charles Stanley argues that Jesus' description of the "outer darkness" of "weeping and wailing and gnashing of teeth" refers not to hell but to a region of heaven occupied by carnal Christians (*Eternal Security: Can You Be Sure?* [Nashville: Nelson, 1990], 121–29).

27. "Final Perseverance" in *Lutheran Cyclopedia*, eds. Erwin L. Lueker, Luther Poellot, and Paul Jackson (St. Louis: Concordia, 2000). The article points out that while Lutherans stress the assurance of all who trust in Christ, the severe warnings of the law should be borne in mind, to guard against "carnal security."

28. A regenerate believer may apostatize, "but the cause is not as though God were unwilling to grant grace for perseverance to those in whom He has begun the good work ... [but that these persons] willfully turn away" (Formula of Concord: Solid Declaration, art. xi, par. 42).

Chapter Six: Calvinism and the Christian Life

1. Westminster Confession of Faith, chap. 16.6 in *The Trinity Hymnal* (Atlanta: Great Commission, 1990) 857.
2. Ibid., chap. 19.5, 859.
3. The Heidelberg Catechism, Lord's Day 44, Q. 113, *The Psalter Hymnal*, 56.
4. The Belgic Confession, Art. 24, *The Psalter Hymnal*, 80.
5. See, e.g., the Belgic Confession, Art. 22–23, *The Psalter Hymnal*, 80; Westminster Confession of Faith, chap. 11, *Trinity Hymnal*, 855.
6. The Westminster Confession of Faith, chap. 13, *Trinity Hymnal*, 856.
7. Wilhelm Niesel, *The Theology of John Calvin*, trans. Harold Knight (Philadelphia: Westminster, 1956), 99.
8. Calvin, *Institutes* 3.19.5.
9. The Heidelberg Catechism, Lord's Day 26, Q. 69, in *The Psalter Hymnal*, 33.
10. "Of Christian Liberty, and Liberty of Conscience," The Westminster Confession of Faith, chap. 20, *Trinity Hymnal*, 859–60.
11. For an excellent summary of how Christ rules both the kingdoms of this age and his kingdom of grace, see David VanDrunen, *Living in God's Two Kingdoms* (Westchester, IL: Crossway, 2010).
12. John Wesley, *The Works of John Wesley* (Grand Rapids: Baker, repr. 1996), 7:376–84.
13. Ibid., 8:336.
14. Calvin, *Institutes* 3.11.13; 3.16.7.
15. John Calvin, "Reply to Sadoleto" in *Tracts*, 1:41.
16. John Calvin, *Commentary on the Psalms*, 5:251.
17. Calvin, *Institutes* 2.5.15.
18. Ibid., 3.11.2.
19. Calvin, *Commentary on Romans*, xxix–xxx.
20. Ibid., 180.
21. Ibid., 186.
22. Geneva Catechism (1536), in *Tracts*, 2:132.
23. Calvin, *Institutes* 3.2.7.
24. Ibid., 3.13.5.
25. Calvin, *Commentary on Romans*, 159.
26. Calvin, *Institutes* 3.2.4.
27. Calvin, *Commentary on the Synoptic Gospels*, 2:325.
28. Calvin, *Institutes* 3.11.1.
29. Ibid., 3.16.1.

30. Ibid.
31. Calvin, *Commentary on Habakkuk to Haggai*, 351.
32. Calvin, *Institutes* 3.3.4.
33. Calvin, *Commentary on the General Epistles*, 209.
34. Calvin, "Prefatory Address to King Francis I," 6 (in *Institutes*, p. 25).
35. Calvin, *Institutes* 4.1.9.
36. Calvin, *Commentary on Ezekiel*, 2:294.
37. Calvin, *Commentary on the Four Last Books of Moses*, 2:329–30.
38. Calvin, *Commentary on the Pastoral Epistles* (on Tit. 2:15), 323.
39. Calvin, *Commentary on the Synoptic Gospels*, 2:245.
40. Calvin, *Commentary on the Psalms*, 5:229.
41. Ibid., 1:336.
42. Calvin, *Institutes* 3.20.2.
43. Calvin, *Commentary on Genesis*, 1:489.
44. Ibid., 2:238.
45. Donald Alexander, ed., *Christian Spirituality: Five Views of Sanctification* (Downers Grove, IL: InterVarsity Press, 1988).
46. Laurence W. Wood, in his contributions to *Christian Spirituality*, 37.
47. Ibid., 38.
48. Ibid., 86.
49. Ibid., 38–39.
50. Ibid., 98.
51. Ibid., 39.
52. Russel P. Spittler, in his contributions to *Christian Spirituality*, 42–43.
53. E. Glenn Hinson, in his contributions to *Christian Spirituality*, 46.
54. Ibid., 46.
55. Hinson, in his contributions to *Christian Spirituality*, 93.
56. Spittler, in his contributions to *Christian Spirituality*, 89.
57. Hinson, in his contributions to *Christian Spirituality*, 180.
58. Gerhard Forde, in his contributions to *Christian Spirituality*, 191–92.
59. Ferguson, in his contributions to *Christian Spirituality*, 194.
60. Ibid., 195.
61. See Melvin E. Dieter et al., *Five Views on Sanctification* (Grand Rapids: Zondervan, 1987).
62. Robert McQuilkin, in *Five Views on Sanctification*, 55.
63. Ibid., 154.
64. Ibid.,155.
65. Ibid., 156.
66. Ibid., 161.
67. Ibid., 163.
68. Ibid., 167.
69. Ibid., 168.
70. Ibid., 170.
71. Ibid., 171.
72. Ibid., 180.
73. Ibid., 181.
74. Melvin E. Dieter, in *Five Views on Sanctification*, 186.
75. John Walvoord, in *Five Views on Sanctification*, 223.
76. McQuilkin, in *Five Views on Sanctification*, 237.

Chapter Seven: Calvinism and Christian Missions

1. William R. Estep, "Doctrines Lead to 'Dunghill,' Prof Warns," *Texas Baptist Standard* (March 26, 1997).

2. Ruth Tucker, *From Jerusalem to Irian Jaya: A Biographical History of Christian Missions* (Grand Rapids: Zondervan, 1983), 67.
3. Fred Klooster, "Missions, The Heidelberg Catechism, and Calvin," *Calvin Theological Journal* 7/2 (1972): 183.
4. Tucker, *From Jerusalem to Irian Jaya*, 67–68.
5. Philip E. Hughes, ed., *The Register of the Company of Pastors of Geneva in the Time of Calvin* (Grand Rapids: Eerdmans, 1966), 25.
6. Frank A. James III, cited in Keith Coleman, "Calvin and Missions," *WRS Journal* 16:1 (February 2009): 29–30.
7. John Calvin, *Commentary on the Epistle to the Hebrews*, 135.
8. John Calvin, "Sermon on 1 Tim. 2:3–5," *Calvin's Sermons: The Mystery of Godliness* (Grand Raids: Eerdmans, 1950).
9. D. W. Torrance and T. F. Torrance, eds., *Calvin's New Testament Commentaries* (Grand Rapids: Eerdmans, 1972), 251.
10. Timothy George, *Faithful Witness: The Life and Mission of William Carey* (Birmingham, AL: New Hope, 1991), 135.
11. Quoted in Tucker, *From Jerusalem to Irian Jaya*, 84.
12. Ibid., 89.
13. Ibid., 89–90.
14. Quoted in ibid., 93.
15. Quoted in ibid., 153.
16. Ibid., 141.
17. For this part of the story, I am dependent on the excellent essay by Kenneth J. Stewart, "Calvinism and Missions: The Contested Relationship Revisited," *Themelios* 34, no. 1 (April 2009): 63–78.
18. Tucker, *From Jerusalem to Irian Jaya*, 162–63.
19. Ibid., 168–71.
20. Ibid., 172.
21. Ibid., 188–89.
22. Ibid., 193.
23. Ibid.
24. Quoted by Kenneth Stewart, from N. Carr Sargant, "Calvinism, Arminianism and Missions," *London Quarterly and Holborn Review* 176 (1951): 340–44. From the same era, note J. Van den Berg, "Calvin's Missionary Message: Some Remarks about the Relation between Calvinism and Missions," *Evangelical Quarterly* 22 (1950): 174–87; and S. M. Zwemer, "Calvinism and the Missionary Enterprise," *Theology Today* 7 (1950): 206–21.
25. Sargant, "Calvinism, Arminianism and Missions," 51. We will shortly return to the question of Protestant mission in the eighteenth century and earlier. The point being established initially here is simply that twentieth-century judgments about Calvinism and mission have been subject to wide variation.
26. For an excellent history of these sources, see Kenneth J. Stewart, *Restoring the Reformation: British Evangelicalism and the Francophone 'Réveil' 1816–1849*; Paternoster Studies in Evangelical History and Thought (Eugene, OR: Wipf & Stock, 2006).
27. J. Herbert Kane, *A Concise History of the Christian World Mission* (Grand Rapids: Baker, 1978), 85.
28. George, *Faithful Witness*, 24.
29. Ibid., 37.
30. Ibid., 53.
31. Ibid., 54.
32. Tucker, *From Jerusalem to Irian Jaya*, 134–35.
33. *World Christian Encyclopedia: A Comparative Survey of Churches and Religions in the Modern World*, ed. D. B. Barrett, G. T. Kurian, and T. M. Johnson (Oxford: Oxford Univ. Press, 2001), 559.

34. Ibid., 683.
35. Ibid., 252.
36. S. M. Zwemer, "Calvinism and the Missionary Enterprise," *Theology Today* 7 (1950): 215.
37. *World Christian Encyclopedia*, 96.
38. Ibid., 380.
39. Ibid., 384.
40. Ibid., 394, 437, 568.
41. Ibid., 446.
42. Stewart ("Calvinism and Missions") refers to the comment made by T. M. Lindsay (1843–1914) in the Glasgow 1896 General Council Meeting of the Reformed and Presbyterian Alliance, as quoted by S. M. Zwemer, "Calvinism and the Missionary Enterprise," *Theology Today* 7 (1950): 215.
43. *PCA News*, "Does Calvinism Hinder Missions?": http://70030.netministry.com/articles_view.asp?articleid=32260&columid+3844.
44. Ibid., citing www.sbc.net/aboutus/default.asp.
45. *PCA News*, "Does Calvinism Hinder Missions?"
46. "Briefing," *Christianity Today* (February 2011), 7.
47. Reported by Joel Belz, "Our 2 Cents' Worth," in *World Magazine* (Oct 27, 2007), at World Archives: www.worldmag.com/articles/13429.
48. George, *Faithful Witness*, 171.
49. Ibid., 172.
50. Canons of Dort, Second Head of Doctrine, Art. 5, in *The Psalter Hymnal*, 99.
51. C. H. Spurgeon, *Autobiography*, vol. 1: *The Early Years*, rev. ed. (Edinburgh: Banner of Truth Trust, 1962), 172.

Chapter Eight: Calvinism Today: A SWOT Analysis

1. Brian McLaren, *A Generous Orthodoxy* (Grand Rapids: Zondervan, 2004), 188.
2. C. S. Lewis, *The Screwtape Letters* (New York: Macmillan, 1961), 115–19.
3. Abraham Kuyper, "Conservatism and Orthodoxy: False and True Preservation," in *Abraham Kuyper: A Centennial Reader*, ed. John Bratt (Grand Rapids: Eerdmans, 1998), 67.
4. Ibid.
5. Ibid.
6. Ibid., 71.
7. Ibid., 72.
8. Ibid.
9. Ibid., 74.
10. Ibid.
11. Ibid., 75.
12. Ibid., 76.
13. Ibid.
14. Ibid., 78.
15. Ibid., 79.
16. Ibid., 80–81.
17. Ibid., 81.
18. Ibid., 82.
19. Ibid., 85.
20. McLaren, *A Generous Orthodoxy*, 127.
21. Jaroslav Pelikan, interviewed in *U. S. News & World Report* (July 26, 1989), 25.